Organizational Learning II

Theory, Method, and Practice

Chris Argyris
Harvard University

Donald A. Schön
Massachusetts Institute of Technology

ADDISON-WESLEY PUBLISHING COMPANY
Reading, Massachusetts • Menlo Park, California • New York
Don Mills, Ontario • Amsterdam • Bonn
Sydney • Singapore • York St John *• Juan • Milan • Paris*

Library of Congress Card No. 77-81195

This book is in the Addison-Wesley Series on Organizational Development.
Editors: Edgar H. Schein, Richard Beckhard

Reprinted with corrections August, 1996

ISBN 0-201-62983-6
  4 5 6 7 8 9 10-BA-9897

Other Titles in the Organization Development Series

Integrated Strategic Change: How OD Builds Competitive Advantage
Christopher G. Worley, David E. Hitchin, and Walter L. Ross
1996 (85777)
This book is about strategic change and how firms can improve their performance and effectiveness. Its unique contribution is in describing how organization development practitioners can assist in the effort. Strategic change is a type of organization change that realigns an organization's strategy, structure and process within a given competitive context. It is substantive and systemic and therefore differs from traditional organization development that produces incremental improvements, addresses only one system at a time, or does not intend to increase firm-level performance.

Team Building: Current Issues and New Alternatives, Third Edition
William G. Dyer
1995 (62882)
One of the major developments in the field of organization redesign has been the emergence of self-directed work teams. This book explains how teams are most successful when the team becomes part of the culture and structure or systems of the organization. It discusses the major new trends and emphasizes the degree of committment that managers and members must bring to the team-building process. It is written for managers and human resource professionals who want to develop a more systematic program of team building in their organization or work unit.

Creating Labor-Management Partnerships
Warner P. Woodworth and Christopher B. Meek
1995 (58823)
This book begins with a call for changing the social and political barriers existing in unionized work settings and emphasizes the critical need for union-management cooperation in the present context of international competition. It demonstrates the shift from confrontational union-management relationships toward more effective and positive systems of collaboration. It is written for human resource management and industrial relations managers and staff, union officials, professional arbitrators and mediators, government officials, and professors and students involved in the study of organization development.

Organization Development: A Process of Learning and Changing, Second Edition
W. Warner Burke
1994 (50835)
This text presents an overview of OD and looks at OD in part as a change of an

organization's culture. It looks at the organization and factors that will influence structure and development in the future. The author also introduces new topics such as information management and strategy implementation.

Competing with Flexible Lateral Organizations, Second Edition
Jay R. Galbraith
1994 (50836)

This book focuses on creating competitive advantage by building a lateral capability, enabling a firm to respond flexibly in an uncertain world. The book addresses international coordination and cross business coordination as well as the usual cross functional efforts. It is unique in covering both cross functional (lateral or horizontal) coordination, as well as international and corporate issues.

The Dynamics of Organizational Levels:
A Change Framework for Managers and Consultants
Nicholas S. Rashford and David Coghlan
1994 (54323)

This book introduces the idea that, for successful change to occur, organizational interventions have to be coordinated across the major levels of issues that all organizations face. Individual level, team level, inter-unit level, and organizational level issues are identified and analyzed, and the kinds of intervention appropriate to each level are spelled out.

Total Quality: A User's Guide for Implementation
Dan Ciampa
1992 (54992)

This is a book that directly addresses the challenge of how to make Total Quality work in a practical, no-nonsense way. The companies that will dominate markets in the future will be those that deliver high quality, competitively priced products and service just when the customer wants them and in a way that exceeds the customer's expectations. The vehicle by which these companies move to that stage is Total Quality.

Parallel Learning Structures: Increasing Information in Bureaucracies
Gervase R. Bushe and A. B. Shani
1991 (52427)

Parallel learning structures are technostructural interventions that promote system-wide change in bureaucracies while retaining the advantages of bureaucratic design. This text serves as a resource of models and theories built around five cases of parallel learning structures that can help those who
create and maintain them be more effective and successful. For those new to parallel learning structures, the text provides practical advice as to when and how to use them.

Managing in the New Team Environment: Skills, Tools, and Methods
Larry Hirschhorn
1991 (52503)
This text is designed to help manage the tensions and complexities that arise for managers seeking to guide employees in a team environment. Based on an interactive video course developed at IBM, the text takes managers step by step through the process of building a team and authorizing it to act while they learn to step back and delegate. Specific issues addressed are how to give a team structure, how to facilitate its basic proccesses, and how to acknowledge differences in relationships among team members and between the manager and individual team members.

Leading Business Teams: How Teams Can Use Technology
and Group Process Tools to Enhance Performance
Robert Johansen, David Sibbett, Suzyn Benson, Alexia Martin,
Robert Mittman, and Paul Saffo
1991 (52829)
What technology or tools should organization development people or team leaders have at their command, now and in the future? This text explores the intersection of technology and business teams, a new and largely uncharted area that goes by several labels, including "groupware," a term that encompasses both electronic and nonelectronic tools for teams. This is the first book of its kind from the field describing what works for business teams and what does not.

Becoming a Learning Organization: Beyond the Learning Curve
Joop Sweiringa and André Wierdsma
1991 (62753)
As organizations evolve with time, the ability to learn and change is becoming increasingly more important. The future poses numerous obstacles and challenges for all organizations, and having the proper learning tools will provide a necessary competitive advantage. This text not only analyzes what a learning organization is, it also explores practical approaches and tools that teach a company to "learn to learn." The aim of this book is to identify and define the learning process, but also to begin the implementation of it in order to gain an advantage in a highly competitive environment.

The Conflict-Positive Organization: Stimulate Diversity and Create Unity
Dean Tjosvold
1991 (51485)
This book describes how managers and employees can use conflict to find common ground, solve problems, and strengthen morale and relationships. By showing how well-managed conflict invigorates and empowers teams and organizations, the text demonstrates how conflict is vital for a company's continuous improvement and increased competitive advantage.

Change by Design
Robert R. Blake, Jane Srygley Mouton, and Anne Adams McCanse
1989 (50748)
This book develops a systematic approach to organization development and provides readers with rich illustrations of coherent planned change. The book involves testing, examining, revising, and strengthening conceptual foundations in order to create sharper corporate focus and increased predictability of successful organization development.

Organization Development in Health Care
R. Wayne Boss
1989 (18364)
This is the first book to discuss the intricacies of the health care industry. The book explains the impact of OD in creating healthy and viable organizations in the health care sector. Through unique and innovative techniques, hospitals are able to reduce nursing turnover, thereby resolving the nursing shortage problem. The text also addresses how OD can improve such bottom-line variables as cash flow and net profits.

Self-Designing Organizations:
Learning How to Create High Performance
Susan Albers Mohrman and Thomas G. Cummings
1989 (14603)
This book looks beyond traditional approaches to organizational transition, offering a strategy for developing organizations that enables them to learn not only how to adjust to the dynamic environment in which they exist, but also how to achieve a higher level of performance. This strategy assumes that change is a learning process: the goal is continually refined as organizational members learn how to function more effectively and respond to dynamic conditions in their environment.

Power and Organization Development:
Mobilizing Power to Implement Change
Larry E. Greiner and Virginia E. Schein
1988 (12185)
This book forges an important collaborative approach between two opposing and often contradictory approaches to management: OD practitioners who espouse a "more humane" workplace without understanding the political realities of getting things done, and practicing managers who feel comfortable with power but overlook the role of human potential in contributing to positive results.

Designing Organizations for High Performance
David P. Hanna
1988 (12693)
This book is the first to give insight into the actual processes you can use to translate organizational concepts into bottom-line improvements. Hanna's "how-to" approach shows not only the successful methods of intervention, but also the plans behind them and the corresponding results.

Process Consultation, Volume 1:
Its Role in Organization Development, Second Edition
Edgar H. Schein
1988 (06736)
How can a situation be influenced in the workplace without the direct use of power or formal authority? This book presents the core theoretical foundations and basic prescriptions for effective management.

Organizational Transitions: Managing Complex Change, Second Edition
Richard Beckhard and Reuben T. Harris
1987 (10887)
This book discusses the choices involved in developing a management system appropriate to the "transition state." It also discusses commitment to change, organizational culture, and increasing and maintaining productivity, creativity, and innovation.

Organization Development: A Normative View
W. Warner Burke
1987 (10697)
This book concisely describes and defines the theories and practices of organization development and also looks at organization development as change in an organization's culture. It is a useful guide to the field of organization development and is invaluable to managers, executives, practitioners, and anyone desiring an excellent overview of this multifaceted field.

The Technology Connection: Strategy and Change in the Information Age
Marc S. Gerstein
1987 (12188)
This is a book that guides managers and consultants through crucial decisions about the use of technology for increasing effectiveness and competitive advantage. It provides a useful way to think about information technology, business strategy, and the process of change in organizations.

Stream Analysis: A Powerful Way to Diagnose and Manage Organizational Change
Jerry I. Porras
1987 (05693)
Drawing on a conceptual framework that helps the reader to better understand organizations, this book shows how to diagnose failings in organizational functioning and how to plan a comprehensive set of actions needed to change the organization into a more effective system.

Process Consultation, Volume II: Lessons for Managers and Consultants
Edgar H. Schein
1987 (06744)
This book shows the viability of the process consultation model for working with human systems. Like Schein's first volume on process consultation, the second volume focuses on the moment-to-moment behavior of the manager or consultant rather than the design of the OD program.

Managing Conflict: Interpersonal Dialogue and Third-Party Roles, Second Edition
Richard E. Walton
1987 (08859)
This book shows how to implement a dialogue approach to conflict management. It presents a framework for diagnosing recurring conflicts and suggests several basic options for controlling or resolving them.

Pay and Organization Development
Edward E. Lawler
1981 (03990)
This book examines the important role that reward systems play in organization development efforts. By combining examples and specific recommendations with conceptual material, it organizes the various topics and puts them into a total systems perspective. Specific pay approaches such as gainsharing, skill-based pay, and flexible benefits are discussed, and their impact on productivity and the quality of work life is analyzed.

Work Redesign
J. Richard Hackman and Greg R. Oldham
1980 (02779)
This book is a comprehensive, clearly written study of work design as a strategy for personal and organizational change. Linking theory and practical technologies, it develops traditional and alternative approaches to work design that can benefit both individuals and organizations.

Organizational Dynamics: Diagnosis and Intervention
John P. Kotter
1978 (03890)
This book offers managers and OD specialists a powerful method of diagnosing organizational problems and of deciding when, where, and how to use (or not use) the diverse and growing number of organizational improvement tools that are available today. Comprehensive and fully integrated, the book includes many different concepts, research findings, and competing philosophies and provides specific examples of how to use the information to improve organizational functioning.

Career Dynamics: Matching Individual and Organizational Needs
Edgar H. Schein
1978 (06834)
This book studies the complexities of career development from both an individual and an organizational perspective. Changing needs throughout the adult life cycle, interaction of work and family, and integration of individual and organizational goals through human resource planning and development are all thoroughly explored.

Matrix
Stanley M. Davis and Paul Lawrence
1977 (01115)
This book defines and describes the matrix organization, a significant departure from the traditional "one man-one boss" management system. The author notes that the tension between the need for independence (fostering innovation) and order (fostering efficiency) drives organizations to consider a matrix system. Among the issues addressed are reasons for using a matrix, methods for establishing one, the impact of the system on individuals, its hazards, and what types of organizations can use a matrix system.

Feedback and Organization Development: Using Data-Based Methods
David A. Nadler
1977 (05006)
This book addresses the use of data as a tool for organizational change. It attempts to bring together some of what is known from experience and research and to translate that knowledge into useful insights for those who are thinking about using data-based methods in organizations. The broad approa of the text is to treat a whole range of questions and issues considering the various uses of data as an organizational change tool.

Designing Complex Organizations
Jay Galbraith
1973 (02559)
This book attempts to present an analytical framework of the design of organizations that apply lateral decision processes or matrix forms. These forms have become pervasive in all types of organizations, yet there is little systematic public knowledge about them. This book helps fill this gap.

Organization Development: Strategies and Models
Richard Beckhard
1969 (00448)
This book is written for managers, specialists, and students of management who are concerned with the planning of organization development programs to resolve the dilemmas brought about by a rapidly changing environment. Practiced teams of interdependent people must spend real time improving their methods of working, decision making, and communicating, and a planned, managed change is the first step toward effecting and maintaining these improvements.

Organization Development: Its Nature, Origins, and Prospects
Warren G. Bennis
1969 (00523)
This primer on OD is written with an eye toward the people in organizations who are interested in learning more about this educational strategy as well as for those practitioners and students of OD who may want a basic statement both to learn from and to argue with. The author treats the subject with a minimum of academic jargon and a maximum of concrete examples and others' experience.

Developing Organizations: Diagnosis and Action
Paul R. Lawrence and Jay W. Lorsch
1969 (04204)
This book is a personal statement of the author's evolving experience, through research and consulting, in the work of developing organizations. The text presents the authors' overview of organization development, then proceeds to examine the issues at each of three critical interfaces: the organization-environment interface, the group-group interface, and the individual-organization interface, including brief examples of work on each. The text concludes by pulling the themes together in a set of conclusions about organizational development issues as they present themselves to practicing managers.

About the Authors

Donald A. Schön is currently Ford Professor Emeritus and Senior Lecturer in the Department of Urban Studies and Planning at the Massachusetts Institute of Technology (MIT).

Educated initially as a philosopher, he has been an educator, organizational consultant, government administrator, and president of a nonprofit social research consulting organization. He has worked as a researcher and practitioner on problems of technological innovation, organizational learning, and professional effectiveness and education. He was invited in 1970 to deliver the Reith Lectures on the BBC.

In recent years, Dr. Schön's research and consulting interests have centered on three main fields: practice knowledge and reflective practice, design research, and organizational learning.

Since he joined MIT in the early 1970s, Dr. Schön has studied the kind of "knowledge" that makes practitioners good at what they do. These studies which began with architecture and branched out to include many other professions such as engineering, management, medicine, law, psychotherapy, and city planning resulted in a book, *The Reflective Practitioner* (1983). Here Dr. Schön described the tacit knowing-in-action that practitioners bring to their everyday lives; the capability for "reflection-in-action" through which skilled practitioners often think about what they are doing while they are doing it on-the-spot in situations of uncertainty, uniqueness, and conflict; and the capability for reflecting on knowing- and reflecting-in-action, through which practitioners can formulate and criticize their action strategies and their ways of framing problems and roles. A second book about practice knowledge, *Educating the Reflective Practitioner* (1987), drew out the implications of these ideas for the education of practitioners and for education in general. It advocated the importance of the "reflective practicum," based on the tradition of the design studio in architectural education. In 1991 Dr. Schön edited a book of case studies of reflection in and on (mainly educational) practice, *The Reflective Turn*; and in 1994 with Martin Rein, he published *Frame Reflection: Toward the Resolution of Intractable Policy Controversies* which explores how policy practitioners can reflect, in concrete practice predicaments, on the frames that underlie their stubborn disputes. Dr. Schön devotes much of his time to workshops, lectures, and consulting engagements with practitioners and educators who are trying to work out their own approaches to reflective practice.

Dr. Schön has a long-standing interest in research on designing—the design of both physical objects and environments, as in the "design professions," and the broader sense in which designing is more widely understood as the process of making things under conditions of complexity and uncertainty. In this area Dr. Schön's work is influenced by John Dewey's theory of inquiry, which was the subject of his doctoral dissertation and by his early studies of generative metaphor (*Displacement of Concepts*, 1963). His recent publications on designing deal with the significance of prototypes, the construction of "design worlds," and the idea of designing as "reflective conversation with the materials of a situation." Increasingly, in recent years, Dr. Schön has become interested in software design, the possible roles of the computer in designing, and the uses of design games to explore and develop capability for designing.

Dr. Schön's interest in organizational learning goes back to his first experience as an organizational consultant at the industrial research firm of Arthur D. Little, Inc., where he was greatly influenced by his friend and colleague, Dr. Raymond M. Hainer. His research in this field, built mainly on his consulting experience, was presented in two early books: *Technology and Change* (1967), and *Beyond the Stable State* (1971). Since the early 1970s Dr. Schön has worked in close teaching, research, and consulting collaboration with Dr. Chris Argyris. Their coauthored books include *Theory in Practice: Increasing Professional Effectiveness* (1974) and *Organizational Learning: A Theory of Action Perspective (1978).*

Chris Argyris is James Bryant Conant Professor of Education and Organizational Behavior at Harvard University. He received his A.B. degree (1947) from Clark University in psychology, his M.A. degree (1949) from Kansas University in economics and psychology, and his Ph.D. degree (1951) from Cornell University in organizational behavior. Argyris has also earned honorary doctorate degrees from McGill University (1977), the University of Leuven, Belgium (1978), the Stockholm School of Economics (1970), DePaul University (1987), and IMCB of Buckingham, England (1987). The School of Industrial and Labor Relations at Cornell University awarded him the Judge William B. Grant Alumni Award for scholarly contribution. From 1951 to 1971, he was a faculty member at Yale University, serving as Beach Professor of Administrative Sciences and as chair of the Administrative Sciences department during the latter part of this period.

Argyris' early research focused on the unintended consequences for individuals of formal organizational structures, executive leadership, control systems, and management information systems—and how individuals adapted to change those consequences (*Personality and Organization*, 1957; *Integrating the Individual and the Organization*, 1964). He then turned his attention to ways of changing organizations, especially the behavior of executives at the upper levels of organization (*Interpersonal Competence and Organizational Effectiveness*, 1962; *Organization and Innovation*, 1965).

This line of inquiry led him to focus on the role of the social scientist as a researcher and interventionist (*Intervention Theory and Method*, 1970; *Inner Contradictions of Rigorous Research*, 1980). During the past decade he has also been developing, with Donald Schön, a theory of individual and organizational learning in which human reasoning—not just behavior—becomes the basis for diagnosis and action (*Theory in Practice*, 1974; *Organizational Learning*, 1978). Argyris' other books include *Strategy, Change and Defensive Routines* (1985), *Overcoming Organizational Defenses* (1990), *On Organizational Learning* (1992), and *Knowledge for Action* (1993).

Argyris is currently working on a long range project to integrate features of managerial functional disciplines with concepts from his theory of action. The current focus is on finance and governance, activity-based accounting, information science and technology, and operations.

Foreword

The Addison-Wesley Series on Organizational Development originated in the late 1960's when a number of us recognized that the
rapidly growing field of "OD" was not well understood or well defined. We also recognized that there was no one OD philosophy, and
hence one could not at that time write a textbook on the theory and
practice of OD, but one could make clear what various practitioners
were doing under that label. So the original six books launched what
has since become a continuing enterprise, the essence of which was
to allow different authors to speak for themselves instead of trying to
summarize under one umbrella what was obviously a rapidly growing and highly diverse field.

By the early 1980s, the series included nineteen titles. OD was
growing by leaps and bounds, and it was expanding into all kinds of
organizational areas and technologies of intervention. By this time,
many textbooks existed as well that tried to capture core concepts of
the field, but we felt that diversity and innovation were still the more
salient aspects of OD.

Now as we move towards the end of the century, our series includes over forty titles, and we are beginning to see some real con-
vergence in the underlying assumptions of OD. As we observe how
different professionals working in different kinds of organizations
and occupational communities make their case, we will see that we
are still far from having a single "theory" of organizational development. Yet, a set of common assumptions is surfacing. We are beginning to see patterns in what works and what does not work, and we
are becoming more articulate about these patterns. We are also seeing
the field increasingly connected to other organizational sciences and
disciplines such as information technology, coordination theory, and
organization theory. In the early 1990s, we saw several important
themes described with Ciampa's *Total Quality* showing the important

link to employee involvement in continuous improvement; Johansen et al.'s *Leading Business Teams* exploring the important arena of electronic information tools for teamwork; Tjosvold's *The Conflict-Positive Organization* showing how conflict management can turn conflict into constructive action; Hirschhorn's *Managing in the New Team Environment* building bridges to group psychodynamic theory; and Bushe and Shani's *Parallel Learning Structures* providing an integrative theory for large-scale organizational change.

We continue this trend with four revisions and three new books. Burke has taken his highly successful *Organization Development* into new realms with an updating and expansion. Galbraith has updated and enlarged his classic theory of how information management is at the heart of organization design with his new edition entitled *Competing with Flexible Lateral Organizations*. And Dyer has written an important third edition of his classic book on *Team Building*. In addition, Rashford and Coghlan have introduced the important concept of levels of organizational complexity as a basis for intervention theory in their book entitled *The Dynamics of Organizational Levels*. Woodworth and Meek in *Creating Labor-Management Partnerships* take us into the critical realm of how OD can help in labor relations, an area that's of increasing importance as productivity issues become critical for global competitiveness. Organization development is making important links with related fields. In *Integrated Strategic Change* by Worley, Hitchin and Ross, they powerfully demonstrate how the field of OD must be linked to the field of strategy by reviewing the role of OD at each stage of the strategy planning and implementation process. Finally, an important link to organizational learning is provided by a new version of the classic book by Argyris and Schön entitled *Organizational Learning II: Theory, Method, and Practice*.

We welcome these revisions and new titles and will continue to explore the various frontiers of organization development with additional titles as we identify themes that are relevant to the ever more difficult problem of helping organizations to remain effective in an increasingly turbulent environment.

New York, New York   Richard H. Beckhard
Cambridge, Massachusetts   Edgar H. Schein

Preface

Twenty or twenty-five years ago organizational learning was a rare species among ideas, relegated along with such closely allied notions as "societal," "public," and "institutional" learning to the popular literature of social change. With few exceptions—among the more notable of whom were Michel Crozier, Philip Herbst, and Herbert Simon—organizational learning was largely absent from the scholarly literature of organizational research. As late as 1978 when our *Organizational Learning* was first published, such well-respected scholars as Tom Burns and Geoffrey Vickers found the idea confusing and, in some ways, repugnant.

Now in the mid-1990s, it is conventional wisdom that business firms, governments, nongovernmental organizations, schools, health care systems, regions, even whole nations and supranational institutions need to adapt to changing environments, draw lessons from past successes and failures, detect and correct the errors of the past, anticipate and respond to impending threats, conduct experiments, engage in continuing innovation, build and realize images of a desirable future. There is virtual consensus that we are all subject to a "learning imperative," and in the academic as well as the practical world, organizational learning has become an idea in good currency.

The sources of this dramatic shift in views and attitudes are somewhat different in each of the fields of social action. Clearly much of the shift is attributable to a greatly amplified awareness that business firms, economic regions, governments, and all of the groups dependent on them, are caught up in a global economy where the pace of competition is savage and swift, where the most apparently solid companies and, indeed, whole industries can disappear or suffer decline because they fail to detect and respond to early warning signals that call for rapid change. By the 1980s competitive shocks to giants in the automotive and computer industries had given managers of large multinational companies a visceral sense that the nature of the competitive game in which they were involved had radically changed. They were going to have to remake their organizations in a more fundamental way than they had imagined, and the demand for organizational transformation would be continual in a business world that had moved "beyond the stable state."

At the same time, in the schools of business and management, strategic planning and competitive analysis were becoming established as disciplines; and already-established disciplines such as finance, accounting, manufacturing, and management information systems, were becoming more sophisticated and rigorous in their diagnostic methods. As these fields developed, the implementation of their principles and techniques became a problem. And as their focus expanded to include implementation, they, too, began to adopt organizational learning as an idea in good currency. In the field of strategy, for example, leading thinkers began to realize that strategic planning had to be rethought in terms of organizational change. In his *Managing the Resource Allocation Process,* Joseph Bower described how win-lose games of interests and powers, played at the middle-management level, were critical to the shaping of corporate strategy; he identified the equivalent of what we call "limited learning systems"—treating them as fixtures of the status quo. The recent writings of authors such as Russell Ackoff, Igor Ansoff, Edward Bowman, and Andrew Pettigrew reflect a growing agreement that the development of strategy would have to become an active, iterative process involving whole organizations—hence, requiring organizational learning.

In other organizational spheres it was also becoming apparent by the 1980s that change and turbulence, long-familiar features of the language of management and organization theory, had now become salient features of the organizational environment, requiring dramatic increases in organizational capability for adaptation. In fields such as public administration, health care, social services, environmental management, and education, demands for cost reduction were causing severe cutbacks, while rising dissatisfaction with the outputs of these services were provoking attempts at radical restructuring. The effects of these changes and demands for change were felt at the levels of individual action, organizational systems, and interorganizational fields.

In all areas of social action, there has evolved a powerful image of organizations caught up in reciprocal transactions with the environments in which they are embedded. Organizational success, however defined, is seen as depending on the organization's ability to see things in new ways, gain new understandings, and produce new patterns of behavior—all on a *continuing* basis and in a way that engages the organization as a *whole.*

The burgeoning literature that has grown up around organizational learning in the past twenty-five years can be divided into two separate branches. One branch of the literature—prescriptive, practice-oriented, value-committed, sometimes messianic, and largely uncritical—treats the phrase, "learning organization," as catchword for whatever it is the front-running Japanese, or other, organizations are doing and whatever the rest of the world needs to do to catch up with them. The second branch, also probably stimulated by the ideas in good currency triggered by the wave of the new global competition, treats organizational learning as a research topic for scholars, mainly in schools of management and business. The second branch tends to be distant from practice, skeptical of first-branch claims, nonprescriptive, and neutral with respect to its definition of learning—that is, open to the view that learning may be good or bad, linked or not linked, to effective action or desirable outcomes.

Although the communities of practice that make up the two branches of the bifurcated field of organizational learning tend to be insulated from each other, they converge on certain key ideas, some of which they have drawn from our earlier writings. Both branches tend to pick up, for example, our emphasis on the importance of recognizing, surfacing, criticizing, and restructuring organizational theories of action (or the closely related term, "mental models.") Both branches tend to pick up our distinction between single- and double-loop learning; they speak, for example, of lower- and higher-level learning or of paradigm-constrained and paradigm-breaking learning. Even scholars who have been highly skeptical of the possibilities of higher-level organizational learning have recently evinced a cautious movement toward its acceptance.[1] The two branches of the field also converge on a certain blindness toward, or avoidance of, the factors we regard as most critical to the successful achievement and maintenance of higher-level organizational learning: the behavioral world of

---

[1] For example, Barbara Leavitt and James March in their 1988 review article on "organizational learning" (Ann. Rev. Sociol. 1988. 14:319–40) observe that "...there is adequate evidence that the lessons of history as encoded in routines are an important basis for the intelligence of organizations. Despite the problems, organizationals learn." (p. 336)

the organization and the theories-in-use of individuals that reinforce and are reinforced by it.

From our point of view, which cuts across the two branches, four questions lie at the center of the field of organizational learning:

1. What is an organization that it may learn?
2. In what ways, if at all, are real-world organizations capable of learning?
3. Among the kinds of learning of which organizations are, or might become capable, which ones are desirable?
4. By what means can organizations develop their capability for the kinds of learning they consider desirable?

The two branches have worked out an informal division of intellectual labor according to which questions taken up by one branch are ignored by the other. The proponents of the "learning organization" do not, for the most part, ask what an organization is that it may learn. They do not seem to think that the task of developing a learning organization requires a fundamental rethinking of what an organization is in the first place. Nor do they appear to worry about what kinds of organizational learning are desirable. They describe desiderata of the learning organization—flat organization, local autonomy, trust and cooperation across functional boundaries—but they seldom go deeply into the meanings of these terms or the nature of the change processes to which they refer. Most advocates of the learning organization do not puzzle over these questions because the advocates start from *answers* to them.

The scholarly students of organizational learning, intending to be distant from practice, nonprescriptive, and value-neutral, focus on those questions the first branch ignores: What does "organizational learning" mean? How is organizational learning at all feasible? What kinds of organizational learning are desirable, and for whom and with what chance of actual occurrence? The scholars of organizational learning generally adopt a skeptical stance toward these questions; their skepticism revolves around three main challenges that correspond to three of the four questions we place at the center of the field:

1. Some researchers argue that the very idea of organizational learning is contradictory, paradoxical, or devoid of meaning.
2. Other researchers who accept organizational learning as a meaningful term doubt that real-world organizations actually engage in it, or can be capable of doing so.

3. A third challenge accepts organizational learning as a meaningful notion and agrees that organizations do sometimes learn; what it denies is that organizational learning is always, or ever, beneficent.

In contrast to the polar positions of learning-advocates and learning-skeptics, we try to combine a practice-oriented, value-committed stance with a skeptical attitude toward many of the claims and tacit assumptions of those who currently promote a version of the learning organization. These are the main elements of our approach:

1. We recognize an overarching sense of organizational learning that refers broadly to an organization's acquisition of understandings, know-how, techniques, and practices of any kind and by whatever means. In this sense organizational learning is pervasive and, in and of itself, neither good nor bad. Indeed, much of what would count as organizational learning, in the overarching sense, works counter to the kinds of organizational learning we consider most desirable.

2. Our approach to organizational learning is normative and practice-oriented. We are mainly interested in *productive* organizational learning, recognizing that the meaning of this term can be defined only in general outline and requires specification in each particular context in which it may occur. We want to understand how this kind of learning can be generated in real-world organizations and how practitioners can help to foster it. But we are also skeptical of many of the claims made by advocates of the learning organization, and we acknowledge many of the threats to productive learning that skeptical researchers have identified. Our normative interests lead us, however, not only to describe the patterns of behavior that threaten productive organizational learning but to learn how to change them.

3. Because we attempt to combine the two branches of the field of organizational learning, we adopt a method of research that combines elements and attitudes that are often kept apart. Our research method proceeds from directly observable behavior in particular cases *and* it aims at producing generalizable, empirically disconfirmable propositions. We strive for a general theory of organizational learning useful to practitioners who seek to enhance the kinds of

learning we regard as productive. For this reason our approach deals with patterns of behavior common to all organizations, while it also incorporates a theory of rare events. Indeed, it must take the form of action research that aims at generalizable understandings of organizational phenomena through the attempt, in collaboration with practitioners, to *produce* the rare events associated with productive organizational learning.

4. We take individual practitioners as centrally important to organizational learning, because it is their thinking and acting that influence the acquisition of capability for productive learning at the organizational level. Unless we begin at this point, we have no chance of producing knowledge useful to practitioners.

5. We recognize the complex interactions that occur between individual and organizational learning. We see the causal arrow pointing in both directions: the learning of individuals who interact with one another is essential to organizational learning, which feeds back to influence learning at the individual level. "What is an organization that it may learn?" We answer in the first instance by reference to the political conditions under which individuals can function as agents of organizational action. Within this political framework, we recognize the importance of organizational cultures that serve as holding environments for knowledge, attitudes, and values. And we include in "culture" the critically important organizational artifacts of maps, memories, and programs.

6. Hence, our focus is on organizational *inquiry*. We use this term in the Deweyan sense as a highly general characterization of the exercise of human intelligence in the world—the intertwining of thought and action by which we move from doubt to the resolution of doubt. Organizational inquiry occurs when individuals in organizations inquire, in interaction with one another, in an effort to produce productive organizational learning outcomes.[2]

---

[2] See John Dewey, *Logic: The Theory of Inquiry* (New York: Holt, Rinehart and Winston, 1938).

conflict!

Within the process of inquiry, we give special importance to the experience of *surprise,* the mismatch of outcome to expectation,which we see as essential to the process by which people can come to see, think, and act in new ways.

7. Organizational inquiry, in our usage, is broad enough in scope to include kinds of inquiry central to a variety of types of learning usefully distinguished by recent scholars, as well as to forms of organizational intelligence that are sometimes distinguished from learning in a narrow sense of the term.

8. We recognize the importance of distinguishing between coming to see things in new ways and coming to *act* on the basis of insight. Threats to productive organizational learning can undermine valid inference as well as productive action. But such threats are of interest not only to researchers but to practitioners, whom we see as inquirers capable of reflecting on their own inquiry ("inquiring into inquiry," as Dewey put it). Because we regard practitioners as reflective inquirers, we are also attentive to their implicit views of causality and causal inference, which differ from the uses of these terms in normal social science.

learning to learn

9. Our approach to productive organizational learning focuses on both single- and double-loop learning: some kinds of learning take place within existing systems of values and the action frames in which values are embedded, while other kinds involve changes in values and frames and call for reflective inquiry that cuts across incongruent frames.

10. At the levels of interpersonal and organizational behavior, we emphasize the distinction and the complex interactions that occur between types of single- and double-loop learning.

One kind of double-loop learning consists of restructuring values and fundamental assumptions built into an organization's theory-in-use, which includes its strategy, values, views of its environment, and understandings of its own competences. This kind of learning may include the kinds of transformations toward increased openness, flexibility, local autonomy, and inquiry-orientation envisaged by the advocates of the learning organization.

We believe that the organizational double-loop learning involved in such transformations depends on the organization's *learning system,* the behavioral world "draped over" its stucture, information network, and systems of incentives. Learning systems may promote or inhibit organizational double-loop learning. Their transformation depends on double-loop learning in processes of organizational inquiry, a shift from inquiry-inhibiting to inquiry-enhancing theories-in-use. In the kind of collaborative action research that we advocate, researchers and practitioners inquire into such first-order errors as competence traps and superstititous learning (Leavitt and March, 1988), as well as into the second-order errors in processes of organizational inquiry that lead to the production and reproduction of first-order errors.

> 11. We distingish analytically between these two kinds of double-loop learning in order to explore their causal interactions. We think we detect in both branches of research on organizational learning a tendency to avoid noticing, or giving sufficient importance to, these interactions. In our view the ability of real-world organizations to engage in productive organizational learning, to achieve their own learning objectives or implement the principles and techniques advanced by learning-oriented organizational researchers, is primarily constrained by the inquiry-inhibiting theories-in-use that shape normal patterns of organizational inquiry under conditions of threat or embarrassment.

Nevertheless, we see that interesting questions may be raised about the possibility of bypassing double-loop learning in organizational inquiry. For example, advanced information technology makes it possible to collect and distribute data about the relative contribution of an organizational unit to corporate costs or profits. Can such information systems facilitate productive organizational learning in ways that sidestep the restructuring of limited learning systems? Are there structures of incentives, in the sense described by Albert Hirschman (1970), that tend to call forth the kinds of behavior essential to double-loop organizational learning? May organizational ecologies tend toward certain patterns of selective adaptation in ways that require no special reference to individual or interpersonal inquiry?

These questions, among others, we pursue throughout the four parts of this book. In Part I we introduce our conceptual framework, both for organizational learning and for the relationship between research and practice, and illustrate these concepts in a case that describes the long-term evolution by an industrial firm and the roles played in that evolution by organizational inquiry. In Part II we introduce and illustrate concepts central to limited learning—defensive reasoning and Model I theory-in-use; organizational defensive routines and limited (O-I) organizational learning systems. Part III presents a brief classroom-based example, and a sustained organizational example of the shift from defensive to productive reasoning, from Model I to Model II theory-in-use, and from limited to more productive organizational learning systems. In Part IV we review the recent history of the field of organizational learning, and frame controversial issues and challenges that have arisen within it. We analyze these issues from our perspective on organizational learning, arguing for a collaborative action-research approach and for the fundamental importance of a view that links individual and interpersonal inquiry, and their underlying theories-in-use, to patterns of productive and unproductive learning at higher levels of aggregation.

Acknowledgments

We would like to thank Michael Beer, Robert Burgelman, and Andrew Van de Ven for reading and responding to drafts of our commentary on their case studies.

Cambridge, Massachusetts	C.A.
Cambridge, Massachusetts	D.A.S.

Contents

Part I   An Introduction to Organizational Learning   1

1   What Is An Organization That It May Learn?   1
Some Preliminary Distinctions   3
Individual and Organizational Learning   4
Organizations As Collectivities   6
Organizational Action   8
Organizational Inquiry   11
Organizational Knowledge   12
Organizational Learning Again   15
Near Misses   17
Productive Organizational Learning   18
Single- and Double-Loop Learning   20
Additional Considerations   25
Organizational Deuterolearning   28

2   Turning the Researcher/Practitioner Relationship On Its Head   30
Deweyan Inquiry   30
Detecting and Correcting Error   31
Organizational Inquiry   33
The Researcher/Practitioner Relationship   34
Practitioners As Inquirers   35
Causality and Causal Inference   37
Practitioner/Researcher Collaboration in Action Research   43
Appropriate Rigor in Collaborative Action Research   46

3   The Mercury Case: What Facilitates or Inhibits Productive Organizational Learning   52
Inquiring into the Process of New Business Development   53
Perspectives On Organizational Learning   64

Part II Defensive Reasoning and the Theoretical Framework that Explains It—Model I and O-I   73

4 Defensive Reasoning In Individuals   75
A Generic Dilemma In Double-track Research   75
Features of Our Research Method   76
A Relatively Simple Paper-and-Pencil Method for Obtaining Valid Information About Individual Theories of Action   78

5 The Case of the CIO: Primary and Secondary Inhibitory Loops   85
Case Description   85
Reflecting on the Action of the CIO and His Reports   88
The Primary Inhibitory Loop   89
The Secondary Inhibitory Loop   97
How the Technical-Objective Dimension of Organizational Life Is Smothered By Individual-Organizational Defensive Routines   103
Conclusion   106

Part III Inquiry-Enhancing Intervention and Its Theoretical Basis   109

Prologue   Intervention Toward O-II Learning Systems   111
O-II Learning Systems   111
Model II Theory-in-Use   117

6 The Classroom: Intervention for Learning and Research   122
The Focus of the Testing   122
The Class As A Setting for Relevant Tests   124
Transcript of Class Discussion: Dealing with the Left-hand Column   125
Intervening for Testing and Learning: Class II   140
Conclusions   147

7 A Comprehensive Model II Intervention   150
Design of the Research/Intervention Activities   151
The Feedback Process   154
Constructing the Action Map   156
The Directors' Action Map   158
Discussions During the Feedback Session   165
Summary of the First Seminar   168
The Second Seminar   171
Analysis of the Discussion of the Cases   172
Conducting Learning Experiments   175

Part IV Strengths and Weaknesses of Consultation and Research in the Field of Organizational Learning 177

Prologue 179

8 The Evolving Field of Organizational Learning 180
The Literature of "The Learning Organization" 180
The Scholarly Literature of Organizational Learning 188
Conclusion 198

9 Making Sense of Limited Learning 200
Controversial Issues of Organizational Learning 200
Research Studies of Organizational Adaptation and Learning 202
Studies of Interventions Aimed At Promoting Productive Organizational Learning 222
Lessons from the Two Sets of Studies 242

10 Strategy and Learning: Making Prescriptions Actionable by Wim Overseer 251
The Split in the Field of Strategic Management 251
Realizing Strategy As Probing the Environment 256
Requirements for Organizational Learning 258
Learning Strategically: The Contributions of the Theory of Action Perspective to Strategic Management 273
An Action-based Research Agenda for Strategic Management 277

Afterword 280
The Learning Paradox 280
Directions for Future Research 286

References 289

Name Index 296

Subject Index 299

Part I

An Introduction
to Organizational Learning

1

What Is An Organization That It May Learn?

Some Preliminary Distinctions

"Learning" may signify either a *product* (something learned) or the *process* that yields such a product. In the first sense, we might ask, "What have we learned?" referring to an accumulation of information in the form of knowledge or skill; in the second sense, "How do we learn?" referring to a learning activity that may be well or badly performed. When we speak of "drawing lessons from experience," for example, we implicitly treat "lessons" as learning product and "lesson drawing" as learning process. The product/process ambiguity, which cuts across the many different meanings scholars and practitioners give to learning in general and "organizational learning" in particular, is important to every other question with which we shall be concerned—for example, what forms of organizational learning are desirable, and what constitutes evidence for their existence.

Generically an organization may be said to learn when it acquires information (knowledge, understanding, know-how, techniques, or practices) of any kind and by whatever means. In this overarching sense, all organizations learn, for good or ill, whenever they add to their store of information, and there is no stricture on how the addition may occur. The generic schema of organizational learning includes some informational content, a *learning product;* a *learning process* which consists in acquiring, processing, and storing information; and a *learner* to whom the learning process is attributed. Learning may be attributed to an agent inside or outside the organization, or even to the information itself, as when one says that "new ideas invade an organization." We may also speak of the particular kind of learning that consists of "unlearning:" acquiring information

3

that leads to subtracting something (an obsolete strategy, for example) from an organization's existing store of knowledge.

Within this generic schema, an important species of organizational learning consists in an organization's improvement of its task performance over time. Such *instrumental learning* also rests on a schema, which refers to an action's effectiveness in achieving its intended objectives and to criteria and measures for assessing that effectiveness. The action must be of an identifiable type (for example, filling an order, sending a bill, or producing an airplane), for otherwise we could not speak sensibly of its repetition, implicit in the idea of improved performance. There must be an agent that deliberately seeks to improve performance and an intermediate process of deliberate thought and action ("trial and error," for example) through which improvement is achieved. Evidence of improvement consists in data that permit a comparison of performance at different points in time. Instrumental learning is the species of organizational learning favored by economists, implicit in their "learning curves," which originated in the field of industrial engineering.

From a normative perspective, however, instrumental organizational learning should be taken only as a point of departure. Instrumental learning may be good or bad depending on the values used to define "improvement." The distinction between single- and double-loop learning, which we introduce later in this chapter, differentiates instrumental learning within a constant frame of values from learning to change the values that define "improvement." The distinction also differentiates the values of learning outcomes from values inherent in the learning process.

Individual and Organizational Learning

To the distinguished social scientists who were repelled by the idea when we first broached it in the early 1970s, "organizational learning" seemed to smell of some quasi-mystical, Hegelian personification of the collectivity. Surely, they felt, it is *individuals* who may be said to learn, just as to think, reason, or hold opinions. To them, it seemed paradoxical, if not perverse, to attribute learning to *organizations.*

Yet in everyday conversation, as well as in scholarly discourse, it is increasingly common to find people attributing to teams, departments, or whole organizations, such activities as thinking, reasoning, remembering, or learning. They say, for example, "The marketing department realized that sales were about to decline," or "The administration learned to consult the faculty before announcing a re-organization." In everyday conversation, such statements may be taken as shorthand for more complex, perhaps tacit, processes. But when scholars treat organizational entities as knowers or learners, they seem to be consciously sidestepping the problem of relating individual to organizational phenomena.

How can it seem natural and unproblematic to attribute thinking, knowing, or learning to an organization? Two strategies seem to be involved:

1. adopt the stance of a distant spectator so that the organizational unit or subunit can be seen as a monolithic entity and
2. treat that entity as an impersonal agent.

To treat an organizational entity as an impersonal agent is to adopt a kind of machine language, as when one says, for example, that "an organizational routine survived and established dominance over other routines," or that "general management selected one of the proposals generated by R&D." The increasing use of such language seems to reflect the rising influence of the computer. With the pervasiveness of computers in organizations comes a tendency to employ computer language to refer to phenomena that used to be attributed to thought, will, deliberation, feelings, or habits. People in organizations now say familiarly, "I am in sales mode," "I'm not programmed for this task," "This is our default option." If computers may be said to act, think, remember, or know, and if computational systems may be casually treated as intelligent or stupid, then why not organizations or parts of organizations? The power of the computer metaphor may underlie the growing tendency to treat organizations and their parts as impersonal agents. — *reflects customer attitude to Public Sector*

A spectator's distant stance toward an organization is consistent with, and perhaps necessary for, its treatment as a monolithic, impersonal agent. For example, economists concerned with the theory of the firm and theorists of business strategy tend to see the business organization as though from a great distance, enabling them to see it whole, but also as a black box. They speak of firms as agents competing with other firms, adopting or changing strategies in order to gain competetive advantage in a market environment. All such distant theories of organizational behavior, operating at high levels of social aggregation, may make useful contributions to economic theory or even to policy analysis. What they do not do or seek to do is to describe and explain the processes within an organization that give rise to patterns of activity seen, in the aggregate, as the organization's knowing, thinking, remembering, or learning. Nor do such theories say anything about how to achieve "productive learning," however that term may be defined.

If theorists of organizational learning seek to be of use to practitioners, they must somehow link organizational learning to the practitioners' thought and action. And even if they do not wish to be of use to practitioners, as we shall argue in Chapter 9, they should explore these linkages if only to provide a coherent and robust theoretical account of the aggregate organizational phenomena they *do* seek to explain.

If we shift from a distant spectator's viewpoint, from which organizations and their parts can be seen as impersonal agents, and come close enough to become aware of the individual and interpersonal processes that underlie an organization's behavior, we reawaken the paradox of organizational learning. Perhaps this term is a metaphor, on a par with "organizational" force or entropy. Does it make sense to say that organizations *literally* know, remember, think, or learn? How could we test whether they do so? A literal understanding of organizational learning requires that we spell out these processes and conditions.

However troublesome it may be, the paradox that hovers around the notion of organizational learning constitutes its potential interest to organization theory, for it pushes against the boundaries of our usual understandings. In order to explore organizational learning, we must rethink what we mean by organization. We must ask what an organization is that it may be said to learn.

Organizations As Collectivities

One might begin such a quest by arguing that, since organizations are collectivities made up of individuals, they learn something when their individual members, or a substantial fraction of them, learn it. But a moment's thought suggests that such an equivalence cannot hold.

In many cases when the knowledge held by individuals fails to enter into the stream of distinctively organizational thought and action, organizations know *less* than their members do. For example, a social service bureaucracy may continue to operate on the basis of categories of clients, such as "single parents," "abused children," or "dysfunctional families," even though social workers in the agency know very well that these categories fail to capture critically important characteristics of the people they serve. In some cases an organi-

Groupthink

zation cannot seem to learn what *all* of its members know. When a mistake becomes "too big to admit"—in the case of large-scale investments in technology or massive projects of economic development in the Third World—an organization may persist in a course of action that all of its members recognize as foolhardy. Conversely, there are situations in which an organization seems to know far *more* than its individual members. Structures, procedures, and memories built into the fabric of organizations such as the army or the telephone company may permit an organization to perform brilliantly, at least for a time, even when its individual members seem far from brilliant.

Such considerations may suggest that we should think of organizational learning in terms of the "organizational environments" within which individuals think and act. Organizations have been conceived as behavioral settings for human interaction, fields for the exercise of power, systems of institutionalized incentives that govern individual behavior, or socio-cultural contexts in which individuals engage in symbolic interaction. From one or more of these perspectives, we may be able to describe the conditions under which, within an organizational environment, the thought and action of individuals yield organizational learning. But such an approach still leaves us with the problem of linking individual to organizational processes.

We might consider solving this problem by treating organizational learning as the prerogative of a person at the top who learns "for" the organization as a whole. But the bosses of large and complex organizations often complain of being unable to communicate to their subordinates the lessons they themselves have acquired. Bosses may follow one another in rapid succession, while the organization beneath them remains very much the same. And when something that looks like organizational learning occurs, it seems, not infrequently, to have little to do with the person at the top.

Alternatively, we might think of clusters of individual members as the agents who learn "for" the larger organization to which they belong. For example, groups of middle-level employees may discover, in interaction with one another, how to solve a production problem or improve product quality. Yet the learning outcome generated by a group of individuals may not be diffused throughout the larger organization. And even when the results of a group's investigation are broadly diffused, they may not enter into the stream of debates and deliberations that affect an organization's policies, programs, or practices.

We are still left with the problem of determining under what conditions the thought and action of individuals become distinctively organizational.

Organizational Action

The idea of organizational action is logically prior to that of organizational learning, because learning itself—thinking, knowing, or remembering—is a kind of action, and because the performance of an observable action new to an organization is the most decisive test of whether a particular instance of organizational learning has occurred. How can we know what it means for an organization to learn, then, unless we know what it means for it to take action?

Does an organization "act" whenever one of its members acts? If so, there would appear to be very little difference between an organization and the collection of individuals who comprise its members. Yet it is clear that some collections of people constitute organizations and others do not. Furthermore, even when a collection of individuals clearly belongs to an organization, these individuals may do many things (such as eat, sleep, go for walks, gossip with their friends) which do not qualify as instances of organizational action.

Organizations are not merely collections of individuals, yet there is no organization without such collections. Organizational action cannot be reduced to the actions of individuals, even of all the individuals that make up the organization, yet there is no organizational action without individual action. When, then, does it make sense to say that a collection of individuals constitutes an organization that acts?

Consider a mob of students who are holding a spontaneous protest against their university's financial aid policy. At what point do they cease to be a mob and begin to be an organization? The mob is a collectivity, a collection of people who may run, shout, and mill about together. But it is a collectivity that cannot make a decision or take an action in its own name, and its boundaries are vague and diffuse. The mob begins to resemble an organization as it begins to meet three conditions. The individual members of the mob must

1. devise agreed-upon procedures for making decisions in the name of the collectivity,

2. delegate to individuals the authority to act for the collectivity, and

3. set boundaries between the collectivity and the rest of the world.

As these conditions are met, members of the collectivity begin to become a recognizable "we" that can make decisions and translate their decisions into action.

When the members of the mob become an identifiable vehicle for collective decision and action, they become, in the ancient Greek sense of the term, a *polis.* Before an organization can be anything else, it must be "political," because it is as a political entity that the collectivity can take organizational action. Then it is the individuals who decide and act, but they do these things on behalf of the collectivity, as its agents. And in order for individuals to be able to decide and act in the name of the collectivity, there must be rules that determine the boundaries of the collectivity, when a decision has been made and when authority for action has been delegated to individuals. Insofar as members of a collectivity create such rules, which we call "constitutional," and become a *polis,* they have organized.

The rule-making that brings organizations into being need not be conscious, and constitutional rules need not be explicit. What is essential is that the members' behavior be *rule-governed* in the crucial respects. If the students milling about in front of the dean's office know how to organize, something they probably learned to do as children playing in a neighborhood, they will spontaneously work out enacted rules for decision, delegation, and membership. Their rules may well remain tacit; there will be no reason to make them explicit unless something happens (a surprise, a crisis, an influx of new people) that calls them into question. So long as there is continuity in the rules that govern the behavior of individual members, the organization will persist, even though some of its members may come and go. And the organization's existence need not be compromised (might even be enhanced) by the presence of vagueness, ambiguity, or inconsistency in those rules.

By establishing rule-governed ways of deciding, delegating, and setting the boundaries of membership, a collectivity becomes an organization capable of acting. But if we wish to apply this theory of organizational action to the familiar organizations of our society, we must make some further distinctions.

The group of protesting students may form an organization that lasts no longer than their protest; their organization may come to an end, for example, when the dean agrees to hold a university-wide meeting on financial aid. Gian-Francesco Lanzara (1985) used the term, "ephemeral," to describe such temporary, informal organizations. Ephemeral organizations may arise spontaneously in response to a crisis, such as the Abruzzi earthquake in Lanzara's example, springing up overnight and disappearing just as quickly. Yet they function for a time as cooperative systems.

As Chester Barnard pointed out (1938), organizations are a species that belong to the genus of systems in which individuals cooperate to perform tasks that arise repetitively (such as making coffee and distributing it to the victims of an earthquake). Every cooperative system embodies a strategy for dividing up, according to one principle or another, the tasks it regularly performs and delegating the components to individual members, thereby establishing organizational roles. The organization's "task system," its pattern of interconnected roles, is at once a division of labor and a design for the performance of work. This design shares the properties of other designed artifacts. It is more or less complex; it involves a multiplicity of variables, values, and constraints; it is subject to variation and change; and it may be represented prior to its enactment—"planned in advance"—or designed and redesigned while in operation.

In contrast to ephemeral organizations, an *agency* is a collection of people that makes decisions, delegates authority for action, and monitors membership, all on a continuing basis. It is a collective vehicle for the regular performance of recurrent tasks. Households, the exemplar of organizations, are agencies, as are the durable, cooperative systems formed by individuals in folk societies. Amish communities, for example, form cooperative building teams that are regularly entrusted with building houses, silos, or corn sheds. Usually they operate without a formal plan or identified leaders. They work out their situation-specific task systems through talk and gestures on the spot, in the presence of site and materials. Such informal agencies are especially interesting because they suggest the existence of culturally specific schemas of organizing that are familiar to all members of the culture and capable of being reproduced again and again, with infinite variation.

Agencies also include the entities we more familiarly treat as organizations: business firms, churches, schools, armies, manufacturing plants, labor unions, social service institutions, or government bureaus. These are formal organizations, whose rules are to some degree explicit and grounded in the legal system of the society. These organizations are formally identified as "legal persons." Their task systems are complex, and they possess in varying degrees the properties that Max Weber attributed to bureaucracies: a clear distinction between persons and the roles they occupy, a complex and detailed

Project Teams

articulation of roles and rules, proceduralized task systems, hierarchical and pyramidally organized layers of authority (Weber, in A.M. Henderson and Talcott Parsons, 1957). Such complex task systems may be tightly or loosely coupled, rigid or variable. All of them, however, fall within our basic definition of the conditions for organizational action: they are cooperative systems governed by the consitutional principles of a polis.

Organizational Inquiry

If a collectivity meets these conditions, so that its members can *act* for it, then it may be said to learn when its members *learn* for it, carrying out on its behalf a process of inquiry that results in a learning product.

We use "inquiry" here not in the colloquial sense of scientific or juridical investigation but in a more fundamental sense that originates in the work of John Dewey (1938): the intertwining of thought and action that proceeds from doubt to the resolution of doubt. In Deweyan inquiry (which we discuss more fully in the following chapter), doubt is construed as the experience of a "problematic situation," triggered by a mismatch between the expected results of action and the results actually achieved. Such a mismatch—a surprise, as we experience it—blocks the flow of spontaneous activity and gives rise to thought and further action aimed at re-establishing that flow.

Inquiry does not become organizational unless undertaken by individuals who function as agents of an organization according to its prevailing roles and rules. Individuals may also inquire in ways that remain separate from the organization to which they belong. Consider, for example, an agency that produces television programs for use in schools. Some of the agency's staff members may wonder what classroom teachers actually do with their programs. Nevertheless, their explorations may remain unconnected to the stream of distinctively organizational activity because their superiors display no interest in learning what happens to the agency's programs so long as schools continue to pay their yearly fees. Conversely, what an organization learns may remain inaccessible to any particular individual, as when staff members are kept ignorant of the reasons for a change in programming policies.

When individual and organizational inquiry do intersect, individual inquiry feeds into and helps to shape organizational inquiry, which then feeds back to shape the further inquiry carried out by individuals. If, for example, members of the educational television agency get their managers interested in probing how teachers use their programs, the agency may adopt new practices for deciding on program content, which may lead agency staff, in turn, to involve teachers in collaborative program design.

Organizational Knowledge

The output of organizational inquiry may take the form of a change in thinking and acting that yields a change in the design of organizational practices. For example, a telecommunications company may experience a large-scale network failure. Its investigation of the causes of the failure may result in redesigned procedures for developing and maintaining network software or for new ways of detecting threats to network reliability.

Under what conditions does such knowledge become "organizational?" We recognize two distinct but complementary answers to this question.

First, organizations function in several ways as *holding environments for knowledge,* including the knowledge gained through organizational inquiry. Such knowledge may be held in the minds of individual members. If it is held in only this way, it may well be lost to the organization when the relevant individuals leave; an organization may be devastated, for example, by the departure of the one person who really knows how the budget works. But knowledge may also be held in an organization's files, which record its actions, decisions, regulations, and policies as well as in the maps, formal and informal, through which organizations make themselves understandable to themselves and others. Finally, organizational knowledge may be held in the physical objects that members use as references and guideposts as they go about their business. Roger Barker's study of behavioral settings (1960) showed how everyday knowledge is embedded in once-familiar places, such as the corner drugstore—in the presence of the soda fountain, the prescription counter, the candy display. Everyone who belongs to the culture in which that setting has its place knows how to deliver the appropriate behavior. More recent studies by Sylvia Scribner and her colleagues (1982) show how workers may use objects in the workplace as things to think with. Scribner describes how veteran milkmen perform the calculations required to fill complicated orders far more rapidly than their school-trained coworkers by making use of visual patterns they discern in standard milk containers. The results of inquiry carried out by individuals may be embedded in an organization's holding environment for knowledge in any or all of these ways.

Second, *organizations directly represent knowledge* in the sense that they embody strategies for performing complex tasks that might have been performed in other ways. This is true not only of an overall task system but of its detailed components. Organizational knowledge is embedded in routines and practices which may be inspected and decoded even when the individuals who carry them out are unable to put them into words. For example, a sugar-refining company embodies in its practices particular answers to questions such as how to grow, harvest, and refine cane, or how to distribute and market refined sugar. In this sense, any given organization represents answers to a set of questions or solutions to a set of problems.

Such organizational task knowledge may be variously represented as systems of beliefs that underlie action, as prototypes from which actions are derived, or as procedural prescriptions for action in the manner of a computer program. We have chosen to represent such knowledge through what we call "theories of action," which have the advantage of including strategies of action, the values that govern the choice of strategies and the assumptions on which they are based. We define a theory of action in terms of a particular situation, S, a particular consequence, intended in that situation, C, and an action strategy, A, for obtaining consequence C in situation S. The general form of a theory of action is: If you intend to produce consequence C in situation S, then do A. Two further elements enter into the general schema of a theory of action: the values attributed to C that make it seem desirable as an end-in-view and the underlying assumptions, or model of the world, that make it plausible that action A will produce consequence C in situation S.

Theory of action, whether it applies to organizations or individuals, may take two different forms. By "espoused theory" we mean the theory of action which is advanced to explain or justify a given pattern of activity. By "theory-in-use" we mean the theory of action which is implicit in the performance of that pattern of activity. A theory-in-use is not a "given." It must be constructed from observation of the pattern of action in question. From the evidence gained by observing any pattern of action, one might construct alternative theories-in-use which are, in effect, hypotheses to be tested against the data of observation. In the case of organizations, a theory-in-use must be constructed from observation of the patterns of interactive behavior produced by individual members of the organization, insofar as their behavior is governed by formal or informal rules for collective decision, delegation, and membership.

We can say that the values, action strategies, and assumptions embedded in the sugar refining company's routine activities constitute its theory-in-use for cane growing, for distributing and marketing, and for its other functions. Taken together, these components make up the organization's *instrumental theory-in-use*. This instrumental theory includes norms for corporate performance (for example, margin of profit or return on investment), strategies for achieving values (for example, strategies of plant location or selection of manufacturing technology), and assumptions that bind strategies and values together (for example, the assumption that maintenance of a high rate of return on investment depends on the continual introduction of new technologies). An organization's instrumental theory of action includes in its scope communication and control, allocating resources to particular functions, rewarding or punishing individual performance, constructing career ladders and regulating the rates at which individuals climb them, and recruiting new members and instructing them in the ways of the organization.

Like the rules for collective decision and action, organizational theories-in-use may be tacit rather than explicit and tacit theories-in-use may not match the organization's espoused theory. An organization's formal documents, such as organization charts, policy statements, or job descriptions, not infrequently contain espoused theories of action incongruent with the organization's actual patterns of activity.

Organizational theory-in-use may remain tacit because it is indescribable or undiscussable. It may be indescribable because the individual members who enact it know more than they can say and are unable, rather than unwilling, to describe the know-how embedded in their day-to-day performance of organizational tasks. It may be undiscussable because any attempt to reveal its incongruity with the organization's espoused theory would be perceived as threatening or embarrassing.

Whatever the reasons for its tacitness, an organization's theory-in-use largely accounts for its identity over time. Consider a large and enduring organization, such as the United States Army. Over a period of fifty years or so, the Army's personnel turn over completely. Still, we speak of "the Army." If it no longer consists of the same people, in what sense does it remain the same? In an attempt to answer this question, we might examine artifacts such as uniforms and weapons. Over a period of fifty years these are likely to have undergone radical change. We might examine the societal functions carried out by the Army. But even if we discover that these functions have remained substantially in force for fifty years, we leave open the possibility that the organization now fulfilling them is radically different from its earlier counterpart. If, on the other hand, we study the fifty-year evolution of the theory-in-use implicit in the Army's military practices and discover that certain of its strategies, values, and assumptions—say, for command and control, promotion, and training—have remained relatively constant throughout that period, then we would have to treat these as most central to the Army's continuity of identity. The Army's theory-in-use, seemingly an abstract idea, would then be the "realest" thing about it.

One may describe an organization's theory-in-use from the point of view of an outsider or an insider to the organization. An outsider would have to observe how the organization's task system is enacted through the rule-governed behavior of its members. Insiders (as we will discuss at greater length in Chapter 8) have some access to the know-how through which they generate and control the practices appropriate to the organization's task system. This know-how may take the form of procedural knowledge, such as rules of thumb or the members' grasp of various categories of situations and behavior appropriate to them or their spontaneous perceptions of "the right thing to do now." Such representations constitute the organization's theory-in-use as seen from the inside.

Organizational Learning Again

Drawing on these ideas of organizational action, inquiry, and knowledge, we can now describe more precisely what we mean by organizational learning.

Each member of an organization constructs his own representation of the theory-in-use of the whole, but his picture is always incomplete. He strives continually to complete his picture by redescribing himself in relation to others in the organization. As conditions change, he remakes his descriptions; other individuals do likewise. There is a continual, more or less concerted meshing of individuals' images of their activity in the context of their collective interaction.

An organization is like an organism, each of whose cells contains a particular, partial, changing image of itself in relation to the whole. And like such an organism, the organization's practice stems from these very images: its theory-in-use is dependent on the ways in which its members represent it. Hence, our exploration of organizational learning must deal not with static entities called organizations but, as Karl Weick pointed out (1969), with active processes of organizing. The members' evolving images of the organization shape the very object of their investigation.

Organizational continuity would not be understandable if it depended exclusively on multiple, parallel, private imaging. When organizations are large and complex, their members cannot rely entirely on face-to-face contact to help them compare and adjust their private images of organizational theory-in-use. Even in face-to-face contact, private images of organization often diverge. Individuals need external references to guide their private adjustments.

Such reference functions are fulfilled by organizational maps, memories, and programs. Examples of maps include diagrams of work flow, organization charts, and drawings or photographs of the workplace. An actual building may serve as a map of groupings of individuals and patterns of communication among them. Organizational memories include files, records, data bases, and financial accounts, as well as the physical objects (tools, products, or working materials) that hold organizational knowledge. Programs are procedural descriptions of organizational routines; they include work plans, policies, protocols, guidelines, scripts, and templates. Artifacts such as these describe existing patterns of activity and serve as guides to future action.

> *Organizational learning occurs when individuals within an organization experience a problematic situation and inquire into it on the organization's behalf. They experience a surprising mismatch between expected and actual results of action and respond to that mismatch through a process of thought and further action that leads them to modify their images of organization or their understandings of organizational phenomena and to restructure their activities so as to bring outcomes and expectations into line, thereby changing organizational theory-in-use. In order to become organizational, the learning that results from organizational inquiry must become embedded in the images of organization held in its members' minds and/or in the epistemological artifacts (the maps, memories, and programs) embedded in the organizational environment.*

The learning products of organizational inquiry may take many forms, all of which, to qualify as learning must include evidence of a change in organizational theory-in-use. Often such changes are mediated by lessons drawn from inquiry. These include

a. interpretations of past experiences of success or failure;

b. inferences of causal connections between actions and outcomes and their implications for future action;

c. descriptions of the shifting organizational environment and its likely demands on future performance;

d. analysis of the potentials and limits of alternative organizational strategies, structures, techniques, information systems, or incentive systems;

e. descriptions of conflicting views and interests that arise within the organization under conditions of complexity and uncertainty;

f. images of desirable futures and invention of the means by which they may be achieved;

g. critical reflections on organizational theories-in-use and proposals for their restructuring; and

h. description and analysis of the experiences of other organizations.

All such intermediate outcomes of inquiry qualify as products of organizational learning when they are accompanied by changes in behavior that signify changes in organizational theory-in-use and when they are embodied in the individual images (the memories, maps, or programs) that store organizational knowledge.

Near Misses

It may help, at this point, to clarify our intended meaning by considering some examples that are "near misses"—almost but not quite organizational learning. We have already mentioned the case in which members of an organization gain new insights that are not converted to action. There are also cases in which individuals' inquiry leads to both new understandings *and* action but remains outside the stream of distinctively organizational activity and produces no change in organizational theory-in-use; for example, an individual or small group becomes an underground champion of an innovation in organizational policy, technology, or practice. A case in point was McLain's unauthorized, secret development of the first prototype of the Sidewinder missile in a shed at the Naval Research Station at Indio, California, in the 1950s. Such a development may become organizational and its learning product an organizational one, if (eventually as happened with McLain) the covert project is discovered, publicly legitimized, and formally adopted by the organization.

There are instances in which organizational inquiry produces a temporary change in organizational theory-in-use, but the new understandings associated with that change, held only in the minds of certain individual "carriers," are lost to the organization when they leave. This often happens in small professional organizations, such as research and development firms, design offices, or software companies, where staff members habitually move in and out of organizational homes, taking their ideas and capabilities with them. Sometimes members of the host organization recognize the risk of loss and seek deliberately to uncover and document the special insights and skills of these organizational birds of passage.

Finally, it is worth noting that not all changes in organizational theory-in-use qualify as learning. For example, changes in an organization's environment (such as a slackening of product demand) may trigger patterns of response that undermine organizational norms. Members may lose enthusiasm, become sloppy in task performance, or lose touch with one another. These kinds of changes are forms of deterioration. On the other hand, as in an example we will describe in Chapter 9, an episode of organizational inquiry may provoke deterioration in some regions of organizational theory-in-use even as it generates learning in another.

All such near misses suggest that our category of organizational learning has fuzzy edges. There are boundary instances in which it is difficult to determine with precision whether interactive inquiry is truly organizational or has truly changed organizational theory-in-use or whether its results have been truly embedded in the organization's memories, maps, and programs. Such vagueness may be inherent in organizational phenomena that are ill-formed or emergent or may reflect, on the other hand, a lack of information sufficient to permit a clear determination. They do not invalidate our definition as long as many examples do clearly fall inside it and as long as what information we would need in order to make a definite attribution of organizational learning is clear.

Productive Organizational Learning

There are several ways in which instrumental learning may be for ill rather than for good. Some of these are particular to organizational learning; others, applicable to learning by agents of any kind.

First, the *ends* of action may be reprehensible. The value we attribute to an increase in effectiveness or efficiency depends on how we answer the question, Effectiveness or efficiency for what? and how we evaluate the "what." This issue is critically important when the action in question emanates from an organization whose members are eager or unthinkingly compliant participants. During World War II, Eichman's bureaucracy learned over time to become more efficient at sending its victims to the gas chambers.

The value attributed to a particular instance of learning also depends on how we judge its validity. Learning seems to suggest the acquisition of valid, workable knowledge or know-how. But when we treat organizational learning as inquiry that leads to a change in theory-in-use, we open up the possibility that any given change may be based on a lesson that turns out to be false or unworkable. James March (1988) uses the term "superstitious learning" to refer to one such class of lessons: those based on the belief that because events have followed one another in time they are also related to one another as cause to effect. For example, corporate managers' may believe that a rise in profits following the institution of a new policy must have been caused by that policy, though it may have been due to nothing more than an improvement in market conditions. March suggests that managers are drawn to superstitious learning because it reinforces the myth of managerial control—a belief congenial to the norms of managerial stewardship but often contrary to fact.

Organizational learning that is valid or workable at the time of its first occurrence may lead to effects that are negative overall. To take a notable example, "competence traps" (also March's term) are situations in which an experience of perceived success leads an organization to persist in a familiar pattern of thought and action beyond the time and conditions within which it yields successful outcomes. The behavior that yields success at time, t, may not yield it at t + 1. Yet an organization lulled by its success and misguided by the lessons drawn from it, may persist in a familiar pattern of behavior long after it has ceased to work. In business strategy, General Motors, IBM, and Digital Equipment Corporation come to mind as recent examples of firms that persevered in following a once-winning strategy that had become a losing strategy, apparently blind to the fact that the competetive environment had shifted out from under it. Such examples should be understood in terms of the webs of interest organizations build up around familiar strategies, technologies, or structures, and the "dynamically conservative" processes (Schön, 1967) that reinforce an organization's adherence to the lessons it has drawn from past experience.

Later we will have opportunity to see how people can learn collectively to maintain patterns of thought and action that *inhibit* productive organizational learning. For example, they may learn to respond to error by the use of scapegoating, games of unilateral control and avoidance of control, systematic patterns of deception, camouflage of intentions, and maintenance of taboos that keep critical issues undiscussable. Such patterns of thought and action, learned from experience, often have the effect of inhibiting the kinds of productive learning that yield improved performance or restructured values for performance. Yet members of the organization may develop an attachment to these patterns, even to the point of exclaiming, "It has taken us years to learn to live in this screwed-up world; don't make waves!"

If we were to use learning only in a positive sense, then we would have to qualify the learning involved in all such negative examples with adjectives like dysfunctional, pseudo, or limited. These semantic devices are misleading, since they tend to be applied to learning products after the fact; whereas we are often uncertain in any given situation of action, whether an alleged instance of productive organizational learning is valid and workable. The crucial point is that, as we try to understand or enhance organizational learning, we should keep in mind the variety of ways in which any particular example of it may prove to be invalid, unproductive, or even downright evil.

For these reasons, it is useful to distinguish three types of productive organizational learning:

1. *organizational inquiry,* instrumental learning that leads to improvement in the performance of organizational tasks;
2. inquiry through which an organization explores and restructures the values and criteria through which it defines what it means by improved performance; and
3. inquiry through which an organization enhances its capability for learning of types (1) or (2).

Single- and Double-Loop Learning

By **single-loop learning** we mean instrumental learning that changes strategies of action or assumptions underlying strategies in ways that leave the values of a theory of action unchanged. For example, quality control inspectors who identify a defective product may convey that information to production engineers, who, in turn, may change product specifications and production methods to correct the defect. Marketing managers, who observe that monthly sales have fallen below expectations, may inquire into the shortfall, seeking an interpretation they can use to devise new marketing strategies to bring the sales curve back on target. Line managers may respond to an increase in turnover of personnel by investigating sources of worker dissatisfaction, looking for factors they can influence, such as salary levels, fringe benefits, or job design, to improve the stability of their work force.

In such learning episodes, a single feed-back loop, mediated by organizational inquiry, connects detected error—that is, an outcome of action mismatched to expectations and, therefore, surprising—to organizational strategies of action and their underlying assumptions. These strategies or assumptions are modified, in turn, to keep organizational performance within the range set by existing organizational values and norms. The values and norms themselves (related in the previous examples to product quality, sales level, or work force stability) remain unchanged.

By **double-loop learning,** we mean learning that results in a change in the values of theory-in-use, as well as in its strategies and assumptions. The double loop refers to the two feedback loops that connect the observed effects of action with strategies and values served by strategies. Strategies and assumptions may change concurrently with, or as a consequence of, change in values.[1] Double-loop learning may be carried out by individuals, when their inquiry leads to change in the values of their theories-in-use or by organizations, when individuals inquire on behalf of an organization in such a way as to lead to change in the values of organizational theory-in-use.

---

[1] We borrow the distinction between single- and double-loop learning from W. Ross Ashby's *Design for a Brain* (New York: John Wiley and Sons, Inc., 1960). Ashby formulates his distinction in terms of (a) the adaptive behavior of a stable system, "the region of stability being the region of the phase space in which all the essential variables lie within their normal limits," and (b) a change in the value of an effective parameter, which changes the field within which the system seeks to maintain its stability. One of Ashby's examples is the behavior of a heating or cooling system governed by a thermostat. In an analogy to single-loop learning, the system changes the values of certain variables (for example, the opening or closing of an air valve) in order to keep temperature within the limits of a setting. Double-loop learning is analogous to the process by which a change in the setting induces the system to maintain temperature within the range specified by a new setting. See especially pp. 71–75.

Organizations continually engaged in transactions with their environments regularly carry out inquiry that takes the form of detection and correction of error. Single-loop learning is sufficient where error correction can proceed by changing organizational strategies and assumptions within a constant framework of values and norms for performance. It is instrumental and, therefore, concerned primarily with effectiveness: how best to achieve existing goals and objectives, keeping organizational performance within the range specified by existing values and norms. In some cases, however, the correction of error requires inquiry through which organizational values and norms themselves are modified, which is what we mean by organizational double-loop learning.

In any particular instance of double-loop learning, the resulting changes in values and norms may not be judged to be desirable: their desirability can be determined only through a situation-specific critique of the changes themselves and of the inquiry through which they are achieved. Nevertheless, it is through double-loop learning alone that individuals or organizations can address the desirability of the values and norms that govern their theories-in-use.

Consider a chemical firm which has set up a research and development division charged with the discovery and development of new technologies (an example we consider at greater length in Chapter 3). The firm has created its new R&D division in response to the perceived imperative for growth in sales and earnings and the belief that these are to be generated through internally managed technological innovation. However, the new division generates technologies that do not fit the corporation's familiar pattern of operations. In order to exploit some of these technologies, the corporation may have to turn from the production of intermediate materials, with which it is familiar, to the manufacture and distribution of consumer products with which it is unfamiliar. This, in turn, requires that members of the corporation adopt new approaches to marketing, managing, and advertising; that they become accustomed to a much shorter product life cycle and to a more rapid cycle of changes in their pattern of activities; that they, in fact, change the very image of their business. And these requirements for change come into conflict with another sort of corporate norm, one that requires predictability in the management of corporate affairs.

Hence, the corporate managers find themselves confronted with conflicting requirements. If they conform to the imperative for growth, they must give up on the imperative for predictability. If they decide to keep their patterns of operation constant, they must give up on the imperative for growth, insofar as that imperative is to be realized through internally generated technology. A process of change initiated with an eye to effectiveness under existing norms turns out to yield a conflict in the norms themselves.

If corporate managers are to engage this conflict, they must undertake a process of inquiry which is significantly different from the inquiry characteristic of single-loop learning. To begin, they must become aware of the conflict. They have set up a new division that has yielded unexpected outcomes; this is an error, a surprise. They must reflect upon this surprise to the point where they become aware that they cannot deal with it adequately by doing better what they already know how to do. They must become aware that they cannot correct the error by getting the new division to perform more efficiently under existing norms; the more efficient the new division is, the more its results will plunge the managers into uncertainty and conflict. The managers must discover that it is the norm for predictable management which they hold, perhaps tacitly, that conflicts with their wish to achieve corporate growth through technological innovation.

Then the managers must undertake an inquiry that resolves the conflicting requirements. The results of their inquiry will take the form of a restructuring of organizational norms and very likely a restructuring of strategies and assumptions associated with those norms; these must then be embedded in the images and maps that encode organizational theory-in-use. There is in this sort of episode a double feedback loop which connects the detection of error not only to strategies and assumptions of effective performance but to the values and norms that define effective performance.

In such an example of organizational double-loop learning, incompatible requirements in organizational theory-in-use are characteristically expressed through a conflict among members and groups of members. One might say that the organization becomes a medium for translating incompatible requirements into interpersonal and intergroup conflict.

For example, some managers of the chemical firm may become partisans of growth through research; while others, committed to familiar and predictable patterns of corporate operation, become opponents of the new, research-based conception of the business. Double-loop learning, if it occurs, will follow from the process of inquiry by which these groups of managers confront and resolve their dispute. They may respond in several ways, not all of which meet the criteria for organizational double-loop learning.

First, the members may treat the conflict as a fight in which choices among competing requirements are to be made, and weightings and priorities are to be set on the basis of dominance. The R&D faction, for example, may include the chief executive who is able to win out over the old guard because of his greater power, or the two factions may fight it out to a draw, settling their differences in the end by a compromise that reflects nothing more than the inability of either faction to prevail over the other. In both of these cases, the conflict is settled for the time being but not by a process that could be appropriately described as learning. If the conflict ends with a power play or a stalemate, neither side is likely to emerge with a new sense of the nature of the conflict, its causes and consequences, or its meaning for organizational theory-in-use.

On the other hand, the adversaries may engage their conflict through inquiry in any of the following ways:

a. They may invent new strategies of performance that circumvent the perceived incompatibility of requirements; they may succeed in defining a kind of research and development addressed solely to the existing patterns of business that offer the likelihood of achieving existing norms for growth. They will then have succeeded in finding a single-loop solution to what at first appeared a double-loop problem.

b. They may carry out a trade-off analysis that enables them to conclude jointly that so many units of achievement of one norm are balanced by so many units of achievement of another norm. On this basis, they may decide that the prospects for R&D payoff are so slim that the R&D option should be abandoned, and with that abandonment there should be a lowering of corporate expectations for growth. Or they may decide to limit R&D targets so that the disruptions of patterns of business operation generated by R&D are confined to particular segments of the corporation. Here there is a compromise among competing requirements, but it is achieved through inquiry into the probabilities and values associated with options for action.

c. The incompatible requirements may be perceived as incommensurable. In such a case, the conflict may still be resolved through inquiry that gets underneath the members' initial commitments. Participants must then ask why they hold the positions they do and what the positions mean. They may ask what factors have led them to adopt particular standards for growth in sales and earnings, with what rationales, and what are likely to be the consequences of attempting to meet the standards by any means whatever. Similarly they may ask what kinds of predictability in operations are of greatest importance, to whom they are important, and what conditions make them important.

Inquiry of type B or C may lead to a restructuring of corporate values and norms. Or it may lead to the invention of new patterns of incentives, budgeting, and control that take greater account of requirements for both growth and predictability.

In this type of organizational double-loop learning, individual members resolve interpersonal and intergroup conflicts that express incompatible requirements for organizational performance. They do so through organizational inquiry that creates new understandings of the conflicting requirements—their sources, conditions, and consequences—and sets new priorities and weightings of norms, or reframes the norms themselves, together with their associated strategies and assumptions. In such a process the restructured requirements for organizational performance become more nearly compatible and more susceptible to effective realization. And the resulting understandings, priorities, and reframed norms become inscribed in the images, maps, and programs of the organization and are thereby embedded in organizational memory.

Additional Considerations

The distinction between single- and double-loop learning is complicated by several factors. As we consider these, we identify gradients of significance in organizational learning, become aware of zones of ambiguity at the boundaries of these two types of learning, and identify a variety of patterns of inquiry through which organizations may engage in double-loop learning.

First, the distinction between single- and double-loop learning is complicated by organizational size and complexity.

Organizational theories-in-use are structures composed of many interconnected parts. Some of these are local and peripheral, while others are core elements fundamental to the structure as a whole. In a chemical firm, for example, norms governing requirements for growth and predictability are fundamental to the theory-in-use of the whole organization. If these norms were to change, a great deal of the rest of the theory-in-use would also have to change; this secondary change is why their conflict is so important for the whole firm. On the other hand, a particular norm for product quality could change without affecting much of the rest of the the organization's theory-in-use. From such observations, we infer that double-loop organizational learning may be of greater or lesser significance for the organization as a whole, depending on the degree to which core values and norms are involved.

Furthermore, large organizations are composed of many layers. Such organizations can be described in terms of a *ladder of aggregation* that proceeds from individuals to small groups, to departments made up of many small groups, to divisions that are clusters of departments, to the organization as a whole, to the larger field in which the organization interacts with other organizations. These organizational layers exist not only as abstractions but as living entities each of which may be described as having interests, intentions, values, and theories-in-use of its own. From the point of view of each such entity, the rest of the organization is environment. An organization may be said to act, interact, inquire, and learn; so may the groups, departments, and divisions at different levels of aggregation within it.

Often the actions of intraorganizational units are crucial to organizational inquiry and consequential for single- and double-loop learning. Learning may be more or less contained within an organizational unit, depending on how tightly or loosely that unit is is coupled with others. For example, a change in the technology of a production line may change values that guide behavior in that workplace without repercussions on the larger organization's theory-in-use. In contrast, a bank's decision to introduce just-in-time paper processing in one of its divisions may provoke a shift in the norms by which the bank's control system perceives, evaluates, and rewards production in all of its divisons. In this instance, what begins as single-loop learning at one level of aggregation stimulates double-loop learning at all levels. More generally, the type of organizational learning that occurs may vary with the level of aggregation at which it occurs and the tight or loose coupling of units within or across levels.

A second factor that complicates the distinction between single- and double-loop learning is the relationship between learning products and processes. We have so far defined single- and double-loop learning in terms of the *products* of organizational inquiry, distinguishing a change in organizational theory-in-use that affects only strategies of action and assumptions from one that affects values. But we are also concerned with values and norms that govern *processes* of organizational inquiry, for these are critical to an organization's capability for improving its performance and restructuring the values that define improvement.

As we try to determine whether an instance of organizational learning is single- or double-loop, it is important to notice not only where inquiry begins but where it goes. For example, the managers of a firm may decide that in order to gain market share, their organization needs to become far more nimble and proactive in its responses to threats and opportunities. Starting with this goal, they may propose to create a flatter and more decentralized organization in which local units take on much greater freedom of action and display higher levels of initiative. As the managers begin to implement the new organizational plan, they may well discover that its success depends on creating an organizational climate tolerant of public dissent and debate, risk-embracing, and hospitable to decision making under uncertainty. These values may have been included in the organization's espoused theory of action but not in its theory-in-use. The original initiative, framed as one of increasing organizational effectiveness, turns out to have critical implications for double-loop changes in core values that govern theory-in-use for the conduct of organizational inquiry.

Consider a related example, which we will take up at greater length in Chapter 9: an organization introduces a program of Total Quality Management (TQM) (Argyris, 1994). As individuals working within this program search out the "root causes" of defects in a product or process, they may identify two different kinds of problems. Inefficiencies in production represent one kind of problem; the other is illustrated by a group of employees who stand passively by and watch inefficiencies develop and persevere. TQM may produce the simple learning necessary to effect a solution to the first problem, but it is not likely to prevent a recurrence of the second or cause the supervisors to wonder why they never acted.

Double-loop learning in organizational inquiry calls for an additional step or even several additional steps. It turns the question back on the questioner, exploring not only the objective facts surrounding an instance of inefficiency, but also the reasons and motives behind those facts. For example, a CEO who discovers in his organization the practice of requiring 275 sign-offs for the approval of an innovation, might ask, "How long have you known about these requirements?" "What prevented you from questioning these practices?" Such double-loop learning depends on questioning one's own assumptions and behavior.

The distinction between double-loop learning outcomes for organizational theory-in-use and double-loop learning in processes of organizational inquiry is correlated with the distinction between *first- and second-order errors*. First-order errors in organizational theory-in-use are illustrated by excessive costs or too many sign-offs. The second-order errors that arise in processes of organizational inquiry, such as a failure to question existing practices, allow such first-order errors to arise and persist. Double-loop learning in organizational inquiry consists in the questioning, information-gathering, and reflection that get at second-order errors. When it is successful, it results in change toward values for inquiry that yields valid and actionable learning about second-order error. As we shall show in Part II, such changes are closely linked to an organization's "learning system" and the individual theories-in-use that both reinforce it and are reinforced by it.

Organizational Deuterolearning

An organization's *learning system* is made up of the structures that channel organizational inquiry and the behavioral world of the organization, draped over these structures, that facilitates or inhibits organizational inquiry. Together, structural and behavioral features of an organizational learning system create the conditions under which individuals interact in organizational inquiry, making it more or less likely that crucial issues will be addressed or avoided, that dilemmas will be publicly surfaced or held private, and that sensitive assumptions will be publicly tested or protected.

By "organizational structures," we mean

- channels of communication (forums for discussion and debate, formal and informal patterns of interaction);
- information systems, including their media and technologies (the computer, for example);
- the spatial environment of the organization insofar as it influences patterns of communication;
- procedures and routines that guide individual and interactive inquiry; and
- systems of incentives that influence the will to inquire.

Insofar as such structures facilitate organizational inquiry, we speak of them as *enablers*.

By the "behavioral world" of the organization, we mean the qualities, meanings, and feelings that habitually condition patterns of interaction among individuals within the organization in such a way as to affect organizational inquiry—for example, the degree to which patterns of interaction are friendly or hostile, intimate or distant, open or closed, flexible or rigid, competetive or cooperative, risk-seeking or risk-averse, error-embracing or error-avoiding, productive or defensive. A key feature of the behavioral world of an organization is the degree to which organizational inquiry tends to be bound up with the win/lose behavior characteristic of organizational games of interests and powers. These games are usually intertwined with organizational inquiry. At the extreme, as Michel Crozier demonstrated (1963), surprises that might trigger productive organizational learning may be overwhelmingly interpreted in the light of their meaning for the status of players within games of interests and powers.

An organization's learning system is interdependent with the theories-in-use that individuals bring to its behavioral world. Individual theories-in-use help to create and maintain the organization's learning system; this system, in turn, contributes to the reinforcement or restructuring of individual theories-in-use. For example, when individuals operate in terms of "mystery and mastery," keeping their intentions and strategies private while they seek to master their interactions with others, they tend to engender distrust, which may then be widely perceived as a consistent feature of the organization's behavioral world. And a behavioral world characterized by distrust tends to reinforce the disposition of individuals to act according to theories-in-use that feature win/lose behavior and unilateral self-protection.

A critically important kind of organizational double-loop learning, therefore, is the second-order learning through which the members of an organization may discover and modify the learning system that conditions prevailing patterns of organizational inquiry.

This is the organizational equivalent of what Gregory Bateson (1972) calls **deuterolearning** by which he means second-order learning, or "learning how to learn," organizational deuterolearning. We shall describe this in terms of a shift from O-I to O-II learning systems. Organizational deuterolearning is critically dependent on individual deuterolearning, which we shall describe in terms of a shift from Model I to Model II theories-in-use. These correlated shifts are at the heart of the concerns that have led us to write this book.

2

Turning the Researcher/ Practitioner Relationship On Its Head

What does an inquiry-based view of organizational learning imply for the relationship between practitioners and researchers? If we see practitioners as inquirers who are called upon in their day-to-day work to detect and correct errors in organizational performance, how should we think about their relationship to those who do academic research on organizational learning? Depending on our answer to this question, what are the implications for the appropriate roles, attitudes, and methods of academic researchers?

In this chapter we argue that when we see both organizational practice and academic research as forms of inquiry, we can reframe the conventional view of their relationship in a way that promotes both usable knowledge and robust research. We will no longer see this relationship in terms of practitioners' application of knowledge generated by researchers but as a collaboration between types of inquirers who occupy different roles and rely on different but complementary skills and methods. Central to this reframing is the Deweyan idea of inquiry and, within it, a recognition of the different ways in which researchers and practitioners treat causality and causal inference.

Deweyan Inquiry

Dewey's idea of inquiry derives in part from the writings of Charles Peirce, the founder of American Pragmatism; but whereas Peirce (1877) treated doubt as a property of individual consciousness, Dewey (1938) believed we doubt because we are in a situation that is inherently doubtful. He thought that inquiry begins with an indeterminate, problematic situation, a situation whose inherent conflict, obscurity, or confusion blocks action. And the inquirer seeks to make that situation determinate, thereby restoring the flow of activity.

Inquiry for Dewey combines mental reasoning and action. The Deweyan inquirer is not a spectator but an actor who stands within a situation of action, seeking actively to understand and change it. When inquiry results in a learning outcome, it yields both thought and action, at least in some degree new to the inquirer.

Both doubt and its resolution are transactional properties of the relationship between the inquirer and the situation; the inquirer participates in constructing the situation to which he also responds. For example, an artist makes the painting in which, at any given moment, she finds requirements and possibilities that call for further making. The problems and potentials in an interpersonal relationship that generate feelings and call for new thought and action, are always, at least in part, of the participants' making.

The transaction between inquirer and situation is continuing and inherently open-ended. As inquirers seek to resolve what is problematic about a situation of action, they bring new problematic features into being. Inquiry "does not merely remove doubt by recurrence to a prior adaptive integration," as Dewey put it, but "institutes new environing conditions that occasion new problems." Within such a dialectic (a term whose organizational counterpart we shall explore in the following chapter), there is, in Dewey's words, "no such thing as a final settlement." Inquiry is to be tested by its success in resolving a problematic situation and by the value inquirers come to attribute to the new problems their resolution creates.

Detecting and Correcting Error

It is the detection of error, which we define as the mismatch of outcomes to expectations, that triggers awareness of a problematic situation and sets in motion the inquiry aimed at correcting the error. When the outcomes of our action are mismatched to expectations, the inquirer gets an experience of surprise—an experience essential, as Israel Scheffler wrote (1987), to the process of coming to think and act in a new way. The attempt to resolve a problematic situation frequently generates new sources of surprise.

Consider what happens when a telephone network suddenly breaks down. In the company responsible for the network, people look for ways to restore it to full operation. If they do not immediately figure out how to do so, they try to devise methods of experimentation that will not make things worse. They investigate the causes of the breakdown and explore ways of preventing the future occurrence of such disruptions. How they understand the causes and how they frame the problem of reliability guide their invention of short-term fixes and longer-term strategies of prevention.

Not infrequently, their attempts to carry out their problem-solving strategies reveal flaws in their initial framing of the problem. If they locate the immediate cause of the breakdown in an error buried deep in millions of lines of network software, they may first direct their attention to the process of software-testing. Further inquiry may lead them to frame a deeper problem. They may discover that as they have tried to improve network performance, they have introduced systems that increase the complexity of the network software, making it more vulnerable to error. The discovery of this more fundamental problem, an inconsistency in the objectives for network design, may call for a more fundamental solution. Inquiry, triggered in the first instance by surprise, generates new surprises that call for new rounds of error detection and correction.

It is important to note, however, that the term, "error," which we define as "a mismatch of outcomes to expectations," tends in ordinary usage to suggest a *mistake,* an invalid strategy of action or assumption, for example, the mistaken belief that better software-testing tools will assure network reliability. Getting from an error to the mistake that underlies it requires a further process of inquiry, as in the telecom staff's analysis of the causes of the network breakdown. Errors are not in themselves mistakes; rather, they signal the presence of mistakes.

It is also important to notice that although error tends in ordinary usage to suggest a negative outcome, it may actually have a positive meaning. A surprising outcome of action is perceived, on occasion, as desirable. In the realm of science, a researcher may stumble onto a surprising phenomenon, such as the unexpected bloom of mold on a petrie dish that led to Alexander Fleming's discovery of penicillin, and thereby detect an error that leads to the development of a new technology. In the interpersonal domain, a manager may be pleasantly surprised to find a colleague actually receptive to direct confrontation on a threatening issue.

Whether inquirers perceive a surprising outcome of action as negative or positive, they try to correct the error, to realign outcomes and expectations so as to convert a mismatch to a match. In one case, they try to reshape what they perceive as an undesirable outcome in order to make it conform to their original expectations; in the other, they realign their expectations and intentions in order to conform to the happy outcome. Hence, when we describe inquiry in terms of the detection and correction of error, we are not claiming that one learns more readily from failure than from success; we are emphasizing the role of surprise as a stimulus to new ways of thinking and acting.

Organizational Inquiry

Dewey saw inquiry as a social process. He meant not only that people usually think and act together in a social setting, but that the very process of inquiry, individual or collective, is conditioned by membership in a social system that establishes inquiry's taken-for-granted assumptions. Like Peirce, Dewey saw individual inquirers as members of a "community of inquiry," bound by contractual responsibilities. He wrote that an inquirer enters into a "contract such that...he is committed to stand by the results of similar inquiries." In just this way, we see organizational learning as a process carried out by members of an organization, working alone or in interaction with one another, within an *organizational* community of inquiry.

> *Inquiry becomes organizational when individuals inquire on behalf of the organization, within a community of inquiry governed, formally or informally, by the roles and rules of the organization.*

It follows that individuals may inquire and learn in ways that are connected to and, at times, disconnected from the organization to which they belong.

When organizational inquiry leads to learning, its results are manifested in thought and action that are in some degree new to the organization. In instrumental learning, organizational inquiry yields new ways of thinking and acting that enable the improved performance of an organizational task. In this sense, the attribution of organizational learning is contingent on the presence of an observable change in behavior. To be sure, behavior may change in ways other than through learning, for example, through deterioration, forgetting, or random variation. But such observations show only that change in behavior is not a sufficient condition for learning. We argue that it is a *necessary* one, however. The action that resolves a problematic situation is what Dewey would call the "end-in-view" of inquiry, the purpose that sets it in motion; and it is by reference to such an action that we can judge whether organizational inquiry has been effective. It is not easy to imagine how we could confirm an occurrence of organizational learning without observing a change in behavior. It is true that individuals who puzzle over a phenomenon may gain important insights that remain dormant for long periods of time. For example, members of a consumer product company may detect changes in the marketplace that portend a shift in the ground rules governing competition for market share, yet their insights may lie fallow for months or may never find their way into the design of new product strategies. Such insights fall short of learning, since they do not result in new forms of organizational action. They are best seen as representing a *potential* for organizational learning.

The Researcher/Practitioner Relationship

When we define organizational learning in terms of the inquiry practitioners carry out within an organizational setting, we point toward what they and academic researchers hold in common: both are inquirers, concerned with detecting and correcting errors, making sense of confusing and conflictual problematic situations. This is in contrast to a more conventional emphasis on a critical difference between the two groups. According to the conventional view, which emanates mainly from the research universities, research gives rise to special expertise of the sort that Everett Hughes (1959) called "esoteric knowledge." The relationship between researchers and practitioners is governed by "the Veblenian bargain" (Schön, 1983): from the practitioners, their problems; from the researchers, the expert knowledge whose application to those problems enables practitioners to solve them in a distinctively professional way. This view tends to take one of two forms, depending on whether the researcher's claim to expertise rests on

1. research-based theory or
2. expert intuitions.

Each of these interpretations leads to difficulties. When researchers see themselves mainly as sources of research-based knowledge, the consequence of their interactions with practitioners is likely to be rejection or dependency. Dependency is the likely outcome if practitioners pick up the experts' esoteric knowledge and become little scientists—most often, "little social scientists"—who use fragments of theories as ritual clichés, floating, without palpable connection to the ways in which work is actually done. This condition, which in organizations holds for much of the current use of such terms as "organizational culture," has been described (DeMonchaux, 1992) as the "loss of the innocent eye." Rejection is the likely outcome if practitioners question how well researchers' theories fit the practice situation, how they stand in relation to theories held by the practitioners themselves, or whether the researchers' actual behavior is consistent with the theories they profess.

In the case of researchers seeing themselves as operating on expert intuition, rejection or dependency is again the likely outcome, but for somewhat different reasons. The researcher's intuitive expertise tends to be opaque to the practitioner, who must then choose, more or less blindly, whether to "buy" it on a dependent basis or reject it. We cannot easily imagine how a practitioner can learn from expertise that presents itself as intuitive. It is true that athletes and artists do seem at times to learn from one another by observation and imitation alone; but even if we grant that organizational practitioners may sometimes learn from researchers in this way, neither the practitioner nor the researcher is likely, so long as the expertise remains tacit, to reason critically about it, hence to make a reasoned choice to accept it within limits, in certain respects and not in others.

Whether research-based expertise takes the form of esoteric theory or intuition, the conventional model of expert-practitioner interaction ignores the *practitioners'* inquiry, their own theories and ways of reasoning or testing ideas. What the practitioner already knows is ignored, just as conventional models of good teaching ignore the pupil's spontaneous understandings. How, then, is a practitioner's capability for inquiry thought to be enhanced as a result of interaction with a research-based expert?

Practitioners As Inquirers

We propose to turn the conventional relationship between researcher and practitioner on its head. We see practitioners not as passive recipients of expertise, but as Deweyan inquirers. Hence, we ask, "What do these practitioners already know?" "How do they inquire and learn?"

We perceive striking similarities between the issues of greatest interest to those who practice and those who conduct research on organizational learning. Both groups have an interest in making sense of organizational experience in instrumental terms: they want to know what makes for effective organizational action. Because they share an interest in understanding how organizations work and how they may be changed, they want to learn about the causal connections between organizational actions and outcomes. They have an interest in discovering what patterns of thought and action account for past experiences of organizational success or failure, and how individuals contribute to either outcome. If they are impressed by the surprises and puzzles that arise in the course of organizational experience, they seek to make sense of them, as well as of patterned regularity.

Organizational practitioners may be curious about the processes through which they carry out the day-to-day business of organizational inquiry. Often they are capable of reflection *on* organizational practice, which researchers tend to see as their special prerogative. Practitioners are sometimes curious about how success and failure are defined in organizational terms, how goals and priorities are set, and, how ends of action are chosen as desirable. Practitioners, as well as researchers, may be interested in threats to the validity of organizational learning, that is, the kinds of reasoning and the forms of behavior that lead them to draw distorted lessons from past experience. Often they see that by focusing on immediate issues of local importance they may become blind to the larger significance of their actions. Increasingly they suspect that existing structures and incentive systems may undermine their ability to function well in a changing environment. Many of them want to learn how to create new structures and incentives and how to acquire new skills, enabling them to increase the learning capability of their organizations.

The ways in which practitioners and academic researchers inquire into such issues are in some ways alike and in other ways radically unlike.

Geoffrey Vickers describes two types of inquirers, each representing a distinctive stance toward inquiry (Vickers, 1975). He uses the term "spectator-manipulator" to refer to distant observers who keep their subjects at arms' length, exempting themselves from the worlds they study, only occasionally perturbing those environments under carefully controlled conditions in order to observe their subjects' responses. In contrast, "agents-experient" locate themselves within the problematic situation as concerned actors "whose actions and appreciations may be partly guided and changed by better understanding of the situations which prove to be relevant to [their] concerns."

Organizational practitioners are, of necessity, agents-experient. Only in fantasy or by way of retreat can they afford the luxury of becoming spectators. They are in the situations they try to understand, and they help to form them by coming to see and act in them in new ways. Through their perceptions, words, and thoughts as well as their actions, they help to construct the objects of their inquiry. They are designers, not in the special sense of the design professions but in a more inclusive sense: they make things under conditions of complexity and uncertainty. The objects they design include products and services, policies, marketing strategies, information systems, organizational roles and structures, jobs, compensation schemes,and career ladders. They may even become designers of whole organizations. Not least, they design their day-to-day strategies of action.

Practitioners share with academic researchers an interest in building explanatory models of organizational worlds. Like researchers, practitioners try to account for the data they consider relevant, and they often show a decent respect for disconfirming evidence. But practitoners' models must also serve the purposes of designing. However appealing models may be as tools of exploration or explanation, they are judged by how well they "work," in the sense of enabling practitioners to do something they wish to do. This decisively affects what criteria apply to the reasoning of practitioners, in what sense they experiment, and in what sense their experimentation may be appropriately called "rigorous." Like academic researchers, organizational practitioners have a lively interest in forming and testing hypotheses about their environments. But because practitioners are agent-experient designers whose actions serve the dual function of probing and influencing their situations of action, their inquiry is subject to a different "stopping rule." In at least one view of science (Popper, 1968), the scientific cycle of hypothesis forming and testing should continue for as long as members of the community of inquiry bring forward plausible competing hypotheses. For practitioners, on the other hand, that cycle comes appropriately to a close when their inquiry enables them to achieve their intended results and when they like, or can live with, the unintended side effects inherent in their designing.

In these respects, the norms of practice inquiry differ from those of academic research even though in other respects the two forms of inquiry hold fundamental processes and criteria of adequacy in common. Nowhere is this more evident or more significant than with respect to the meaning of causality and the nature of causalinference.

Causality and Causal Inference

Researchers and practitioners alike are unavoidably concerned with issues of causality and causal inference. When organizational researchers try to understand variations in patterns of organizational growth and deterioration or when they study how technological innovation works, how incentive systems function, how risks are managed, or how ideas circulate and evolve, their understandings hinge on causal connections. Practitioners, for their part, try to understand things so that they can change them or adapt to them. They seek to discover the features of context and action that caused past successes or failures in order to design more effective systems and strategies. They are continually engaged in detecting and correcting error, as we shall see in the following chapter and throughout the rest of this book. They are vitally interested in both the causes of error and the causal efficacy of the actions they design to correct error. But researchers and practitioners characteristically operate on different models of causality and reason about causes in different ways—a fact of great significance for the nature of their possible collaborative inquiry into organizational learning.

The model of causality conventionally adopted by normal scientists centers on the idea of a "variable," a named attribute extracted from the complexity of observed phenomena which is treated as essentially the same in whatever local context it occurs. It is this presumed constancy of meaning that allows scientists (social scientists, in this instance) to speak of variations in the local values of a variable. If variables were not seen as having constant meanings, we could not speak sensibly about variation in the values or arguments of the same variable; we would have to speak of a different variable whenever a variable assumed a different value. Herbert Simon expresses a similar idea when he writes that each value of variables, X and Y, standing for cause and effect, defines a "class of events," and that each variable, therefore, comprises a set of classes of events (Simon, 1977). Building on this conception, Simon treats causality as a function of an effect, Y, on one or more causes, X, as expressed by the formula, $Y = F(X)$. Simon calls such a function "self-contained" when "one and only one value of Y is associated with each value of X."

According to this model of causality, researchers who investigate a causal relationship aim at formulating general causal propositions in the form of "covering laws." Examples of covering laws are: "The occurrence of aggressive behavior always presupposes the existence of frustration and, contrariwise, the existence of frustration always leads to some form of aggression," or "State anxiety, defined as 'subjective, consciously perceived feelings of tension, apprehension, and nervousness,' is caused by perceptions of role overload" (quoted in James, Mulaik, and Brett, 1982). Researchers look for evidence to show that the values of Y (state anxiety) can be determined completely by the values of X (role overload), given the values of X and the knowledge that X has occurred, independent of any other features of the contexts in which X and Y occur.

According to the normal-social-science model of causality, probabilistic covering laws may be inferred from data provided by either of two empirical methods: "contrived experiment" or "natural experiment." In both cases researchers try to determine whether values of the effect variables are uniquely determined by values of the cause variables, relying on one or more of Mill's methods: Agreement (X is regularly followed by Y), Difference (without X, no Y), or Concomitant Variations (variations in X are regularly followed by analogous variations in Y) (Mill, 1843). In a contrived experiment the researchers construct a setting in which they can control variations in the value of X in order to observe changes in the value of Y. In the method of natural experiment, or "quasi-experimental method" (Campbell and Stanley, 1963), the researchers observe a number of settings in order to measure the naturally varying values of X and Y, relying on observation of many local settings in order to avoid being misled by the peculiarities of any particular one. In both cases researchers try to maintain a respectful "research distance," lest they contaminate their data or become affected by their subjects' biases. They avoid referring to their subjects' intentions, which they regard as subjective, idiosyncratic, and qualitative—unsuited to the generality, quantitativeness, and context-independence that are essential to the normal-social-science model of rigorous causal inference.

In everyday practice, on the contrary, organizational practitioners think in terms of "design causality:" the causal relation that connects an actor's intention to the action he or she designs in order to realize that intention. To explain the cause of an action in terms of design causality, we describe the intention we believe the actor is trying to achieve by means of the action. To put the same idea in different terms, we describe the reasoning that led up to the action, not the reasoning by which that action might be justified after the fact. Olafson (1967) calls this type of causality "cause by reason," and Von Hayek (1948) calls it "sufficient reason." Practitioners make reference to a second type of simple causalilty, "efficient cause": the causal connection between an act and its consequences, intended or unintended. Furthermore, when individuals habitually interact with one another in an organizational setting, their designed behaviors, together with the first- and second-order consequences of which those behaviors are the efficient causes, tend to create complex organizational systems that display "pattern causality."

Consider the behavior of grant-making officers in a philanthropic foundation. They know that funds are made available to them on a "use-it-or-lose-it" basis. Hence, they make sure they spend their allocated funds (design causality), no matter how shoddy the grants they may support in order to do so. In aggregate, such grant-making behavior produces a high level of questionable grants (efficient causality). Taking notice of this effect, the director of the foundation institutes increasingly rigorous systems of external evaluation (design causality), by which grant makers feel unfairly constrained (efficient causality) and which they seek to elude (design causality) with the further result that evaluations come to be considered unreliable (efficient causality). Once such patterns have been created, they tend to maintain themselves (pattern causality) through feedback loops that influence how individuals in the system think and act.

Consider a factory in which top management has instituted a system of "pay- for-performance." Supervisors in that factory learn to soften their criticisms of their workers, in order to avoid the complaints and grievance actions they have come to expect in response to their honest evaluations (design causality). As a first-order consequence (efficient causality), workers' performance ratings become inflated; as a second-order consequence (efficient causality), the wage bill grows. The rising wage bill, the unintended aggregate effect of each supervisor's deliberate actions, may alarm upper-level managers and become, in turn, a trigger for their new attempts to drive the wage bill down (design causality), meeting a fate similar to the one described previously. The system of pay-for-performance, originally intended to improve productivity, turns out to have the cumulative effect of rewarding mediocre performance and increasing the cynicism of the supervisors (pattern causality).

A practitioner-inquirer who operates on such a model of organizational causality tries to infer component causes of organizational events and to construct and test models of their interaction in causal patterns. The practitioner uses the method of *causal tracing*, observing how one phenomenon leads to another. Causal tracing depends for its feasibility on the inquirer's having a background model of the system's pattern causality. The process is like the reasoning of a skilled plumber: given a broad understanding of a system of pipes and how liquid flows through them, the plumber tries to identify the cause of a leak by tracing it back (in space and time) to its sources within the system. Like plumbers, organizational inquirers can test their causal hunches by carrying out on-the-spot experiments. For example, the plumber may close a valve and observe whether the leak stops. In the instance of the foundation, an organizational inquirer might institute a change of policy (eliminating the "use-it-or-lose it" rule, for example) in order to observe consequent changes in the grant makers' behavior. Inquirers into organizational or plumbing systems can also test their pictures of a whole causal pattern by considering alternative models of it and trying to discriminate among them by finding data that only one of the competing models can explain. In the last analysis, practitioners test their causal inferences by determining whether they can use them to get design results they intend and like.

The normal social-science model of causal inference aims at generalizability: it employs general cause- and effect-variables and calls for observation of multiple instances in which those variables take on different values. The practitioner's model of causality is situation-specific. It deals with named phenomena, for example, "softening evaluations of subordinates," that need not (and usually do not) take the form of general, quantifiable variables. The normal social scientist employs contrived or natural experiments that cut across many different contexts. The practitioner traces causes in the light of a background model of a particular system and tests causal inferences in that system through on-the-spot experiment.

The general covering laws established through normal social science tend to have relatively little utility in practice because of the characteristic representation of a covering law. The functional relationships of variables that result from normal-social-science research tend to be precise, quantitative, probabilistic, abstract, and complex, making it difficult for practitioners to form images of research results that can be used to guide action in a particular local context. There is also a "gap of valid application" between the contexts of research and practice. In order to establish that the general causal relationships among variables, established in a research context, will hold at a particular time in a particular practice setting, the practitioner will have to recreate in that setting the conditions under which the research results were obtained in the first place. This means that he or she will have to construct operational definitions of the key terms and show that observers who do not know the propositions to be tested can use these definitions to make reliable observations of the relevant phenomena across a suitable range of variance. Moreover, the practitioner will need to minimize threats to internal and external validity through the use of suitable controls, including keeping the experimental strategy secret from the subjects lest their awareness of it confound its results. Under practice conditions of real time, confusion, and pressure, such actions are difficult to carry out. Moreover, when implemented they are not neutral. As Argyris has shown (1980), actions of this kind imply an approach to management that is reminiscent of the managerial climate of hierarchical organizations. Such an approach places subordinates in a submissive, dependent role that is very likely to create strong feelings of ambivalence or outright hostility.

Finally, we have been impressed with the step-function difference between what happens when people discover problems and invent strategies of action, and when they actually try to produce their inventions under everyday conditions of real time and pressure—especially when it comes to situations of embarrassment or threat. Under these conditions, individuals frequently produce actions contrary to their inventions and are unaware of the discrepancy. A manager may want to persuade the middle-managers under her to stop witholding negative evaluations of their workers. But in order to avoid upsetting her subordinates, she may actually smooth over the negative attributions she makes about them. Her unawareness in such a case is likely to be due not so much to ignorance as to skillful adherence to theories-in-use learned early in life.

In ordinary organizational practice, phenomena like these are the rule rather than the exception. It is a rare normal social scientist who takes them into account or focuses on the skills practitioners would actually need in order to produce inventions based on normal science research. Hence, normal scientists are unlikely to generate research results that practitioners can actually use to produce inventions derived from those results.

The practitioners' causal inquiry does not yield general covering laws. Their situation-specific inferences of design, efficient, or pattern causality can be generalized only by a process we call "reflective transfer"—"transfer," because the model is carried over from one organizational situation to another through a kind of seeing-as; "reflective," because the inquirer should attend critically to analogies and disanalogies between the familiar situation and the new one. In reflective transfer, causal stories play roles similar to the roles of legal precedent in judicial decision making or precedents in architectural design. The utility of the prototype lies in its ability to generate explanation and experimentation in a new situation. When it is carried over to a new situation, its validity must be established there by a new round of inquiry through which it is very likely to be modified. And the modified prototype that results from the new round of inquiry may serve, in turn, as a basis for reflective transfer to a new situation.

Practitioner/Researcher Collaboration in Action Research

What shall we say about the roles, methods, and attitudes appropriate to research on organizational learning once we recognize that the process of organizational learning is carried out by practitioners who are inquirers in their own right, that the topics of interest to organizational inquirers and academic researchers have large areas of overlap, and that the patterns of causal reasoning characteristic of the two groups of inquirers are in some respects alike yet in other respects, radically unlike?

For researchers who hope to produce knowledge useful to practitioners, the implications of our analysis are straightforward. These researchers should join with practitioners who seek to promote productive organizational learning and to understand the nature of their own learning processes and systems. The researchers should try to discover what practitioners already know how to do and to learn to appreciate the inquiry in which practitioners are already enaged, including the questions they know how to ask and the knowing-in-action they may take for granted and be unable to describe. These researchers should join with practitioners to help discover the hidden rationalities that are often built into everyday organizational practice, the productive forms of pattern causality of which practitioners themselves are often unaware. But this research function should be coupled with helping practitioners extend and enhance the inquiry they already know how to carry out. This means helping them to discover how they get stuck and what dilemmas underlie their getting stuck; how the same patterns of action that lead to success may also, on occasion, lead to failure; how practitioners can learn from failure; how they can enlarge a focus of attention that may be limited to the local and the immedate, thereby opening the field of design possibilities; how they can become aware of counterintuitive effects masked by their, perhaps tacit, background models; how they can reflect on and explore the impediments to productive organizational learning embedded in their limited organizational learning systems; and how they can become aware of their own contributions to the maintenance of those systems.

There are several reasons for this research focus. First, a researcher who is interested in the study of organizational learning ought to have an interest in studying how practitioners' inquiry contributes to that process. Secondly, an organizational researcher who wants to produce results useful to practitioner-inquirers should want to meet their understandings with his own. He needs to listen to them and get inside their ways of thinking and acting, with respect to both strengths and limits, in order to increase his chances of being listened to and of making his research relevant in their eyes. If practitioners are already inquirers, then an outside researcher's effort to involve them in research must take account of the inquiry in which they are already engaged. Finally, as Kurt Lewin pointed out many years ago (Lewin and Grabbe, 1945), people are more likely to accept and act on research findings if they helped to design the research and participate in the gathering and analysis of data.

Indeed, Lewin's conception of action research is prototypical of the kind of research we have in mind. Lewin's research career had two main sources: his training as a physical scientist and his experience as a Jew driven from his homeland by the Nazi menace. His research revealed his commitment to democracy (as in his studies of democratic versus authoritarian group climates), as well as to creativity, productivity, and inquiry orientation. He was, as Alfred Marrow called him, a practical theorist who often remarked that there was nothing so practical as a good theory. He sought to achieve desirable social results, for example, persuading children to drink orange juice and eat their spinach, promoting the sale of war bonds, and reducing discrimination based on race or religion. The method he evolved was that of involving his subjects as active, inquiring participants in the conduct of social experiments about themselves. He adopted the working hypothesis that people would tend to adopt beliefs in whose development and testing they had been active participants. In the course of such practical experiments, limited to particular social problems and situations, Lewin had the skill and imagination to discover ideas of wide-ranging importance. For example, his invention of the concept of "gatekeeper," which has long since entered into the language of both social scientists and lay persons, grew directly from his experimental studies of influence and persuasion in such contexts as the drinking of orange juice and the buying of war bonds.

A constellation of values and methods, similar to Lewin's, informed the early Tavistock studies and experiments, as at the longwall coal mining operations in Great Britain (Trist and Bamforth, 1951), and at Glacier Metals (Jacques, 1952). The theory and practice of participatory, semiautonomous work groups grew out of these early examples of organizational action research. Nearly a generation before Lewin's and the Tavistock Institute's development of action research, John Dewey advocated similar values of inquiry, participation, and collaboration. However, he based his arguments on philosophical rather than empirical grounds, and he sought to apply his philosophy through social experiments mainly in the fields of citizenship and education.

A researcher who embraces in this spirit a program of collaborative action research on organizational learning becomes, like the practitioners he joins, an agent-experient. He, too, places himself within the situations that he studies and must, in consequence, study himself. His commitment to the organization in question is likely to be less intense than the practitioner's. His interests in inquiry are likely to be overlapping, not identical, with the practitioner's. He is likely to miss some of what the practitioner's local knowledge enables him to see and to retain a partly skeptical stance toward the practitioner's claims to organizational knowledge and learning. Yet he may also attach greater appreciation than the practitioner does to the taken-for-granted practice knowledge that informs his everyday competence.

The action researcher will join the practitioners in their organizations and collaborate with them in conducting their design inquiry, entering into their underlying models of causality and causal inference. At the same time, the action researcher will seek to become aware and help the practitioners become aware of the limits of those models. The theories, models, exemplars, and heuristics that researchers bring to the practice situation they will use as lenses on the situation, to be tested for their use in making sense of it, but not as substitutes for what Kevin Lynch once called "the best kind of theories," those constructed in the situation itself.

Even from the perspective of a skeptical normal social-science researcher who wants only to study the phenomena of organizational learning and has no interest in producing knowledge useful to practitioners, it makes sense to reverse the usual relationship between practitioner and researcher. There are at least two reasons for doing so, which we take up at greater length in Chapter 9, but state briefly here:

1. Scholarly researchers into organizational learning will want to test the insights they gain from simulation studies or

distant empirical research. They have a scientific interest in filling the gaps that now exist between their relatively high-level formulations, for example, the theories of internal variation and selection within organizations which we discuss in Chapter 9, and the fine-grained processes by which such phenomena actually arise. This requires gaining access to the inner workings of organizations through the cooperation of practitioners who are, and often see themselves as, inquirers in their own right. Such cooperation is more likely to take place and to work when outside researchers join practitioner-inquirers in collaborative action research.

2. As a matter of scientific curiosity, scholarly students of organizational learning may wonder whether the patterns of limited learning they discover are law-like, somehow inherent in the structures of organizational life or whether they are, in a sense, artifacts of states of consciousness peculiar to the practitioners they are observing. Could these patterns be changed if practitioners became aware of them? How could such a possibility be tested unless the researcher were to help practitioners design and enact ways of circumventing patterns of limited organizational learning? Robust tests of scholarly models, for example, those that relate to competence traps, superstitious learning, or garbage-can phenomena, call for creating in organizations the conditions under which such models might be confirmed or disconfirmed in action. This, again, requires collaboration with practitioner-inquirers.

Appropriate Rigor in Collaborative Action Research

Practitioners can use their models of causality to make causal inferences, and to engage in reflective transfer of such inferences, because they are agents-experient who live in close proximity to the situations they seek to understand. It is this closeness that enables them to hold usable background models of phenomena, carry out causal tracings, and conduct on-the-spot experiments. On the other hand, the practitioners' closeness to the situation of action also presents a variety of threats to the development of valid, usable knowledge:

- Their busyness may deter them from engaging in inquiry that would otherwise be useful to them; they are often constrained by the need to leave off thinking and begin to "get things done."

- Their familiarity with their own patterns of action may prevent them from seeing what they actually do and leave them unable to describe the action knowledge on which they greatly depend.
- Their biases as interested actors in the situation may blind them to data that might have caused them to change their minds.
- Their focus on pressing business, local and short-term in nature, may prevent them from taking a potentially useful longer-term, wider-ranging view.
- Their very familiarity with their environment may make them blind to it. More specifically, they may be at least partly unaware of causal patterns that constrain productive organizational learning and unaware of how their transactions with the organizational environment contribute to the very impediments that they see as imposed on them from the outside.

What does it mean for practitioners to cope well with these sorts of vulnerabilities? How might they be helped to do so by entering into a collaboration with action researchers based in the academy?

In social psychology there is a long tradition of debate over the trustability of our everyday intuitions into the reasoning—the intentions, throughts, and feelings—that motivate other people's actions. Zajonc (1989) raises this question and concludes that although our own experience

> can be a rich source of ideas and a source of hypotheses...everything we know from the systematic study of social perception indicates that we should be very distrustful of our so-called intuitions.

He cites in support of this position the large number of studies that have revealed

> a substantial self-serving bias in estimating probabilities of causal events.

Even if we take a much more sanguine view of the reliability of our everyday intuitions into human reasoning and intention, it is certainly clear that we sometimes find them to be mistaken. Reasonably competent organizational inquirers, ones who exhibited appropriate rigor, would certainly try to test such intuitions, especially those that played important roles in their construction of causal stories. Consider, for example, the inference that supervisors in the pay-for-performance case smoothed over their negative evaluations "in order to avoid upsetting the workers," or that technical staff in the telecommunications company bypassed software reliability checks "in order to respond to management's pressure for fast installation." How might such inferences be tested? Certainly, one of the principal tests would consist of on-the-spot experiment, namely, asking for information. But this form of experimentation is also vulnerable to error for several different sorts of reasons.

Let us take a situation in which one person asks another, "What led you to do this?" and receives an answer to the question, inferring from it an interpretation of the actor's intentions. First of all, the informant may not be able to make an accurate reconstruction of the before-the-fact reasoning that led to her action. She may not remember it, or, in accordance with the very widespread tendency to engage in instant historical revisionism, she may reconstruct it more or less unconsciously to suit her present ideas, interests, or inclinations. Such distortions might be corrected, perhaps, by inducing the informant to make a careful reconstruction of the incident in which she was involved, or when possible, by comparing the responses of several different informants.

But remedial measures such as these are vulnerable to a second source of error, one that affects any attempt to inquire directly into reasons for action. An inquiry into an actor's reasons for acting in a certain way is itself an intervention, and when it takes place in an organizational setting, it is also an intervention into the life of the organization. Both of these factors can and usually do have powerful effects on the ways in which both inquirer and informant construe the meaning of their interaction, interpret each other's messages, act toward each other, and perceive each other's actions. These effects can complicate and often subvert the inquirer's quest for valid information.

One reason is that the individual who finds herself in the role of informant also seeks to discover the meanings of the situation in which she is involved and acts on the basis of the meanings she constructs. She may answer questions in the light of what she believes the inquirer expects of her. She may construe the situation as one that calls for putting the best possible face on prior actions. Her interaction with the interviewer may be designed, more or less consciously as a form of image management. To the extent that she feels threatened or distrustful in the interview, she may deliberately withold information she feels might be taken in a negative way.

All such interactions are also affected by what George Devereaux (1967), borrowing from quantum physics, once described as "complementarity." The interviewer's questions and his responses, verbal and nonverbal, are also intrusions into the interpersonal situation, affecting the informant's constructions of meanings and her willingness to give valid information. The act of inquiry influences the situation inquired into. So, for example, an investigator into the network failure may convey a threatening, judgmental attitude that makes his informants even more defensive than they might otherwise be.

What is true of the informant is also true of the inquirer. His interpretations of the messages he receives are also affected by the more or less conscious meanings he constructs for his interaction with the informant, his attributions of meanings to her, and his intimations of the way in which she perceives him. If he perceives her as likely to withhold negative information, he may interpret her answers in light of his suspicions about the information he believes her to be withholding.

These interaction effects are by no means peculiar to causal inquiry in organizations. They are also characteristic of the experimental environments of normal social science where they are equally capable of foiling the researcher's quest for valid information. As Harré and Secord (1972) noted, "Social psychological experiments are also social episodes." Indeed, the very controls by which social psychologists strive to make their contrived experiments rigorous are likely, as observed earlier, to introduce sytematic distortions into their research results.

In organizational inquiry, however, all such interaction effects may be exacerbated by certain peculiarities of the organizational context. Organizational inquiry is almost inevitably a political process in which individuals consider, whether they choose to be decisively influenced by such considerations, how the inquiry may affect their standing or their reference group's standing, within an organizational world of competition and contention. The attempt to uncover the causes of a systems failure is inevitably a perceived test of loyalty to one's subgroup and an opportunity to allocate blame or credit. Such an inquiry is likely to trigger familiar games, for example, allocation of blame and avoidance of blame, exercise of control and avoidance of control, winning credit and preventing others from winning credit. Within such games, strategies of deception, pre-emptive blame, stone-walling, fogging, and camouflage, including camouflage of these very strategies, frequently inhibit inquiry into the causes of organizational events and the reasoning of the actors involved in them. We describe such phenomena later in this book from the point of view of what we call "limited learning systems."

Given the personal, interactive, and organizational phenomena that can inhibit the quest for valid information about design causality, how ought one carry out organizational inquiry so as to increase the likelihood of producing valid information? This global question sets a critically important direction for a possible social science that might take seriously the problem of enhancing organizational inquiry. It has at least two main parts. First, how can we build more accurate and usable accounts of the personal, interpersonal, and organizational patterns that inhibit causal inquiry in organizations? Second, from the point of view of the process of inquiry itself, what theories of action, strategies, values, and underlying assumptions are most likely to enable an inquirer to elicit information, interpret it, and test interpretations so as to form valid inferences about design causality?

These questions form the basis of the approach we call "the theory of action perspective" or "action science," a development of Lewinian action research. It focuses on the problem of creating conditions for collaborative inquiry in which people in organizations function as co-researchers rather than merely as subjects. And it does this, as already noted, on the assumption that people are more likely to provide valid information about their own intentions and reasons for action when they share control of the process of generating, interpreting, testing, and using information. The theory-of-action approach posits the existence of a behavioral world created by the parties to an interaction and identifies the characteristics of behavioral worlds that may inhibit or encourage valid inquiry. It explores the features of theories-in-use that are conducive to exchange of valid information in behavioral worlds of interpersonal inquiry, emphasizing the importance of making private attributions public, treating these attributions as disconfirmable, and subjecting them to public test. It operates from the assumption, for which we think there is considerable evidence, that theories-in-use tend to exert a contagion or mirroring effect. We believe that individuals become more effective inquirers when they employ theories-in-use which, if mirrored by their informants and co-researchers, would be likely to produce valid information.

These points, crucial to any future collaboration between organizational practitioners and academic researchers, will be pursued in the remainder of our book, beginning with the following chapter in which we explore the long-term evolution of an industrial firm and a consultant's attempts to foster productive organizational learning at a crucial juncture in that evolution. In the current chapter, we have called attention to questions of method, attitude, and relationship that become central to research into organizational learning once we see it in terms of organizational inquiry, recognize practitioners as inquirers, and turn the researcher-practitioner relationship on its head.

3

The Mercury Case:
What Facilitates or
Inhibits Productive
Organizational Learning

Let us consider the ten-year evolution of an industrial firm, the Mercury Corporation.

This chemical company was established in the 1920s around a single chemical product. It was among the first in its industry to set up a research and development division, and over the decades it generated new businesses in many different fields. By the mid-1960s it had grown to over three billion dollars in sales. But top managers, preoccupied with maintaining the company's rate of growth, began to worry about signs of flagging vitality. They were especially concerned by the declining rate at which the Research and Development Division generated new products that became the basis for new businesses. They framed this problem in terms of an "entrepreneurial gap." Research, they thought, had the capacity to generate new technologies but not to commercialize them. For commercialization, Research depended on existing divisions of the company, and these were often reluctant to take risks on a very new product or process.

Given their diagnosis of the problem, management invented what looked like a workable solution. They would establish a New Business Division (NBD) which would be empowered not only to develop but to "incubate" new technologies. It would be able to make and sell new products, turning them over to existing divisions only when they had already proved their worth. The hope was that existing divisions, freed from the need to shoulder the risks of the first reduction to practice, would no longer resist the new technologies generated by Research.

By the early 1970s Mercury found itself in the midst of a crisis of a different kind. The corporate growth rate had picked up, but vigorous growth was coupled with a declining rate of earnings. Management attributed this problem to the greatly increased scale of the business. They thought that the corporation's success in achieving its targets for growth had created an enterprise whose size and scope exceeded the capacity of the central administration. A business in excess of five billion dollars could not be run in the same old way. There was a decision to decentralize the management of the corporation, creating semiautonomous divisions with their own business charters and presidents, who eventually became known as "the barons."

By the mid-1970s the NBD had accumulated 10 years of experience. It had expended about $20 million dollars on research and development without giving rise to a single new business of any consequence. In spite of this record, the NBD remained in being; indeed, top management had not directly criticized it. But the NBD staff members themselves were becoming uneasy, and they called in an outside consultant.[1] The NBD manager proposed that the consultant help them to explore, as he wrote at the time, "...new venture management in a mature organization in view of the dramatic social, political, and especially economic changes that are taking place in the world today." He asked specifically whether "the pursuit of new ventures is still a viable alternative to growth for a mature corporation in these changing times."

Inquiring into the Process of New Business Development

The consultant's first step was to develop a map of the problem. Characteristically, there turned out to be more than one map. For any problem of consequence, different members of an organization are likely to hold different views, which they often withhold from one another or express incompletely. In the early discussions at Mercury, various members of the organization expressed these different views of the problem of corporate development:

> We're not organized to do the job, not only in development but in the whole technological area...costs of technological development are

---

[1] One of the authors, Donald Schön, took on this consulting task. He had worked with the company we call Mercury in the early 1960s, and he returned to work with the NBD in the mid-1970s.

going up...50 percent of our profits come from 30 percent of the products, the proprietary ones... .We know how to manage capital much better than we do technology.

NBD is constrained by its charter.

NBD tends to take the path of least resistance, placing new technology within existing divisional boundaries.

We have been going for 10 years and have not produced anything of real consequence. Projects that have made it are not NBD projects. We have entertained lots of projects rather than pick an area and try to figure out how to get there.

You need lots of balls in the air, because the odds on any one are so low. You must look at lots of possibilities. Over 10 years, we've looked at more than 200 business opportunities.

Individuals expressed such views in private but not in public. They had never confronted one another with their differences, nor had they pursued their disagreements to the point of exploring how they might test them. The consultant proposed to get underneath these differences by asking his clients—the vice president for technology, the director of research, and members of the NBD staff—to construct case histories of corporate development over the previous decade, paying special attention to the developments they saw as successes and those they saw as failures.

This turned out not to be an easy task. For one thing, the failures tended to remain buried, and people were not eager to exhume them. For another, knowledge of past efforts at development remained scattered among members of the corporation, and individuals who held parts of the development stories in their heads had never sought to compare or reconcile their differing pictures of events. As a result, certain myths of development had arisen. These included such notions as "Good ideas come from the top" and "A good idea will find its own way." Such myths were widely diffused throughout the organization and remained untested. Indeed, they had become self-fulfilling prophecies. Successes were read, after the fact, as good ideas, and failures were read as bad ones. Because failures remained buried, moreover, the quality of the ideas associated with them was never compared with the quality of the ideas associated with perceived successes. Success itself had come to be accepted as the test of a good idea; and because top management support was essential to the achievement of a perceived success, people found it easy to believe that good ideas came from the top.

In spite of such difficulties, members of the corporation came together with the consultant's urging and support to construct case histories of new business development. As they prepared to do so, the consultant suggested that they address the following questions:

1. How have we actually gone about the process of development, particularly in the cases seen as clear successes or failures?
2. What can we learn from a consideration of these histories? How, in particular, do they confirm or disconfirm the theories about effective technological development now held in various quarters in Mercury?
3. What inferences can we draw from these stories about the design of more effective organizational structures and practices for technological development?

This exercise in storytelling was not intended to discover recipes for effective development based on differences between the invariant features of successful and unsuccessful developments. It was intended, rather, to elicit themes of development and to reveal patterns of informal practice that were likely to be more subtle and complex than the theories advanced in Mercury to account for these processes.

The effort at recreating history was based on the assumption that an organization like Mercury can often do more than it can say. With a more accurate and explicit picture of the actual practice of business development, members of the organization should be able to test their existing theories of effective performance, criticize proposed designs for corporate development based on theories they learned to see as inadequate, and construct better designs for development on the basis of theories more firmly grounded in organizational reality. The consultant anticipated, moreover, that, as participants reviewed their stories of development, they would be likely to interpret them in different ways. Attempts to explain these differences could lead to insights into Mercury's learning system, and the members' reactions to the differences could provide useful evidence about Mercury's ways of setting and solving organizational problems.

These, in summary form, are some of the stories that were told. The first was narrated by Participant A (on the next page).

Product X

In the early 1960s, we bought a fabricating company, based on the resin, *R*. We built a division around it. At that time, we had no materials especially developed for this kind of fabrication. We depended on other kinds of materials which were adapted for this purpose. Within one of our materials divisions, however, we had a process for producing materials that looked as though they might offer special advantages for the new fabricating process.

The new division had a good share of market but was up against strong competition. We were aware of needing new market applications, something bigger than our existing market. We set up a task force under a chairman who had both technical savvy and commercial knowledge; the task force came back with a range of possible applications, recommending *X* in particular.

A two-year feasibility study then began. It required collaboration between the fabrication and materials divisions, and their relationship was not the best.

It was not at first evident to the materials division that with this product they could actually lose market for materials they were selling to customers with whom the new fabrication division would compete, although in the long run the division would have materials to sell.

It was decided that the development should not be managed by central research but by the divisions themselves, which would establish a pool of people for this purpose. The corporation funded this effort. In spite of some misgivings, there was a great cooperative atmosphere.

This development represented more than $1,000,000, and existing businesses felt they could have used the money better. Such a new business tends to look like a business that's failing. The project nearly died twice.

Nevertheless, it survived, in part due to corporate funding. No division's P&L was at stake, and a big potential customer became interested within a year of the start of the feasibility study and said, in effect, "If you can make them, I'll buy them."

The managements of the two divisions gave the project their best people and were hurt by the drain on resources. The product is now in test market. It has been an eight-year process, the largest and most expensive we've ever undertaken. Its volume promises to swamp the previous scope of the fabricating division.

The NBD did not have this product, although they thought they should have had it. In the late 1960s, the section had just been formed, and its relations with the operating divisions were worse than now but the chairman of the board was a staunch and dependable advocate of the project.

Participant A told the consultant that they had not told the head of the materials division that he might actually lose market through the new development. The consultant asked why, and the following dialogue took place:

> *Participant A:* If we had told him, given our management policies, he would have been a fool to go along.
>
> *Consultant:* Did you test this assumption about his reaction?
>
> *Participant A:* Of course not. How can you test something like that?
>
> *Consultant:* What happened when he found out that the information had been withheld?
>
> *Participant A:* He blew his top, but he calmed down.
>
> *Participant B:* And some of us there wondered when someone was going to play that game on us.
>
> *Consultant:* Did this make you wary and mistrustful?
>
> *Participant A:* You're right. You have to be that way if you're going to survive.

When information such as this is made public, it not only provides insight into Mercury's learning system but also becomes part of the group's map of the problem which can then be retrieved for later analysis. On the other hand, such discussions are apt to make participants uncomfortable. The consultant, therefore, faces an additional challenge: how to avoid bringing different points of view into collision too early in the process, before the stories are fully told. The participants may feel increasingly uneasy with the complexity and foreignness of the problem they are exploring and with the discussion of things previously considered undiscussable. They may call for closure, rarely in the name of being anxious, but rather in the name of getting on with the task. The consultant may accept their reactions, but he is also responsible for alerting them to the consequences of cutting off the flow of storytelling. If he experiences a great deal of resistance, he can at least test the reasoning that underlies it (asking, for example, "What is it that leads you to conclude that we have enough data?")

A second story of product development was told by a member of the NBD:

Product Y

We had a task force exploring new materials, and we made a chart to show a spectrum of materials properties along a certain dimension.

We asked, "Could you tailor a material to fill the middle region of the chart?"

We had never been in the business represented by that region of the chart, but we knew that several of our existing businesses would be relevant to it. We had a material, Product Y, with many possible markets, rather than one market looking for a special material.

The head of Central Research, presiding over the task force, asked if there was anything worth fighting over. The task force was temporary and part-time. There was significantly less commitment than there had been in the case of Product X. Nobody's job depended on making this one go.

Had we been going to go big, we would have gone after a large-scale materials business, and we were able to identify such a business. Instead, the decision was made to go to a smaller specialty market.

The charter for the larger materials business belonged to another division. NBD couldn't go forward with Product Y unless we looked at it as a fabricated part. And the division thought in terms of intermediate materials. They said, "It's not that different. And the cost of maintaining a separate technology would be high." Meanwhile, they had a plan for the specialty market.

So we gave it to them.

A third story was told by the head of Central Research:

Product Z

One of our old-time investigators had been told that if he took on a disagreeable task, he could devote the rest of his time to anything he chose. He came back with a proposal for Z. This was a technology intriguing to him, a phenomenon he had helped to develop.

He asked, "What have we got?" and "What technology do we bring?"

He thought in terms of the phenomenon, Z, and a business theme, adhesion, shared by many of Mercury's operations. Here we have a tailored material for adhesion, at lower cost than our current materials.

So we looked across the corporation for those instances of adhesion that cost more than a certain amount. We picked internal applications where it would be easier to prove out the applications.

In their reactions to these (much abbreviated) stories, the participants made a number of observations.

They noted that successful technological developments often seemed to involve three distinct processes:

1. exploring the potentials inherent in some technological phenomenon,
2. identifying and describing problems in an existing businesses, and
3. a problem-scanning, or intelligence, function through which problems identified in Mercury's environment could be related to Mercury's capabilities.

Development possibilities seemed to arise out of the matching of the problems and capabilities discerned through these three processes. For example, a technological phenomenon might be matched with an internal business problem or with a problem detected in the external environment. Often these matches seemed to occur through happy accident.

The participants observed that all of these processes required highly developed self-knowledge of organizational capabilities and needs. Useful descriptions of capabilities were those that were readily connectable with descriptions of business themes and needs. The participants felt they were able to recognize "a Mercury problem;" and their recognition seemed to grow out of their ability to keep in mind, at least tacitly, descriptions of internal capabilities and business themes that could be matched, on occasion, with descriptions of troubles or opportunities detected in the outside world. Usually, however, the participants could not make explicit the criteria through which they were able to recognize "our kind of problem."

The phrase, "a Mercury problem," became a take-off point for exploring the participants' sense of their own special business, a sense they felt and strongly shared but had not previously incorporated into their theories of corporate development. Other slogans and metaphors emerged, for example, "a crying baby," for a project whose visibility results from internal trouble rather than inherent potential; or "a flier," a way of entering a business we're not yet in. Images like these resonated with the participants' sense of Mercury's capabilities and market potentials. The ability to make such descriptions seemed to be an important part of the process of mobilizing energy and management commitment for development. It was as though development depended on family-related elements of language that were present in the minds of very useful old-timers. These bits of language and the images related to them were part of the tacit theory of development present in the organization, which the mapping process was designed to surface.

The consultant paid attention to the participants' language for describing phenomena and processes familiar to them. He did not try to convert that language into more apparently rigorous formulations derived from a theory of his own. Rather he stayed as close as possible to the clients' actual descriptions of phenomena, seeking to join them in building a view of development based on their own descriptions of relevant data and avoiding any intervention that might distract them from the problems and processes they themselves described.

As the story telling proceeded, it became apparent that the variety of stories the participants told could be grouped into a small number of basic types. When the stories began to display a high degree of redundancy, the consultant began to work with the participants to construct a model that revealed the themes that underlay the basic story types. The attempt now was to diagnose the complex problem of development and break it into subparts.

The core of the development problem seemed, in the first instance, to be one of mobilizing corporate-wide capabilities. These might be found in any central or operating unit of the corporation, and their nature and location tended to vary from project to project. Moreover, certain capabilities ("a savvy commercially experienced man," "someone who knows the Z business") were likely to be necessary only at particular stages of the process, after which they tended to drop out. The institution of the development task force had been an essential part of Mercury's past ability to achieve temporary fusions of scattered corporate capabilities. Indeed, something like a task-force technology appeared to have developed as an art form. But the task-force approach could not solve the problem of getting embryonic developments to the point where top managers recognized the need to establish a task force.

In each development venture, it was necessary to harness resources and liberate energy, often from those parts of the organizational system least willing to release energy or resources. This generated a dilemma which became clear in the analysis of the differences between stories of success and failure.

The success stories fell into a general pattern. First, there was the perception of a new business opportunity based on the development of a new technology. The technology usually grew out of an existing division; often it was the unexpected consequence of an

R&D project that had been designed to achieve an entirely different target. The exploitation of the new business opportunity represented by that technology required recombining some elements of existing businesses. Members of the corporation might say, for example, "If we could only group these businesses together, we'd have a family of technologies that could help them all to take off." Or they might say, "Here's a technology that would be good for fastening. We don't see ourselves now in that fastening business, but there are pieces of other divisions that have to do with fasteners. If we combined them in a new division, we'd have the marketing vehicle for our new technology."

Promising new businesses (for example, Product X) were those in which Mercury combined and transformed pieces of the existing business. From this point of view, development was a kind of puzzle solving. Existing pieces came to be seen in new ways and were subsequently combined, transformed, and infused with resources that enabled them to grow into new businesses. This dependence on existing pieces can be understood as Mercury's way of building on its strengths, but it is also understandable as a way of generating commitment. Mercury's managers were most likely to grasp and become committed to ventures that contained an element of the familiar. Only the developments based on pieces of the existing puzzle were familiar enough to make Mercury's top management comfortable and significant enough in themselves to make a still bigger business believable. They alone could generate enough top managment support to cause top management to persuade a reluctant baron to see himself, at least for a time, as a piece of the larger corporate puzzle.

Hence the pattern of the successes. Over the previous decade, three such successes had occurred, and they accounted for a major share of the corporate growth. But these successes also had a downside.

The great increase in Mercury's corporate size had led to the decentralization of management. The new scale of the corporation had also set massive requirements for the volume of sales that would have to be delivered by a promising new business. The divisions, with their semi autonomous status, operated under strict incentives to deliver profit. They held fiercely to their business charters, even when they were not fully exploiting them. They were understandably reluctant to give up a piece of themselves for the sake of creating a new business for the corporation.

What figured as a piece of the puzzle, from the perspective of a possible new business, the barons saw as a piece of territory that belonged to their own charter and mandate for growth. As managers of corporate territories, they were subject to conflicting requirements. On the one hand, they were responsible for maintaining and enhancing the integrity of their territory; on the other, they were expected from time to time to regard a part of themselves as a piece of a larger puzzle to be forfeited, combined with something else, and transformed.

Hence, the combinations and transformations inherent in the stories of successful development can also be seen as violations of existing divisional charters. As one participant observed, "In the best marriages, there is at least one unwilling partner!" This was particularly true where the territory in question was profitable and full of potential for more profit. If such territories were the most likely to contain pieces whose combination with other pieces would yield promising new businesses, then the most promising developments would be the ones most likely to encounter vigorous resistance from the heads of existing divisions.

As long as possible, champions of a new business would deal with such resistance by working around it and withholding information. When these strategies no longer worked, the champions would make their bids for top management's support. Sometimes top management would then make a commitment to the new business, provide corporate funds for development, and talk one of the barons into going along. But each success left the barons more mistrustful of central administration, more wary of getting caught up in a losing game.

All of these factors entered into the pattern of the failures.

In these stories, too, technological opportunities were detected, but in these instances they tended to be either "crying babies" or "fliers." When such new business prospects were described to top management, they typically met with one of two responses. Sometimes top management saw them as too small compared to the scale of existing businesses. Promoters of the new business found it difficult to make the case that an entirely new and untried business could achieve the required scale. On the other hand, top management might see the new business as too unfamiliar, "not our kind of thing." Even if the business seemed to promise a large enough volume of sales, the process of getting from here to there seemed too uncertain, and the "flier" into unknown territory would be cut off in mid-flight once the risks of the unfamiliar became fully apparent.

When top management felt uncomfortable with a project, they refused to commit to it. Without top management commitment, although some resources might be made available, there would not be enough to bring the project to fruition. The project would be dropped, and its failure might then be attributed to a bad idea or to someone's incompetence. As a consequence, the best technical people wanted to stay away from such developments, and those who had to stay with them acquired what one participant called a "loser syndrome."

Almost all of the failure stories fell to the New Business Division. The NBD based its operations on a clearly formulated theory of development. As a first step, research would yield new technologies, "balls in the air." The new technologies would then be linked to business opportunities. Finally, they would be screened according to corporate criteria, and the most promising candidates would be selected for further investment. But this espoused theory fell afoul of organizational realities. The NBD existed as an island surrounded by hostile divisional barons, every one of whom saw it as a potential threat to divisional integrity and a potential drain on divisional resources. Seeking to avoid confrontation with the barons, NBD staff tried to protect themselves by limiting their search for new businesses to those that would not infringe on the business charters of existing divisions. Hence, they spent their time exploring opportunities that lay beyond the familiar boundaries of existing businesses. But in order to carry a project forward, NBD depended ultimately on top management support, and top management saw the opportunities it presented as either too small or too unfamiliar. Hence the pattern of the failures.

Taking the patterns of success and failure stories together, the consultant and the client group put together the following picture:

> In its response to the problems of managing a corporation of enormous scale, Mercury managers had created semi autonomous territories whose barons were held accountable for short-term profits and were invited to compete for resources. The corporation had become a kind of oligarchy. But the development process required these barons to function as pieces of a larger puzzle, counter to existing sanctions and incentives. Hence, it was not surprising that the successful developments were those that captured the attention of top management who alone could compel divisional barons to give up resources.
>
> The imperative for increasing R&D productivity had led to the creation of the New Business Division. But the creation of the NBD as a development arm apart from existing divisions was based on a theory of development, "filling the entrepreneurial gap," which ignored both the central dilemma of development and the processes by which the corporation had actually, on rare occasions, resolved it. Given the

dilemma of development, the formal development structure had been doomed to failure.

Moreover, the whole process remained undiscussable. If it were to be discussed, it would have been necessary to bring out into the open the games of control and deception top management played with the divisions as well as the games of competition and exclusion the barons played with the NBD. It would also have been necessary to face publicly the two conflicting requirements of corporate develop- ment and decentralized management. The first reqirement meant that each divisional manager must see himself as a piece of the corporate puzzle, ready to give up resources and markets for the sake of a new corporate business. The second meant that each divisional manager must exploit and protect his business territory and respond only to the demand that he deliver expected earnings, month by month and year by year.

Hence, the absence of direct criticism of NBD. No one was anxious to open that can of worms.

Perspectives On Organizational Learning

The Mercury case presents a story of both productive organizational learning and organizational nonlearning. It illustrates concepts im- portant to the inquiry that we have already introduced and others not yet defined. We intend to pursue these concepts in the remainder of this book.

Framing the Corporate Development Dilemma
At the heart of the story is an inconsistency in Mercury's instrumen- tal theory of action, an inconsistency generated by the company's very success in achieving corporate growth. In the early 1970s, that success gave rise to a problematic situation that management framed in terms of organizational structure, that is, a central administration overwhelmed by the task of managing the greatly increased business. Faced with what it saw as a structural problem, management adopted a structural solution, decentralization into semi-autonomous profit centers. As it implemented that solution over time, Mercury devel- oped a theory-in-use for decentralization that included, as a central norm, retaining central control over corporate performance, even as divisional managers were freed up to manage their own divisional business. The strategy of central control was to set targets for divi-

sional performance as measured by earnings and to use the full array of corporate incentives and sanctions to motivate divisional managers to meet their targets. Divisional managers' theory-in-use for responding to central control included protecting themselves by exercising their own unilateral control wherever they could do so and by defending their charters and territories against all comers. (In Chapter 9, we will have occasion to take a deeper look at the organizational consequences of similar norms and strategies for management behavior in a decentralized structure.)

In the mid-1960s, however, management identified a different sort of worry, a decline in the rate of corporate growth. In this case, the pattern of problem setting and problem solving took more than one form. Top management framed the rate-of-growth problem in terms of an "entrepreneurial gap" and again devised a structural solution, the New Business Division. This structural invention incorporated an espoused theory of business development. New business opportunities were to be generated and screened; the most promising were to be incubated by New Business Division and then passed on to existing divisions for management. But the NBD also developed a theory-in-use for its activities. In order to avoid conflict with the powerful barons, the NBD adopted the strategy of seeking out only those new business opportunities that lay beyond the bounds of existing businesses. In parallel with the creation and operation of the NBD, Mercury evolved another approach to the development of new businesses, one based on a very different theory-in-use. This approach sought to create new business opportunities by transforming and recombining pieces of the existing business, well within the zone that top management would find both credible and comfortable. But this theory-in-use carried with it the requirement that from time to time the barons would give up parts of themselves to serve the purposes of new business development.

Thus, conflicting requirements for decentralized management and corporate development came to a head around the barons' interactions with central management. The internally inconsistent corporate theory-in-use manifested itself in conflicts between divisional managers who saw themseves as unfairly subjected to incompatible demands and the central administration. These conflicts might have been the occasion for organizational inquiry and double-loop learning. The parties to the conflict might have reflected on the conflict and its sources. They might then have explored a restructuring of the corporate norms, strategies, and assumptions that generated the conflict. None of this happened. Instead, the organization responded to the conflict and the inconsistency underlying it through the single-loop learning of some of its component parts. Existing divisions learned to protect their territories more effectively and to become more mistrustful of central; NBD learned to seek business opportunities outside the scope of existing business; and top management learned to criticize particular failures of NBD, yet avoid criticizing NBD itself.

In this process of single-loop learning, the organization functioned as an ecology of subgroups, within which each group responded to other groups within the larger internal environment and, at the same time, became part of the environment to which the other groups responded. At the level of single-loop learning, each subgroup set and solved the problems presented to it by its environment. The net effect of this pattern of a single-loop learning, which we call "ecological adjustment," was to maintain the constancy of organization's theory-in-use. Requirements for development and for decentralized management remained incompatible. Espoused theory and theory-in-use for corporate development remained incongruent.

It is not true, however, that organizational theory-in-use remained entirely constant. Each success in the realm of corporate development made divisional managers more mistrustful, more wary of, and more resistant to central's next incursion. The inconsistency in organizational theory-in-use had begun to take on the character of an organizational dilemma. In light of its conflicting requirements, and its inability to resolve that conflict through inquiry, the organization had begun to find itself in situations of choice where all the options open to it appeared equally bad, and it seemed likely that future development successes would be few and far between.

What was it about the organization that created this dilemma? One answer is that members of the organization had not reflected on the issues underlying the development problem. They had discovered neither the inconsistency in the requirements for development and decentralization nor the incongruity between the organization's espoused theory and theory-in-use for development; they had no map of the problem. In fact, they had treated the whole development process as undiscussable.

But this answer merely shifts the question. What prevented members of the organization from discussing the issue and mapping the problem? What prevented them from doing by themselves what the consultant eventually helped them to do?

Limited Intervention Into A Limited Learning System

Let us consider more carefully how the consultant went about the process of intervention.

> When the consultant found that different members of NBD held different and conflicting views of their problem, he brought them together to confront and discuss their differences.

Within the Mercury Corporation, the norms of the behavioral world induced members to express their diagnoses of sensitive issues in private, never in public. Public discussion of sensitive questions was considered inappropriate. It involved the risk of vulnerability to blame and of interpersonal confrontation. Both were to be avoided. As a consequence, the members of NBD did not realize to what degree they held different views of their common problem.

> The consultant sought to test and explore the different diagnoses by collecting case histories of corporate development which were perceived by NBD staff and other managers as successes or failures, that is, by constructing an organizational history of development.

Perceptions and memories of the development stories were scattered among individuals who kept their views private. No one, for example, had the whole story of the Product X success because no one had experienced that episode from many sides or from beginning to end. The story had to be constructed by piecing together many scattered perceptions, and the norms of the behavioral world militated against such an enterprise.

> The consultant urged the various members of the organization to work together at interpreting the meaning of their stories.

As long as the stories remained scattered and uninterpreted, the map of the development process remained vague, and the diagnoses of the development problem remained ambiguous. But such vagueness and ambiguity were considered normal and appropriate, given the shared wish to avoid exhuming corporate failures which might give rise to blame and to avoid raising in public features of organizational life that were consensually treated as undiscussable.

> The consultant then undertook and supported others in undertaking public confrontation of differing and conflicting views of the problem, testing and exploring of different interpretations of organizational history, concerting scattered perception of organizational events, sharing interpretation of data pertaining to development, and joint modeling of the corporate development problem.

The participant group was surprised by its eventual model of the development problem. The pieces of that model, the stories of development ventures, were not new but they had never before been assembled and considered together. Although the resulting picture was disconcerting, participants found it convincing. It seemed to account for their experiences in the corporation and to make the frustrations they had been experiencing understandable. The vice president for technology, who had been a party to some of the client group meetings, also found the model of the problem convincing.

In constructing this model, the client group had taken a major step toward surfacing what the organization knew about the actual process of development but had been unable to say. For many years, NBD had been operating on its espoused theory of development and had been failing. Its errors were attributed to tactical mistakes or management resistance. Now that resistance had been made a part of a model of the problem, it revealed a fundamental incompatibility between NBD's mode of operation and the corporation's theory-in-use for successful development.

The consultant's interventions had the effect of reducing certain *conditions for error* (scattered perceptions, vague maps, ambiguous diagnoses) so that other conditions for error (inconsistency and incongruity in corporate theory of action) might surface and be subjected to inquiry.

The consultant sought to facilitate a process of double-loop learning in organizational inquiry by reducing the conditions for error which prevented shared perceptions of inconsistency and incongruity in organizational theory-in-use. These conditions for error were reinforced by certain prevailing features of the organization's behavioral world, that is, shared strategies in individual theories-in-use which included the following:

- Let buried failures lie.
- Keep your views of sensitive issues private; enforce the taboo against their public discussion.
- Do not surface and test differences in views of organizational problems.
- Avoid seeing the whole picture; allow maps of the problem to remain scattered, vague, and ambiguous.

These strategies, in turn, reflected deeper and more fundamental norms, strategies, and assumptions, for example:

- Protect yourself unilaterally by avoiding both direct interpersonal confrontation and public discussion of sensitive issues which might expose you to blame.

- Protect others unilaterally by avoiding the testing of assumptions where that testing might evoke negative feelings and by keeping others from exposure to blame.
- Control the situation and the task by making up your own mind about the problem and acting on your view. Keep your view private, and avoid the public inquiry which might refute it.

These features of the behavioral world, which the consultant sought to counteract, constrain and guide the character and extent of organizational learning. They determine what will be discussed and what will be left undiscussable, which individual perceptions of organizational experience will be left scattered and which will be concerted. They limit the extent to which organizational maps will be constructed, shared, and tested. They determine whether and in what way conditions of error will be reduced so that inconsistencies and incongruities in organizational theory-in-use may be discovered.

However, the features of the behavioral world that inhibit organizational inquiry into the problems of corporate development also pervade the development process itself. Thus central administrators used strategies of unilateral control and witholding information to protect themselves and deal with divisional managers; divisional managers, with their territoriality and wariness of top management, used similar strategies to protect themselves and resist central control. And both groups sought to avoid confrontation and the negative feelings it might provoke by refraining from publicly testing their assumptions about each other.

Thus features of the behavioral world, which entered into the development process and helped create its perceived difficulties, also constrained inquiry into that process. One might say that the behavioral world protected itself from exposure.

The organization's instrumental theory-in-use is embedded in a behavioral world which shapes and constrains it at the same time that it shapes and constrains the organization's ability to learn about its theory-in-use. This is what we mean by the organization's learning system. In Mercury's learning system, organizational learning about corporate development was limited to the process of ecological adjustment described earlier, a process in which each group carried out single-loop learning so as to cope, within unchanging norms, with the problems created for it by other groups in its environment. For a time the consultant was able to intervene in such a way as to reduce conditions for error and surface the central dilemma of development which the organization's learning system had helped to create and preserve.

As the participants sought to invent solutions to the problem they had mapped, they encountered yet another difficulty. They were strongly tempted to invent solutions acceptable to the present system, but these were the ones least likely to resolve the underlying dilemma.

In this process the consultant took the role of publicly testing proposed solutions and helping the participants to identify in them the potential for unintended consequences. The clients' norms of rationality made them sensitive to the possibility that they might produce consequences they did not intend and suggested that the problem might not be truly solved unless they confronted the dilemma fundamental to it.

In the course of this inquiry, the client group came up with five principles for the redesign of the corporate development process:

1. Find better ways of mobilizing and managing the allocation of existing commercial and technological competences throughout the corporation, instead of setting up parallel structures and resources.

2. The corporate development function must create and manage networks of dispersed corporate competences, oversee the budgeting and management of resources for development, and integrate these functions with ongoing technology planning.

3. The process should start from early top-management commitment to business and technological targets rather than generate many balls in the air for top-management review.

4. There should be a new charter for corporate development that reflects these considerations.

5. It is important that divisional managers understand the conflicting requirements which they experience and that they and top management design incentives and sanctions which would encourage divisional managers to "play the current game well" as well as to function from time to time as a "good piece of the larger puzzle."

The client group recognized that these principles could not be implemented unless top management and divisional managers entered into a dialogue with those presently responsible for corporate development, a dialogue which would begin with the problem mapping the group had undertaken and the dilemma of development that had surfaced.

The prospects for such a dialogue seemed uncertain. Some members of the group worried that "should you ever formalize this process, people might reject it." The vice president for technology felt that such a dialogue was necessary, "but would have to be approached with care."

The Mercury story shows, then, some of the ways in which an organization's learning system may prevent double-loop learning in organizational inquiry, and it illustrates a kind of limited intervention which by-passes that learning system, at least for a time, so as to increase the likelihood of such double-loop learning.

Organizational Dialectic

The Mercury story also suggests the dialectical nature of the larger process of organizational change within which we find episodes of learning or of failure to learn.

The organizational dilemma of corporate development arose as a consequence of a dual process, each part of which took the form of setting and solving an urgent problem. The phenomenal rate of corporate growth led to difficulties that were perceived as a problem of management overload and were solved through decentralization. The wish to maintain that rate of growth, in the face of what was seen as declining R&D productivity, led to the creation of a New Business Division. The working out of these two intertwined solutions led to the creation of a new inconsistency in organizational theory-in-use, an incompatibility between the requirements of decentralization and development that we have described as an organizational dilemma manifested in the conflict between central and divisional management.

We use the term "organizational dialectic" to refer to such processes. In them, problematic organizational situations give rise to organizational inquiry—problem setting and problem solving— which, in turn, creates new problematic situations within which new inconsistencies and incongruities in organizational theory-in-use come into play. These are characteristically manifested in intraorganizational conflict. The organization's ways of responding to such conflicts yields still further transformations of the organization's problematic situation.

We believe that organizational learning occurs within the context of such dialectical processes which stem from two conditions of organizational life. First, organizations are necessarily involved in continual transaction with their internal and external environments which are continually changing in response to both external forces and organizational actions. Second, organizational objectives, purposes, and norms are always multiple and potentially conflicting.

As a consequence, it is no accident that organizational solutions give rise to further problems; they may be expected to do so, given the dialectical context of organizational inquiry.

This, then, sharply raises the problem of criteria for the evaluation of organizational change and learning, a problem central to our inquiry which will occupy us especially in Part III. At this point, however, we may note the following:

- The achievement of stable solutions is not an appropriate criterion for organizational learning; it is in the very nature of organizational problem solving to change situations in ways that create new problems.

- Organizational effectiveness, as measured by the achievement of espoused purposes and norms, is an incomplete criterion for organizational learning. It is appropriate in situations where error correction can occur through single-loop learning alone. It is insufficient where inconsistencies in organizational theory-in-use set requirements for double-loop learning.

"Good dialectic" is the term we use to describe processes of organizational inquiry which take the form of single- and double-loop learning and where both single- and double-loop learning meet standards of high-quality inquiry.

The achievement of good dialectic requires organizational deuterolearning. It requires that the organization's members reflect on and inquire into their organizational learning system and its effect on organizational inquiry.

Part II

Defensive Reasoning and the Theoretical Framework that Explains It—Model I and O-I

4

Defensive Reasoning
In Individuals

In this chapter, we illustrate what we mean by "defensive," in contrast to "productive," reasoning, and we outline in some detail the methods we use to study how individuals reason.

Our methodology operates on an interdependent, double-track strategy through which we attempt to engage with practitioners in collaborative action research.

First, we try to describe the reality of a particular context as accurately as possible, organizing our descriptions in the form of propositions that are generally applicable to many such contexts. In any particular context, we try to test such propositions and, therefore, prove them false. We do not lower the standards of falsification because our tests are conducted in field-organizational settings. We also frame our research propositions so as to make them usable by practitioners, not only to provide an additional test for them but to contribute to the practical effectiveness of knowledge in a world we seek to understand.

Secondly, we try to help practitioners become more reflective inquirers into their practice so that they can monitor it and, by detecting and correcting errors wherever they occur, increase the likelihood of producing what they intend. We seek to help practitioners understand their world in such a way that they can produce conditions for organizational learning, especially double-loop learning.

We see our double-track strategy as a model not only for effective research but for reflective practice especially regarding double-loop learning.

A Generic Dilemma In Double-track Research

Our initial premise is that human beings design their actions and implement their designs. We call these designs theories of action, differentiating, as we pointed out in Chapter 1, between the theories of action individuals espouse and the ones they actually use their theories-in-use.

Both of these types of theories are learned early in life and supported by features of societal and organizational cultures. Although human beings' sense of competence, independence, and self-esteem are based on both types of theories, we consider theories-in-use to be more powerful in explaining and changing behavior, especially in relation to double-loop learning.

Almost all of the individuals we have studied hold theories-in-use that are systematically counterproductive for double-loop learning, especially when the issues are embarrassing or threatening. Moreover, these same theories-in-use, when skillfully used, make the actors unaware of the counterproductive features built into them. Since the theories-in-use are sanctioned and supported by organizational and societal cultures, individuals have little reason to be aware of or to explore this predicament. Indeed, as we shall show, practitioners may even interpret attempts to explore the predicament as bewildering, if not inappropriate.

As researchers, we are therefore likely to be faced with a dilemma: Individuals may unknowingly provide us with distorted information, and these same individuals may hesitate to engage in the dialogue that is required to explore the possibility of such distortions. If we persist in exploring these issues, practitioners may become defensive—their defensiveness leading, in turn, to new distortions, both recognized and unrecognized.

This research dilemma is systematic. It is unlikely to be overcome by the use of better sampling procedures. Nor can it be overcome by the use of the accepted methods of normal social science because embedded in the execution of these methods, with their reliance on research strategies of secrecy and unilateral control, is the same theory-in-use as the one that causes the dilemma in the first place (Argyris 1980, 1993).

Features of Our Research Method

Our approach to the research dilemma begins with the task of constructing the theories-in-use that underlie it, those theories-in-use that inform the reasoning and action of practitioners. This requires the collection of relatively observable data. Observations of actual behavior, especially the tape recording of conversations, is the dominant mode. We may also use questionnaires, projective tests, or structured interviews; but if we use such instruments, we recognize that they are likely to give us insights into espoused theories and not theories-in-use.

The observations made and the conversations recorded should be connected to objectives and actions to which individuals are highly committed, for example, observations of meetings about non-routine issues that tend to stimulate feelings of embarrassment or threat. Such events are intimately tied to an individual's sense of competence, confidence, and self-esteem. A slightly less powerful set of data may be obtained in classrooms and workshops, as long as those activities raise problems that the participants consider important and persistent features of their everyday working lives.

This is one reason why our research methods focus on intervention and change. Practitioners examine such research proposals with care, especially when they deal with double-loop issues. The practitioners realize that research of this kind may generate a variety of costs for them, triggering defenses at all levels of their organizations.

Such defenses should not be avoided or suppressed. When they occur, they become additional data that can be used to test diagnoses of individual, interpersonal, and organizational phenomena. In order to deal with defenses effectively, however, the researcher must possess the necessary skills, the same skills the practitioners will have to learn if they are to deal with defenses in their organization. The theory of action the researcher uses to obtain valid information becomes a model available for use by practitioners.

If a researcher or practitioner is to act effectively in the service of double-loop learning, skills are necessary but not sufficient. The inquirer also needs an *actionable* theory of organizational learning, one that may be used to generate and test specific hypotheses in a wide variety of settings, as well as in the individual case.

"Individual case" typically denotes an *n* of one. In our research, however, the individual case functions as a setting for multiple observations. Most of our research is conducted in one organization, but we treat that organization as a setting in which we conduct many observations of individual and interpersonal behavior.

Our observations are guided by our theories of individual and organizational learning. For example, we are interested in observing behaviors such as evaluating or making attributions. We make a priori predictions about the impact of such behaviors. These predictions vary depending on whether evaluations and attributions are crafted in ways that discourage or encourage inquiry, especially that which leads to double-loop learning. We are able to score transcripts to assess the frequency with which such behaviors occur, making use of interobserver reliability studies and other appropriate measures. We can then make a priori predictions of the behaviors' consequences for such features of inquiry as self-fulfilling or self-sealing processes. These, as we will illustrate in the following chapter, enable us to make a priori predictions about the impact of individuals' behavior on organizational phenomena such as interdepartmental relationships or organizational defensive routines.

A Relatively Simple Paper-and-Pencil Method for Obtaining Valid Information About Individual Theories of Action

Throughout this book, we will illustrate research methods that we claim produce valid knowledge about individual and organizational learning, in such a way as to engage, not bypass, the research dilemma we have described earlier. The first such illustration is a unique type of case that we ask individuals to prepare for classroom or workshop settings.

Typically, we send a letter to each prospective participant in which we describe the format of the case, asking them to send their cases to us at least a week before the seminar. The format instructions are:

1. Identify an important problem that you have tried to solve or will try to solve in the near future. There are no limits on the subject selected except that you should evaluate it as crucial to your own, your department's, and your organization's performance.

2. Describe the steps you took (or plan to take) in order to resolve the problem. With whom did you meet? What was the purpose of the meeting as you recollect it (or as you expect it to be)?

3. Divide the next several pages in half. In the right-hand column, write the conversation, as you can best recollect it. Begin with what you said, what the other(s) said, then what you said, and so on for about three pages. If it is a session that has not yet been held, describe what you plan to say, what you expect others to say, and so on. In the left-hand column, write any thoughts and feelings you had as the conversation proceeded (or that you believe you will have when you meet sometime in the future).

Typically, we receive cases of three to five pages (a few have been as long as ten pages). A brief illustration of a case is presented below. This case was written by a CEO who had been telling his immediate reports that the time has come for "calling a spade a spade." He urged them to be forthright and straightforward with their employees because the firm was in serious financial trouble.

Case Illustration: The Easing-in CEO

Thoughts and Feelings Unsaid	*The Conversation*
I hope we'll work cooperatively. I fear we won't.	CEO: *I'm sure that you and I share the same goals. We need to rethink our latest cost estimates.*
	Other: *The latest estimates are not the most reliable...*
What is wrong with him? He's missing the most important point.	CEO: *I can see that some costs can be reduced (by your recommendation), but that still leaves us with a very large problem.*
	Other: *The original estimates were produced by others. We never really agreed to them.*
He doesn't want to accept ownership; he wants to make me responsible.	CEO: *We will have to use these estimates. That's the reality.*

The participants' cases usually contain several features. First, the left-hand column usually contains important negative evaluations and attributions, indicating that the writers are experiencing the "other" as being ineffective and performing poorly. Second, the case writers typically do not state these evaluations and attributions in a candid and forthright manner as in this example, the writer had advised his subordinates to do for their subordinates. Third, the conversations that are crafted bypass any strong feelings, and the bypass is covered up. Fourth, the writers appear unaware of any discrepancy between what they are espousing and how they actually behave.

Reflecting on the Case Approach in the Light of the Research Dilemma

Our instructions to case writers ask them to identify crucial problems they are experiencing or expect to experience. We ask them to write a short description of the strategy they used (or would use) in order to deal with these problems. The written case tells us what the respondents' objectives are and gives us insight into the processes they state they will use in order to implement their objectives. This information gets at their espoused theory of action.

The conversation the participants write provides directly observable data from which we infer their theory-in-use. The description of thoughts and feelings they did not (or would not) state gives us insight into their self-censoring processes, another key feature of their theory-in-use.

As we shall see, it is possible to use such cases to identify discrepancies between the writers' espoused theories and the theories-in-use built into their actions. Awareness of such discrepancies makes it possible for the writers to assess the degree to which they have been skillfully unaware that their behavior is counterproductive to their intentions. This, in turn, can become the basis for inquiry into the nature of a theory-in-use that leads them to act skillfully yet produces ineffective actions.

We will address the question of the validity of such data as we go along, because we test validity in different ways under different conditions. All we are claiming at this point is the following:

1. The written conversations and thoughts and feelings present what the practitioners wrote. (We are not claiming that these are the words they actually used or would use in the events to which their cases refer. Nor is it necessary for us to make such a claim.)
2. These cases (and the dialogues tape-recorded during their discussion) are adequate to infer the writers' respective theories-in-use as manifested by the data of their cases. (We will eventually answer the question of the generalizing of these inferences to situations beyond the case.)

Case 1: Strategic Case Management Seminar

We draw our first example of the research method described above from a seminar that took place at the Harvard Graduate School of Business Administration in 1993. Thirty-seven upper- and some middle-level financial executives attended. Five were female. Fifteen came from foreign continents (e.g., Africa, Australia, Asia, and South America). The focus of this seminar was on new concepts and procedures used in strategic cost management and on the human problems likely to arise when such concepts and procedures are implemented in organizational settings.

We were not able to discuss all the cases the finanical executives wrote because there was not enough time during the week-long seminar. At the outset, the faculty member (Argyris) used the full set of cases as a vehicle to provide the entire group with an overall picture of the underlying action strategies they used. Three lists were developed. List #1 contained examples of comments quoted verbatim from the "left-hand columns," illustrating the writers' views of the individuals with whom they were dealing:

List #1

1. *Don't let these guys upset you.*
2. *Say something positive.*
3. *This is not going well. Wrap it up and wait for another chance.*
4. *Remain calm. Stick to the facts.*
5. *He is clearly defensive.*
6. *He's playing hardball because he is afraid of losing power.*
7. *She is overblowing the systems issue to avoid having to change.*
8. *He is baiting me now.*
9. *Will he ever be able to change?*
10. *This guy is unbelievable. He will never change.*
11. *You are nowhere as good as you think you are.*
12. *The trouble with you is that you do not really understand accounting as a managerial function.*

These comments illustrate the following patterns, which we find as a general rule in a wide variety of settings whenever we use this case method:

The left-hand columns contain thoughts and feelings that are critical for learning to occur. Yet they are systematically covered up.

Advocating, evaluating, and attributing are the three action strategies subjects most often use in dyadic relationships, in groups or intergroup settings, or when they deal with organizational policies, practices, rules, and norms.

The classroom session began with the executives (all of whom had written cases) reading List #1. After a few minutes, the faculty member asked them to describe their reactions to the list. He asked, "What does this list tell you about the individuals who wrote the comments? What inferences do you make as to what is going on?"

The executives responded easily and quickly. Eight examples of their comments, taken from the transcript, were as follows on the next page.

List #2

1. *They were opinionated.*
2. *They talk as if they are right.*
3. *They are frustrated and angry.*
4. *They are entrenched.*
5. *They are avoiding conflict.*
6. *They are not listening.*
7. *They are fearful.*
8. *They exhibit lack of empathy.*

The faculty member wrote these responses on the board. He then asked the participants to reflect on the nature of their comments. The executives responded that their responses indicated an overall negative reaction. The comments were primarily negative evaluations and attributions of defenses in others. Moreover, the class comments indicated that the executives thought the writers of List #1 (whom they knew to be themselves) appeared closed to learning.

We see in these reactions the following general patterns:

Evaluations and attributions are made in ways that do not encourage testing. The writers appear to act as if their diagnosis is valid and does not require testing.

The writers appear closed to learning or, at least, they see learning as unnecessary. Yet all of them attended the seminar and wrote the case with the expressed purpose of learning how to be more effective in dealing with the human side of enterprise.

The class comments on List #1 led to reflection on a different issue. One executive said that what surprised her was the negativeness of the first list. She recognized her comment in List #1 and it, too, was negative. Yet, she added, she was certain that her intent was to be positive. She guessed that this was probably the intent of others in the class. Several class members responded affirmatively.

The faculty member then asked the executives to analyze List #2, their comments about List #1, as he had written them on the board. The executives responded that these comments, too, were negative. They were evaluations and attributions crafted in ways that did not encourage inquiry. This also surprised them.

Here, we find another general pattern:

There appears to be a systematic discrepancy between the writers' expressed aspirations to learn and help others to learn and their actual behavior, which is largely counterproductive for learning. The individuals are systematically unaware of the ways in which they produce their unawareness.

The faculty member then said that the dialogue so far illustrated some of the main findings that had been obtained worldwide from nearly 6000 individuals of both sexes, ranging widely in majority or minority status, education, wealth, and organizational rank. What the class participants were experiencing was not unique. It seems that individuals throughout the world deal with difficult, embarrassing, and threatening issues in a similar manner. For example, they make evaluations and attributions that are crafted in ways that do not encourage learning. They are predisposed to be unaware of the discrepancies they produce, such as aspiring to be positive yet being negative.

At this point, one executive said that he agreed that a negative pattern did exist in the self-censored left-hand columns and in the responses the faculty member had written on the board. He was certain that part of the "free-flowing negativeness" (as he called it) was due to the fact that the participants thought that they were talking privately. They would have crafted their conversations differently if those they were evaluating were present.

This led to several attempts by the executives to show in roleplaying how they would craft their conversations differently. Indeed, they were different. They were more diplomatic and easing-in. They bypassed the threatening issues and acted as if they were not doing so. The faculty member said that he obtained the same results from all other groups. Unawareness, he suggested, was highly skilled, in that it was in the service of crafting conversations that were intended to be positive; unawareness of this type was not caused by ignorance. The faculty member hoped to show it was caused by a master design in the heads of individuals, through which they attempt to act positively, yet the results of the use of that design are consistently negative.

The faculty member then handed out List #3. This list contained examples from the participants' cases of left-hand column thoughts and right-hand column conversations. The conversations were crafted in ways that were diplomatic and smoothed-over, and they bypassed the meanings in the left-hand columns. Thus their cases written several weeks before were similar to their roleplaying in class. For example,

List #3

Thoughts and Feelings Unsaid	*Conversations*
You guys come up with more excuses that make no sense. You do this all the time.	*You still have the ability to offer different combinations of products.*

If we gave you everything you ask for, we would lose our shirts.	*The research we have done shows that there is a consumer movement toward my views. Your sales will not be harmed.*
How can I convince the group of the necessity to change while we're on top?	*Although we are the leaders, it is becoming more difficult to remain responsive and react quickly enough. Our product development process has to become more effective and efficient.*
Winning the Nobel Prize will not help the company. Perhaps it's time to expand development staff and downsize research staff.	*I am sure that you all realize that we work in a for-profit industry and must be realistic-oriented. Yet, it should be possible to find commercial value even in basic research.*

A further general pattern may be inferred at this point:

Individuals, having realized that features of their actions are counterproductive to learning, are unable to produce actions that encourage learning.

Several members of the class then pointed out that when they are on the receiving end of such positive statements as those in the right-hand column of List #3, they know that the diplomacy is used to cover up negative thoughts (like those shown in the left-hand columns). They also admitted that they themselves keep such thoughts private. Often they try to inquire discreetly, but this rarely seems to work because the other party senses that their discreet inquiry is a cover-up. More often, they bypass inquiry during their meetings but later spend hours holding private conversations to try to find out what was really going on.

Findings such as these have been produced for decades in executive program classrooms and workshops held not only in the United States but in Europe, South America, the Near East, and the Far East. How do we explain them? What are their consequences for organizational learning? We explore these questions in the following chapter.

5

The Case of the CIO: Primary and Secondary Inhibitory Loops

Case Description

The chief information officer (CIO) of a large electronics firm was told by the CEO, his superior, that an important organizational problem existed and had to be corrected.[1] The problem was that the Information Technology (IT) group was too large and too expensive. Moreover, its service to the line organization was inadequate.

The CEO reminded the CIO that this was not the first time he had spoken of this problem. He was becoming impatient. He warned that if costs did not go down and if the quality and efficiency of service did not become better, he would be forced to take drastic action that could include finding a new CIO. The CIO called a meeting of his immediate reports to take corrective action.

CIO and His Immediate Reports

How the Meeting Began

The CIO opened by telling his subordinates that he had received a "read-our-lips" order from line management: cooperation was nonexistent, and the information professionals were providing minimal value added, despite higher budgets.

He then said, "I want to discuss with you our ability to react to users' needs and the fact that we are always having difficulties with line

---

[1] This case was presented and discussed at an executive seminar conducted by Argyris at the Harvard Graduate School of Business Administration in 1993.

management. They are, after all, our customers. We must be concerned about meeting their needs." The information professionals responded as follows:

> *We are concerned about their needs. The big trouble is that they do not know what they want.*
>
> *When they do [know what they want], they have no idea how long it will take to provide them with high-quality services. They want everything yesterday.*
>
> *We have "had it up to here" with line management's complaints. The problem would be easily solved if the line gave us the people and resources we truly need.*

The CIO expressed empathy with their frustration and anger and suggested that they might begin to turn things around by developing "a credible plan to respond to [customer] needs." The professionals responded in the following way:

> *There is no sense in planning; our users don't plan. Anyway, we are convinced that just about the time we think we are on top of things, they will make more demands and complain about what we are failing to do.*

The CIO replied:

> *But since we do not have a solid plan, we cannot review the way we are managing our resources...As I see it, we have two choices. The first is to do what we are doing—and I believe that will be disastrous. The second is to break out of this mold and change the way we do business.*

Members of the group countered by arguing that there was no way to change line management. As one said, "If you want to try, good luck." The CIO replied, "If planning isn't the way to go, how do you propose to solve the problem?"

The information professionals responded with increasing emotion. They said, in effect,

> *1. the problem is not solvable because line management makes impossible requests, and*
>
> *2. the information professionals are already killing themselves.*

"That's why the good people are leaving," said one individual. "I agree," said another, adding, "It is not fixable."

Virtually at the end of his patience, the CIO exclaimed: "We have to fix it because we have no choice! Otherwise we are not being responsible."

What Is Going On Here?

Clearly the information technology professionals are expressing frustration with and mistrust of the line executives, as well as their own superior. Their conversation is crafted in a way that makes a dialogue difficult. For example, they advocate their positions and make evaluations and attributions about line management in ways that do not encourage inquiry or testing. These are examples of their unillustrated, untestable evaluations and attributions about line management:

- *Line does not know what they want.*
- *Line makes demands with unrealistic deadlines.*
- *If we meet their demands, they will follow up with more unrealistic demands.*
- *The problems are unfixable because of line management's recalcitrance.*

The CIO's Reaction.

The CIO wanted to get the subordinates to be cooperative, and he also wanted to minimize the likelihood that they would see him as unfair and judgmental. Unlike his subordinates, he censored his evaluations and attributions and acted as if this were not the case. Asked to write out his private thoughts and feelings, he offered the following:

- *These guys act like a bunch of babies.*
- *They do not realize how insensitive and opinionated they are.*
- *Sometimes I feel that I should read the riot act to them. They've got to wise up or all of us will lose.*

When asked what led him not to make these thoughts and feelings public, he looked astonished, "If I said these feelings and thoughts, all I would have done was add fuel to the fire." He was correct. His private thoughts and feelings were crafted in the same counterproductive manner as were his and his subordinates' public conversation.

The use of self-induced censorship in order to create conditions for dialogue is rarely successful. For example, when some of the professionals were asked if they had any idea of their bosses' private thoughts, they responded with words that were almost identical to the ones the CIO used. When they were asked what led them not to say so, they responded with the same look of astonishment. "Are you kidding," said one of them, "that would make things worse." Quite likely, the subordinates were also carrying on internal monologues that were not vocalized. Thus we have people holding private conversations about each other and thinking that the others do not hear these conversations. In actuality, the others do hear them but act as if they do not.

Reflecting On the Action of the CIO and His Reports

The CIO decided to begin the meeting with a "take charge" attitude. He told his group about negative evaluations by the top, and warned them that the time had come for corrective action. He then requested a constructive dialogue about what could be done to correct the situation. The subordinates also had their own "take charge" attitude. They bypassed the CIO's requests, arguing that the problems were caused by top management.

The CIO responded in two ways. First, he avoided publicly expressing his negative feelings, fearing that doing so could make the situation worse. We would agree. If he were to make public his negative evaluations and attributions, he would be likely to activate the same kind of defensiveness that his subordinates' negative evaluations and attributions had activated in him. The very way he framed his private thoughts and feelings was counterproductive to learning. The irony was that his private thoughts were consistent with the views of the CEO. For example, both saw the IT professionals as uncooperative and acting childishly.

Thus the first action strategy the CIO used in the name of producing a positive dialogue increased the amount of information that was withheld, suppressed his personal feelings, bypassed the feelings of his subordinates, and acted as if he was not doing so.

The second way the CIO responded was to take a rational approach to the problem. He asked the group to develop a credible plan to respond to the needs of line management. The subordinates rejected this suggestion on the grounds that it was irrational: the line managers did not know how to plan, were not likely to be satisfied with a sound plan, and would only escalate their demands and criticisms.

So far, all three levels of participants seem to have the same strategy. All believe that they should take charge and warn the others that their actions are not acceptable. This activates a barrage of evaluations and attributions on all sides, crafted in ways that do not encourage learning. For example, the subordinates evaluate the line as unable to plan and attribute to them the intention of making life difficult for the IT group. The CIO privately felt the same about the IT group but decided that in order to have a constructive discussion, he should remain rational and focus on developing new plans. Again, he appears to be struggling to remain at the rational level of planning, suppressing his private thoughts and feelings, in order to avoid provoking emotional responses that he sees as unconstructive.

This strategy fails to achieve its intended objectives. First of all, the subordinates respond with even more emotion and make more negative evaluations and attributions which they communicate with a sense of certainty. (If the CIO were to ask them openly how they knew their diagnosis was correct, they would probably say, "Trust us, we work with them, we know!") Secondly, when some of the professionals were asked if they had any idea of their boss's private thoughts, they used words that were almost identical to the ones the CIO used about himself. When they were asked, then, what led them not to discuss their views, one of them said, "That would make things worse. All you would get is a blowup." Like the CIO, the subordinates were carrying on private conversations, making private attributions to their boss, which they also covered up.

Reflecting on these consequences, it seems fair to infer the following: The participants experienced an interest in solving the business problem, but their ways of crafting their conversation, combined with their self-censorship, led to a dialogue that was defensive and self-reinforcing. When this happens, the participants have to focus on two major problems:

1. the business problem they set out to solve in the first place and
2. the problem triggered by defensiveness—mistrust, its cover-up, and the cover-up of the cover-up.

The latter problem, we suggest, takes up a lot of the players' span of attention. Not only do they have to listen to the other party and think about their response; they must strive to do all this and at the same time keep track of their cover-ups.

The Primary Inhibitory Loop

We began with a business problem identified as high IT costs and poor IT performance. All three levels of players agreed with this description of the problem, but they disagreed about its causes.

The CIO went into his meeting with three assumptions about the action strategies he should adopt in order to make the meeting effective:

1. I (CIO) should take charge of the meeting, if it is to meet my objectives. The definition of victory is that the subordinates develop a plan that will convince the senior line executives that they intend to cut costs.

2. It is important for me to involve my subordinates in developing a corrective plan. They will then be more committed to its implementation.

3. If my subordinates become emotional and do not act like grown-ups, I must suppress the latter and defuse the former by focusing on rational actions, such as planning. The way to suppress my negative feelings is to experience them privately, censor them from the group, and act as if I am not doing so.

The subordinates appear to have used action strategies based on similar assumptions. They, too, felt that they should take charge of the meeting. Their definition of victory is that the CIO will realize that the major obstacle to solving the problem is the line managers. They, too, seek to involve the CIO so that he will become a more effective spokesman for their views with top management. Finally, they assume that their responses are rational. Whenever they add emotional decibels, it is to make sure the CIO hears what they say.

These shared strategies and assumptions lead each side to craft conversations that upset the other side, leading, in turn, to expression and bypassing of the emotional dimensions of important issues, which then become undiscussable. A conversation that is intended to be positive actually produces defensive reactions in all players who deal with their defensive reactions in ways that reinforce and escalate defensiveness, again, with positive intentions (consequences similar to the ones created by the financial executives in the class described in the previous chapter).

We call these self-reinforcing patterns of action strategies and antilearning consequences **primary inhibitory loops.** The loops are primary in the sense that they are informed by the participants' theories-in-use during face-to-face discussions (especially when these are laced with embarrassment or threat). Within such loops, defensive, dysfunctional responses (based on theories-in-use like those shared by the CIO and his subordinates) are triggered by and, in turn, reinforce **conditions for error**, properties of information that tend to obscure error and make it uncorrectable. Not being able to discuss important issues is one example; other such examples are vagueness and ambiguity. In the CIO's meeting with his subordinates, the actual causes of line/staff troubles remain vague (they are not clearly specified or illustrated) and ambiguous (the different interpretations of line/staff conflict are not clarified or resolved). Attributions that the CIO and his subordinates make to each other or to line management remain untested, and, to the extent that they cannot be tested so long as the issues and feelings associated with them are undiscussable, they become untestable.

A fuller, though not exhaustive, list of conditions for error, together with corrective responses to them, is given below:

Conditions for Error	Corrective Responses
Vagueness	Specify
Ambiguity	Clarify
Untestability	Make testable
Scattered information	Concert
Information withheld	Reveal
Undiscussability	Make discussable
Uncertainty	Inquire
Inconsistency/incompatiblity	Resolve

In organizational settings, conditions for error trigger defensive reactions like those of the CIO and his subordinates; these reactions, in turn, reduce the likelihood that individuals will engage in the kind of organizational inquiry that leads to productive learning outcomes. Vagueness and ambiguity in organizational theory-in-use yield organizational situations that individual members find threatening. Uncertainty over the nature of troublesome situations, over what is to be done and by whom, or over criteria for performance, increase individual feelings of defensiveness and anxiety. When important information is withheld, when important issues are treated as undiscussable, individuals tend to feel mistrust and uneasiness. Incompatibilities in organizational theory-in-use tend to be expressed in interpersonal conflicts, which individuals then live out in terms of win/lose games.

Many readers will not find the existence of such patterns to be news. Indeed, many CIOs who participated in executive programs have confirmed that they have experienced similar situations Executives representing other managerial functions also recognized that the case material illustrates familiar patterns of interdepartmental competitiveness and mutual mistrust between line and staff.

Why do such counterproductive dialogues, with their primary inhibitory loops, occur so systematically? To our knowledge, no one argues for them; and texts and courses on organization design, leadership, conflict resolution, and employee involvement or empowerment, see these loops as violating both the letter and the spirit of management and organization theory. Why, then, do such counterproductive dialogues occur and persist when, most often, the participants go into them with constructive intent to solve a business problem? One answer to this question is related to the assumptions and skills individuals learn to use early in life to deal with issues that are embarrassing and threatening. But individuals are only part of the answer. Organizational phenomena also reinforce such counterproductive dialogues. If we study everyday activity in organizations, we would be hard put to separate the individual from the organizational. The two factors interpenetrate to such an extent that one must conclude there exists a circular relationship of pattern causality where each factor "causes" and reinforces the other.

We believe, then, that there are three levels of explanation for the patterns represented by primary inhibitory loops: the first is individual; the second, organizational; the third, an interaction of the two. Let us begin with the individual level.

Model I Theories-in-Use

As we pointed out in Chapter 4, human beings hold two types of theories of action about effective behavior. One is the theory of action that is espoused; the other is the theory that is actually used, the theory-in-use. We have found that when human beings deal with issues that are embarrassing or threatening, their reasoning and action conform to a particular model of theory-in-use which we call Model I. Model I informs the actions that enter into primary loops, as described above, with the effect of inhibiting double-loop learning. Neither the CIO nor his subordinates espoused such a theory of action, yet all of them used it.

In the table that follows we present a schema of Model I. The first column of the table lists "governing variables," or values, that actors strive to satisfy through their actions:

1. *Define goals and try to achieve them.* Participants rarely tried to develop with others a mutual definition of purposes,

Model I Theory-in-Use

Governing Variables	Action Strategies	Consequences for Behavioral World	Consequences for Learning, Effectiveness
Define goals and try to achieve them.	Design and manage the environment unilaterally (be persuasive, appeal to larger goals, etc.)	Actor seen as defensive, inconsistent, incongruent, controlling, fearful of being vulnerable, withholding of feelings, overly concerned about self and others, or underconcerned about others.	Self-sealing. Decreased long-term effectiveness.
Maximize winning and minimize losing.	Own and control the task (claim ownership of the task, be guardian of the definition and execution of the task).	Defensive interpersonal and group relationship (depending on actor, little help to others).	Single-loop learning.
Minimize generating or expressing negative feelings.	Unilaterally protect yourself (speak in inferred categories accompanied by little or no directly observable data, be blind to impact on others and to incongruity; use defensive actions such as blaming, stereotyping, suppressing feelings, intellectualizing).	Defensive norms (mistrust, lack of risk taking, conformity, external commitment, emphasis on diplomacy, power-centered competition and rivalry).	Little testing of theories publicly. Much testing of theories privately.
Be rational.	Unilaterally protect others from being hurt (withhold information, create rules to censor information and behavior, hold private meetings).		

nor did they seem open to being influenced to alter their perception of the task.

2. *Maximize winning and minimize losing.* Participants felt that once they had decided on their goals, changing them would be a sign of weakness.

3. *Minimize generating or expressing negative feelings.* Participants almost unanimously declared that generating negative feelings showed ineptness, incompetence, or lack of diplomacy. Permitting or helping others to express their feelings tended to be seen as poor strategy.

4. *Be rational.* This is the counterpart to value 3. It is an injunction to be objective, and intellectual, and to suppress feelings. Interactions should be construed as objective discussions of the issues, whatever feelings may underlie them.

The second column identifies action strategies that participants adopted in order to satisfy these governing variables:

1. *Design and manage the environment unilaterally.* Plan actions secretly and persuade or cajole others to agree with your definition of the situation.

2. *Own and control the task.* The CIO privately decides to resolve the task assignment through a full staff meeting and tries to get others to see things his way.

3. *Unilaterally protect yourself.* Keep yourself from being vulnerable by speaking in abstractions, avoiding reference to directly observed events, and withholding the thoughts and feelings that lead you to do what you do. In order to achieve mastery of the situation, keep your own thoughts and feelings a mystery.

4. *Unilaterally protect others from being hurt.* Withholding valuable and important information, telling white lies, suppressing feelings, and offering false sympathy are examples of this strategy. The speaker assumes that the other person needs to be protected and that the strategy of protection should be kept secret; neither assumption is tested. Thus the CIO protects his subordinates from his negative feelings about them, and they do the same for him. In doing so, the CIO also protects himself from their negative reactions to his feelings, and they protect themselves from his negative reactions and feelings.

To the extent that one behaves according to any of the four action strategies, one will tend to behave unilaterally toward others and protectively toward oneself. If successful, such behavior controls others and prevents one from being influenced by them. But as a consequence, the actor tends to be seen as defensive (since he or she is defending), and interpersonal and intergroup relations tend to become more defensive than facilitative, more a matter of win/lose than of collaboration. These effects tend to generate mistrust and rigidity.

Given these governing variables and strategies, there is likely to be little public testing of the assumptions embedded in theories-in-use, because such testing would require confronting one's own defensiveness and the defensiveness of others. Neither the CIO nor his subordinates could test their assumptions about each other's mistrust, for example, without confronting their own defensiveness and without risking the negative reactions that would be likely to follow.

If there is little genuine public testing of one's theory-in-use and if one must nevertheless act, then one will act on an untested theory-in-use. Since behaving according to one's theory-in-use will influence the behavioral world, self-sealing will probably occur. Thus the CIO eventually feels a sense of mistrust, cynicism, and a lack of confidence in his subordinates. The subordinates feel the same about the CIO. None of these evaluations and attributions are tested publicly. Hence, they become sealed in self-reinforcing, defensive loops. In our earlier book, *Theory in Practice* (Argyris and Schön, 1974), we describe the resulting situation as follows:

> ...Lack of such public testing risks creating self-sealing processes...the individual not only helps to create behavioral worlds that are artifacts of his theory-in-use but also cuts himself off from the possibility of disconfirming assumptions in his theory-in-use and thereby cuts himself off from the possibility of helping to create behavioral worlds that disconfirm his starting assumptions about them. However, public testing of theories-in-use must be accompanied by an openness to change behavior as a function of learning. The actor needs minimally distorted feedback from others. If others provide such feedback—especially if they do so with some risk—and if they experience that the actor is not open to change, they may believe that they have placed themselves in a difficult situation. Their mistrust of the actor will probably increase, but this fact will be suppressed. The result will be the creation of another series of self-sealing processes that again make the actor less likely to receive valid information the next time he tries to test an assumption publicly...(p. 78)

Because double-loop learning depends on the exchange of valid information and public testing of attributions and assumptions, Model I tends to discourage it. Because long-term effectiveness depends on the possibility of double-loop learning, Model I tends toward long-term ineffectiveness.

All of these consequences of governing values and action strategies of Model I feed back to reinforce those values and strategies. In a world of defensiveness, escalating errors, and self-fulfilling processes, it is understandable that individuals should protect themselves by striving even harder to be in unilateral control, to win and not lose, to deal with the defensiveness of others by attempting to be, and encouraging others to be, "rational," and to suppress, as best they can, their own and others' negative feelings, as in the left-hand columns of the participants' cases.

Another result of Model I is that social virtues such as concern, caring, honesty, strength, and courage become defined in ways that support Model I theory-in-use. For example, concern and caring come to mean: "Act diplomatically; say things that people want to hear"—meanings that lead to action strategies such as easing-in, covering-up, and telling white lies. Strength becomes defined in terms of winning, maintaining unilateral control of the situation, and keeping private one's feelings of vulnerability.

There is another factor that powerfully reinforces Model I, increasing the likelihood of antilearning processes. Individuals are highly skilled in their execution of Model I. Skillful actions usually "work," in the sense of achieving their intended objectives; they appear spontaneous, automatic, and effortless; they are taken for granted; and they require little conscious deliberation. These features combine to make it less likely that the actors will reflect on and learn about their Model I behavior.

We have found the distinguishing features of Model I theory-in-use not only in executive sessions but in countless meetings in all sorts of organizations. Moreover, in any setting where the actors use Model I theories-in-use, we have never observed consequences opposite to those listed above. And as already noted, the overwhelming majority of the people we have studied (close to 99 percent) use Model I theory-in-use in threatening or embarrassing situations.

This brief sketch of Model I will be illustrated and extended in the cases that follow. The elements of Model I interact in ways that are far more complex than we have so far described. Similarly, there are many ways in which the behavioral world created by Model I behavior feeds back to reinforce that behavior.

The Secondary Inhibitory Loop

We use the term **secondary inhibitory loop** to refer to the behavioral loops—causal connections between action strategies and antilearning consequences—that are supraindividual, pertaining to interactions of groups within organizations. These loops are secondary in the sense that primary loops lead to them, although they become self-reinforcing once they have been set in motion.

Let us return to the case of the CIO to illustrate how face-to-face interactions lead to secondary inhibitory loops that make antilearning actions and attitudes persevere, even though most participants wish they did not.

In the exhibit that follows (on the next page), we present a map of the pattern of relationships among primary and secondary inhibitory loops. We begin with the governing conditions that set the pattern in motion: the dissatisfactions of the users and the tight financial conditions that no longer permit high IT costs. Next we have the action strategies the CIO and his subordinates used during their meeting. These action strategies led to certain first-order consequences. One was that the boss evaluated the subordinates' conclusions as unrealistic and challenged them to come up with a better solution or to use his solution. The subordinates, in turn, evaluated the boss's solution as unrealistic and said that the problem would remain unsolvable unless line management changed.

These interactions led to second-order consequences in the form of two sets of double binds. One affected the group of subordinates; the other affected the CIO and would have affected line managers had they been present.

We now have the beginnings of the transition from primary to secondary inhibitory loops. For example, line managers judge IT staff as unrealistic and lacking in cost-consciousness; the staff attributes the underlying problems to line managers themselves. Both views become embedded in the organizational norms that govern relationships between line and staff. The double binds that follow from such judgments and norms feed into a pattern of intergroup conflict typical of line-staff relationships.

The ramification of secondary inhibitory loops continues. Sensitive issues of intergroup conflict become undiscussable, and their not being discussed becomes undiscussable. Each group sees the other as unmovable, and both see the problem as uncorrectable. Again the literature of line-staff relations is replete with illustrations of such effects.

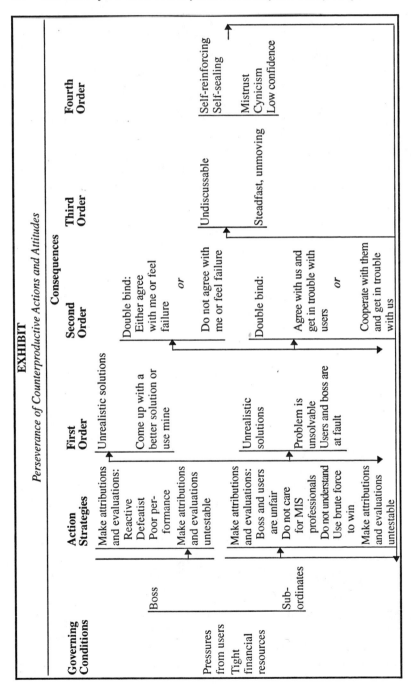

EXHIBIT

Perseverance of Counterproductive Actions and Attitudes

All of these consequences feed back to reinforce the primary inhibitory loops illustrated in the CIO's meeting with his subordinates, creating an organizational pattern that seals in the counterproductive processes. This leads each participant to feel mistrust of the others, low confidence in interactions with others, and cynicism about the likelihood of resolving intergroup conflicts. These feelings are legitimized because they are seen as typical of the organization.

Our map shows that any dialogue around the business problem of reducing IT's costs and improving its performance will be negatively influenced by the primary and secondary inhibitory loops. If the top line management is unaware of the detailed processes shown in our map because they have been shielded from them, they see only the persistence of high costs and poor performance. This leads them to mistrust the CIO and feel doubt, even cynicism, about his ability to solve the business problem. (As it turned out, the CIO in our case was eventually fired and a "tough line officer" was placed in charge.) On the other hand, if the top line management were not shielded from the detailed processes shown in our map, they would probably still have similar reactions. In either case, little corrective action would be taken to improve the organization's capability for double-loop learning. Indeed, several months after his conversation with the CIO, the CEO faced a similar pattern of defensive interactions, this time between Research and Development (R&D) and Finance. Finance claimed that R&D cost too much; R&D counterclaimed that Finance had no real understanding of research and development. Again, the CEO solved the problem by taking a tough stance on controlling research costs.

We have now shown how primary and secondary inhibitory loops can produce consequences counterproductive to learning at all levels of organization. The dynamic interaction within an organizational setting of primary and secondary inhibitory loops, together with their antilearning consequences, is what we mean by a **limited learning system.**

Secondary Inhibitory Loops and Organizational Defensive Routines

Among the most important components of secondary loops are organizational defensive routines. These are actions and policies, enacted within an organizational setting, that are intended to protect individuals from experiencing embarrassment or threat, while at the same time preventing individuals, or the organization as a whole, from identifying the causes of the embarrassment or threat in order to correct the relevant problems.

All organizational defensive routines are based on a logic that is powerful and profound in its impact on individuals and organizations. The logic can be expressed in terms of four rules:

1. Craft messages that contain inconsistencies.
2. Act as if the messages are not inconsistent.
3. Make the ambiguity and inconsistency in the message undiscussable.
4. Make the undiscussability of the undiscussable also undiscussable.

An example of a message conforming to these rules is a chief executive who says to his immediate subordinates,

> We encourage everyone to be innovative and risk oriented. This is what we mean by empowerment. Of course, we also expect you to keep out of trouble.

When individuals communicate mixed messages, they usually do so spontaneously and with no indication that their message is mixed. If they appeared to be hesitant because of the inconsistencies in their message, it could be seen as a weakness. It is rare, indeed, for an executive to design and state a mixed message and then ask, "Do you find my message inconsistent and ambiguous?" The message is made undiscussable by the very naturalness with which it is delivered and by the absence of any invitation or disposition to inquire about it. Moreover, the very undiscussability of a mixed message constitutes a source of threat or embarrassment. In a Model I organizational world (which we call O-I), discussion of the undiscussability of a mixed message would trigger as much defensiveness as the mixed message itself.

Individuals follow such rules all the time, and they do so without having to pay attention to them because they have become highly skilled at enacting them. The irony is that this skillfulness is inextricably intertwined with incompetence, because the skillful use of mixed messages leads to a range of unintended and counterproductive consequences. For example, the CIO and his subordinates created a dialogue in which crucial messages were covered up, and the cover-up was not discussable. This led to increasing emotionality, as well as to double-binds, which, in turn, led to or reinforced existing feelings of mistrust, cynicism, and lack of confidence in the other parties to the dialogue.

We suggest that it is not possible to deal effectively with any subject if it is not discussable and if its undiscussability is also undiscussable. Under the rules that govern defensive routines, individuals with a high sense of integrity and willingness to accept personal responsibility will feel that they are in the following double-bind:

> If we do not discuss the defensive routines, then these routines will continue to proliferate. But if we do discuss them, we are likely to get into trouble.

One colorful senior executive said that in his organization these double binds go under the name of "s--- sandwiches."

The result of such double-binds is that defensive routines are protected and reinforced by the very people who would like to get rid of them. But because their protection is covert and undiscussable, defensive routines appear to other people as self-protective and self-reinforcing.

Whenever actions are self-protective and self-reinforcing, they can easily become self-proliferating. The irony here is that the self-proliferating features of defensive routines are activated especially when someone tries to engage them directly. Once individuals realize that danger, they shy away in the name of progress and constructive action.

Under these conditions, defensive routines flourish and spread into organizational loops that are known to all and manageable by none. Indeed, executives have told us that the thought that defensive loops could be managed is unrealistic, futile, or romantic. A few have wondered if such management might not be dangerous because, as one put it, "Wouldn't it mean that we would have to give up whatever we have to protect us?"

These reactions make sense in the world as it is. They are also self-fulfilling and self-sealing—self-fulfilling because they create the conditions under which it would be naive or dangerous to engage them; self-sealing because they also create conditions under which it is unlikely that the self-fulfilling prophecy will be interrupted.

Hence, we have one of the most important causes of organizational rigidity and stickiness: defensive routines that get stronger and stronger while the individuals responsible for them believe it is unrealistic or even dangerous to do much about them.

Reactions to Defensive Routines. Because defensive routines and the secondary inhibitory loops associated with them, are accepted as inevitable, natural, and immune to management or influence, it is not surprising that the most common reaction to them is a sense of helplessness. Employees in industrialized societies appear as fatalistic about them as peasants do about poverty.

The inevitability of defensive routines, sanctioned by the prevailing culture, also has a personal side. Individuals do not take responsibility for creating or maintaining defensive routines. They are willing to say that they are personally influenced by defensive routines but are unable or unwilling to see how they may create or reinforce them.

One way to live with having little choice about defensive routines is to develop a cynical attitude about them. Cynicism leads to pessimism and doubt. For example,

> Nothing will change around here.
>
> They don't really mean it.
>
> I doubt if anyone will listen.
>
> Hang on. Don't get fooled. Next year there'll be a new fad.

Cynical attitudes make it more likely that individuals will ignore or sneer at evidence of positive intentions. The cynic automatically mistrusts other people and sees the world as full of evidence that nothing will change.

It is a short step from cynicism to blaming other people in the organization for any difficulties that may arise, and people will have plenty of evidence that someone else is to be blamed. They can easily infer the existence of defensive loops, they can see individuals acting consistently with them, they can see the cover-ups, and they can see that promotions often go to individuals who bypass the defensive routines.

Finally, people often give to others advice that reinforces defensive routines. For example, "Be careful. You'll get yourself in trouble if you try to change...That is a legacy from way back." So now we have the very individuals who feel helpless and cynical and disposed to blame others for taking initiative, becoming "positive" by advising others to respect defensive routines and inhibitory loops— the very phenomena that make it difficult for people to take constructive initiatives in organizational life.

To continue the propositions that we began in the previous chapter, we suggest the following:

> Individual and supraindividual unities exist in circular, interdependent relationships with each other. When embarrassment or threat are involved, these relationships interact to create self-fueling, limited-learning processes.

For double-loop learning to occur and to persist at any level in the organization, the self-fueling processes must be interrupted. In order to interrupt these processes, individual theories-in-use must be altered.

How the Technical-Objective Dimension of Organizational Life Is Smothered By Individual-Organizational Defensive Routines

In our research and consulting, we are faced with issues that vary in their degree of objectivity, that is, the degree to which they are seen as matters of fact or as subjects of merely technical theories. Typically, when we deal with issues that are defined by the use of technical theories, we expect that their degree of objectivity will make it difficult for Model I and O-I defensive features to dominate the dialogue. This is not necessarily the case.

Technical theories are theories of action that specify measurable objectives and procedures for achieving those objectives. Some of the technical theories familiarly encountered in organizations include the following:

- accounting
- finance
- economics of the firm
- information technology
- marketing
- competitive strategy
- research and development
- certain theories related to human resource functions, such as incentive schemes, personnel selection, and training.

All technical theories are characterized by a set of common features. First, there is an aspiration to reduce to a minimum the gap between the technical espoused theory and the technical theory-in-use. The technical professional tries to perform in accordance with the prescriptions of established technical theory. Second, there is an explicit emphasis on the use of productive reasoning. Those who construct technical theories aspire to make the premises and inferences from them as explicit as possible. They aspire to derive conclusions that are testable, especially falsifiable. Technical theories are, therefore, written to be causally rigorous because that is required if the procedures are to specify in causal terms what actions will lead to what consequences. Technical theories are causally rigorous in another way. If two professionals follow a set of technical specifications correctly, they will collect the same data, make the same analyses, and produce the same technical conclusions. If this does not happen, it is possible to trace backwards to find where one or both professionals deviated from the established procedures.

It seemed plausible to us that these features of technical theories would be so powerful that they would not succumb easily to the individual-organizational defenses we have described earlier. We thought that the robustness of their intellectual objectivity should make it easier to reduce conditions for error such as vagueness and ambiguity.

So far, however, our expectations have not been confirmed. What often happens is that the objective features of technical theories are bypassed and submerged by Model I defenses. For example, a superior (S) wrote a case about his relationship with a subordinate (O) regarding the latter's inadequate performance around certain technical issues in an information management system.

S and O Case

Thoughts and Feelings	**Actual Conversation**
I am concerned (angry) about what is a continual problem.	S: *We need to find ways to have your group deliver part of the product on time.*
I sense that he is avoiding responsibility for the problem.	O: *It's simple. We cannot test our debugger until the compiler has finished all of its testing.*
My feeling is that the group should accept responsibility.	S: *Are there any tests that can be run before the compiler is ready?*
	O: *There are limited tests that can be run. But the cause of the most difficulties is in the compiler/debugger interaction.*
I again see the avoidance. I want to lead him toward a solution where he can take responsibility.	S: *But it is possible to capture correct compiler output and run your tests against that.*
I feel that he cannot concede the point and will move to other issues as an escape.	O: *Sure, we could do that, but it would not catch places where the compiler has changed. Besides it would also take more disk space. It is simple; we are dependent on the compiler.*
I begin to feel frustration. I'm canceling out the additional excuses.	S: *First of all, disks are cheap. If you need more space, we can get it. Second, there are other components that interact with the compiler that do not have the same problems with delivering.*

I am led in another direction.	O: *The other components do not interact as closely. Look at the last release. The compiler added new features, and we did not find out until the end.*

In reading the right-hand column, the dialogue appears to be about the delays around the compiler and the debugger. The performance of both machines and their interaction is specifiable in technical terms, namely, in terms related to the domain of computer and information technology. Indeed, the disagreement between S and O, as it appears in the right-hand column is crafted primarily in terms of technical issues.

Let us now expand our view. S, who wrote the case, wrote that he was frustrated with O's performance. S doubted O's explanation for delays, namely, that the debugger could not be tested until the compiler finished its testing. This claim could have been tested because the technical theories involved specify the performance features of each machine and their interrelationships. But this technical test was not requested or required by S.

One reason that S did not force such a test was that he believed that the important issue was that O and his group were avoiding their responsibility. S was faced with a leadership and group-performance issue. This claim is illustrated by the left-hand column comments. Yet the case suggests that S acted in ways that suppressed the primacy of the interpersonal-organizational defensive issues. He appeared to hope that by making the technical issues primary he could, through appropriate questioning, eventually surface the leadership and group performance issues. S's strategy was, therefore, to make secondary what he believed was primary and to coverup that he was using such a strategy.

O, on the other hand, crafted his conversation to deal with the technical issues. He was able to distance himself from the interpersonal-organizational dimension that upset S. This resulted in a counterproductive dialogue. S began by noting that disks were cheap (technical). If S would provide more space (technical), and since other components interact with the compiler (technical), then the technical problems could be resolved. O found reasons why S's technically based solution was inadequate. S saw O's emphasis on technical issues as further evidence that O was acting irresponsibly. O could argue that he was doing so because he had not been told of S's view of O's irresponsibility.

S covered up by focusing only on the technical issues, and he acted as if this were not the case (Model I). S never engaged O about his unhappiness over O's avoiding responsibility. O, in his responses, remained at the *technical level and appeared to be designedly sidestepping and acting as if this were not the case (again, Model I).*

It is our hypothesis that each individual in crafting his arguments retrieves knowledge from his mind that is related to technical theories of action (compiler/debugger interaction) and states it forthrightly. Each has little choice but to be forthright in this respect, because it is hard to distort technical features based on publicly stated theories without giving the other party the opportunity to falsify the claim.

S also crafts his conversation in ways that cover up his feelings and acts as if he is not doing so. The difficulty with this strategy is that it makes it easy for O to remain at the technical level and, if he were sidestepping, to act as if he were not.

We have a conversation, therefore, that is unlikely to resolve the problem that S believes is crucial (O's avoiding responsibility). If O is sidestepping because he believes that S's requests are unfair, then that problem will also not be solved. S and O can end the conversation by privately attributing negative evaluations to the other party, each feeling that he is dealing with a difficult individual. What results from such a conversation are the self-fulfilling prophecies and self-sealing processes predicted by Model I, the patterns of an O-I limited learning system.

Conclusion

Individuals are programmed with Model I theories-in-use. When faced with embarrassing or threatening issues, they act in ways that enhance conditions for error. For example, important features of issues become undiscussable, and their undiscussability is also undiscussable. This exacerbates the degree of inconsistency and incongruity, the vagueness, and ambiguity that surround the issues. These consequences lead to organizational behavioral worlds that are dominated by organizational defensive routines. Such defensive routines reinforce the counterproductive learning consequence of Model I theories-in-use and O-I learning systems. At the same time they also create such a degree of interpenetration between individual and organizational defensiveness that it becomes difficult to disentangle the causal roles of these two levels of phenomena. The result is for individuals to experience mistrust, distancing, and cynicism about the potentiality for productive organizational learning around issues that are embarrassing or threatening.

This, in turn, results in a low likelihood that high-quality inquiry will occur. The conditions for what we have called "good dialectic" will be suppressed. There will be a tendency to minimize conflicts and disagreements by bypassing them and covering up the bypassing. It will be difficult to reflect on and produce an accurate history of the problem in question. It is likely that the participants will have difficulty even in agreeing on what actually happened. It is even more likely that they will not try to test their interpretations of events. If they do try, their tests are likely to be poor ones because they will be crafted to avoid threatening the reasoning used by the individuals who made the interpretations in the first place.

At the heart of explaining human behavior are the concepts of reasoning and causality. Human beings use reasoning to diagnose what is going on, to design actions, and to produce their designs. The concept of causality plays a key role in all of these processes because human action is intended to be effective. Effectiveness, in turn, requires having some concept of "If A..., then B...," when diagnosing, inventing, and producing.

Model I theories-in-use and organizational defensive routines combine to sanction the use of defensive reasoning. Defensive reasoning consists in making one's premises and inferences implicit and invulnerable to public testing. This leads to conclusions that are testable only within the constraints of the logic used by the actors who crafted the conclusion. We call this the use of self-referential logic because the testing is not designed to utilize logic independent of the logic used to create the conclusion in the first place. Under these conditions, defensive reasoning becomes sanctioned as the correct reasoning to use. But, as we have seen, this is a recipe for exacerbating conditions for error and for diminishing the condition for good dialectic. We have a paradox: the behavioral strategies that are defined as effective also reduce the likelihood of productive learning at all levels of the organization.

Part III

Inquiry-Enhancing Intervention and Its Theoretical Basis

Prologue: Intervention Toward O-II Learning Systems

In Part III we present a model of an organization learning system (O-II) that can be used to decrease the inhibitions to double-loop learning embedded in Model O-I. We also include several probable scenarios of how organizations would go about double-loop learning.

Next, we address the question of how we get from here to there, and how we help organizations move toward Model O-II learning systems. Our answer to this question is, in effect, our model of intervention. We differentiate between "limited" and "comprehensive" intervention, and note the conditions under which each may be utilized.

O-II Learning Systems

An organization with an O-I learning system is highly unlikely to learn to alter its governing variables, norms, and assumptions, because this would require organizational inquiry into double-loop issues, and O-I systems militate against such inquiry. If we are interested in overcoming the forces that inhibit double-loop learning, we must seek an alternative learning system. But if we are right in asserting that most organizations contain O-I learning systems and that these deter any learning processes incompatible with their basic structure, then we are unlikely to find the new learning system we seek by looking at the world as it presently exists. We will have to create a new learning system as a rare event.

We are unlikely to create such a rare event without a map that provides at least an approximate picture of the end state we are seeking. This new learning system is the one we will map as Model O-II. But if O-II learning systems cannot spontaneously evolve from O-I, as we have argued, then we will also need a map of how to move deliberately from O-I toward O-II. Such a map should inform us of the behavioral conditions that would take us off course if we violated them. For example, if we make statements that are not disconfirmable, or if we unilaterally control others in order to win, in accordance with Model I theory-in-use, then we will reduce the likelihood of achieving an O-II learning system. In order to effect a transition from O-I to O-II, we need not only a "Model O-II learning system" but a "Model II theory-in-use."

These models alone are not sufficient to give us the guidance we need. We also need rules in the form of maxims or heuristics to help us invent and produce Model II processes, such as advocating a position and coupling it with inquiry, making private dilemmas public, and framing attributions so that they can be disconfirmed. Such heuristics provide operational definitions for action without which we cannot reach the guideposts described in Models II and O-II.

There is one other caution. When we speak of Models II and O-II as "end states," we run the risk of suggesting that they may be achieved as final states, fixed and unchangeable. There are at least two reasons why this is not the case. The first is that Models II and O-II represent ideal states that may never be achieved, only approximated; their main value lies in providing models for creating a good organizational dialectic. This leads to the second and more important reason. Models II and O-II will not tend to become fixed and rigid because of their built-in capacity for double-loop learning which continually questions the status quo.

Since O-II learning systems are rare phenomena, we will not be able to provide rich descriptions of actual examples of them as we could do for O-I learning systems. Neither of the authors knows of an organization that has a fully developed Model O-II learning system, nor are we aware of any literature that offers a full description of such a system. In addition, we believe that our intervention theory for the transition from O-I to O-II learning systems is also extremely primitive. The best that we are able to do is to present cases of the beginnings of Model O-II learning systems in various settings in which we have worked.

CIO and His Immediate Reports: A New Scenario

A key component of an O-II learning system is the theory-in-use that people use to deal with conditions for error (e.g., scatteredness, ambiguity, vagueness, and so on). O-II learning systems require conditions under which mis-

taken assumptions can be reformulated, incongruities reconciled, incompatibilities resolved, vagueness specified, untestable notions made testable, scattered information brought together into meaningful patterns, and previously withheld information surfaced. As we have argued, these conditions for productive inquiry are highly unlikely when people use Model I theories-in-use that give rise to primary inhibitory loops. What would it be like to create an individual theory-in-use that helped people confront conditions for error in ways that led to their being reduced and corrected?

Let us return to the case of the CIO, described in the previous chapter. What kind of conversation would he create, if his objective were to reduce interpersonal and organizational defenses and conditions for error?

First, the CIO would carry on a different type of private conversation. The basic thrust of this private conversation would be toward making issues more explicit and testing the validity of assumptions and attributions related to them, in order to enhance productive learning. When the CIO heard his subordinates say that the line managers "do not know what they want," he might carry on the following conversation with himself:

> *These individuals are making evaluations of and attributions about the line's intentions without providing any data that I (or anyone else) could use to make up my own mind about the validity of their claims.*

> *I should ask them to provide data to illustrate their claims. I have learned not to ask them "why" they believe what they do, because that will activate espoused-theory explanations that are likely to be self-serving.*

> *When the subordinates say that line managers don't know what they want, I should say, "What is it that they say or do that leads you to conclude that they do not know what they want?"*

If this question is answered concretely, the CIO can make a judgement as to whether line managers are acting inappropriately. If they are, in his judgment, he can communicate these evaluations upward in order to begin to change line managers' actions.

Let us consider another example from the CIO's dialogue with his subordinates:

> *When the subordinates say that line does not trust them or really care for them, the CIO could say, "Have you tested out your assumptions about their views of us? If so, what did you say to the line? If not, what led you not to do so?"*

If the CIO asks these questions, the subordinates might say, "Are you kidding? That would be disastrous. They would either laugh or get furious." Their response is another attribution about the line management. As such, it should be tested by the use of a logic that is different from the one used by the information technology professionals themselves. If all the CIO hears are further untested assertions, he could say something like, "I ask if you have tested the validity of your assertions about the line. The answer I get is another set of untested assertions. I cannot be an effective representative of our views with line management if I come to the meetings armed with untestable assertions."

If the CIO hears what he believes are incorrect or self-sealing conclusions, he could ask:

> *"If it is true that the users are the problem, because they do not plan and they make last-minute demands and if it is also true that they have been doing this for years, and if we got increased resources, would that not reinforce the very behavior we find frustrating?"*

or

> *"You tell me that our clients are inflexible and insensitive. That may be true. But how do you know? The only answer I get when I ask you this question is that you say they are... (illustrates with examples of what the subordinates have said). I would like these attributions and evaluations to be tested in ways that are independent of your reasoning. Otherwise, I could put myself in the position of being seen as an uncritical carrier of IT ."*

> *"I cannot go along with causal reasoning, yours or mine, when validity is not tested independently of our views, experiences, and logic."*

The CIO could also cite actions that illustrate how his subordinates may be creating the very consequences they condemn. He might say:

> *"You state that our customers are inflexible and insensitive (cites illustrations of such claims). You do not like this behavior, and you use it as evidence that the problems are not correctable."*

> *"You may be right, but I do not hear anyone presenting a compelling argument that is also testable. Whenever I have tried to make some suggestions, the responses that I hear from you include 'good luck to you' and 'trust us, our users are uninfluenceable.'"*

> *"It is difficult for me to trust your diagnosis. If you act toward the line managers the way you are acting toward me, I can see how they would become, in your eyes, uninfluenceable. But I can also see how they may come to a similar conclusion about you."*

and

> *"This leads me to another issue. You may be finding me uninfluence-able. I want to establish conversations that do not require me to distance myself from my responsibility or yours for the problems we are experiencing."*

> *"I want to explore what I am saying or doing that makes me, in your eyes, uninfluenceable."*

Finally, actors should focus on reducing inconsistencies, closing gaps, and surfacing fears. For example,

Instead of	**Act as Follows**
1. judging the players (information technology professionals, line managers, and CIO) as defensive, wrong, and unjust,	*1. request illustrations of evaluations and attributions, and craft tests of their validity.*
2. judging the players as naive, complainers, or crybabies,	*2. request illustrations and tests. Then inquire into how line managers acted (or would act) in response to such attempts to test. If there were no attempt to test, what was the reasoning behind such an omission?*
3. judging the players (e.g., information technology professionals) as self-centered, unfair, and unrealistic,	*3. illustrate how the gaps and inconsistencies in the actors' reasoning processes, if unrecognized, are likely to backfire.*
4. bypassing your tough evaluations about their effectiveness,	*4. State your evaluations and attributions about their counterproductive actions, illustrate, and encourage testing.*

S and O Case: A New Scenario.

Let us turn to the case of S and O which we presented in Chapter 5, and consider a new scenario for their conversation.

What S Could Say	**The Reasoning Behind the Design**
O, I would like to discuss with you a problem that continues between us. (Describes problem.) I am bewildered how to resolve it effectively.	*Seek to test view of the problem. Seek to discover possible personal responsibility.*
Every time I raise the issue about on-time delivery, you claim the cause is due to the computer/debugger interaction.	*Reflect on segments of dialogue that S uses to infer the problem.*
I react in two ways. One way is to attribute that you are avoiding the problem. I do not test this attribution.	*Make private attributions public. Own up that S does not test.*
The other way is that I craft most of my responses at the technical level. This appears, to me, to make it easier for you to respond at the technical level. It also makes it more difficult for me to deal with the issue that troubles me.	*Make his private attributions public in order to test them. Own up to the realization that the process S uses is counterproductive.*
In the name of being positive, I hide all of this, but, as far as I can tell, the results are not positive.	*Make public his covered-up actions. Own up to the dysfunctionality of these actions.*
Does this diagnosis make sense to you? If not, where do you differ?	*Ask for test.*
If it does make sense, would you be willing to join me in redesigning the way we deal with each other?	*Invites the joint design and implementation of more constructive actions.*

We suggest that it is likely that O could respond by cooperating in two ways. First, he could answer S's inquiries and agree to a joint design. Second, he could adapt a similar reasoning process to expand the dialogue so that he would gain insight into his personal responsibility for the problems.

O may admit, for example, that he, too, has been hiding his feelings and thoughts. He was angry at S's attributions that O was avoiding responsibility. He may also admit that he covered up these feelings by focusing on the technical issues and by covering up the cover-up. S could then ask O to describe his fears. Such inquiry often enlarges the issue from an interpersonal one-to-one that includes relevant organizational factors, and shows how the two kinds of factors reinforce each other. The participants are now on their way to more productive learning about the technical, interpersonal, and organizational binds in which they have been caught up.

Model II Theory-in-Use

The scenarios of behavioral strategies and consequences that we have just presented are informed by a model for *individual* theory-in-use which we call Model II (Argyris and Schön, 1974, pp. 85–93).

Briefly, the governing variables or values of Model II are not opposite those of Model I. The governing variables of Model II are valid information, free and informed choice, and internal commitment. The action strategies required to fulfill these values are also not opposite those of Model I. For example, Model I emphasizes that individuals advocate their purposes and simultaneously control the others and the environment in order to assure that the actor's purposes are achieved. Model II does not reject the skill or competence to advocate one's purposes. It does reject the unilateral control that usually accompanies advocacy because the typical purpose of advocacy is to win. Model II couples articulateness and advocacy with an invitation to others to confront the views and emotions of self and other. It seeks to alter views in order to base them on the most complete and valid information possible and to construct positions to which people involved can become internally committed. This means the actor in Model II is skilled at inviting double-loop learning on the part of other individuals.

Every significant Model II action is evaluated in terms of the degree to which it helps the individuals involved generate valid and useful information (including relevant feelings), share the problem in a way that leads to productive inquiry, solve the problem in a way that it remains solved, and do so without reducing the present level of problem-solving effectiveness.

The behavioral strategies of Model II involve sharing power with anyone who has competence and is relevant to deciding about implementing the action in question. Definition of the task and control over the environment are shared with all the relevant actors. Saving one's own face or that of others is resisted because it is seen as a defensive, antilearning activity. If face-saving actions must be taken, they are planned jointly with the people involved. The exception would be with individuals who are vulnerable to such candid and joint solutions to facesaving yet who need to be protected from others (and since it is done unilaterally) from themselves.

Under these conditions individuals will not tend to compete to make decisions for others, to one-up others, or to outshine others for the purposes of self-gratification. Individuals in a Model II world seek to find the people most competent for the decision to be made

Model II Theory-In-Use

Governing Variables for Action	Action Strategies	Consequences of Behavioral World	Consequences on Learning	Consequences on Effectiveness
Valid information	Design situations where participants can be origins of action and experience high personal causation	Actor experienced as minimaly defensive	Disconfirmable processes	Increased long-term effectiveness
Free and informed choice		Minimally defensive interpersonal relations and group dynamics	Double-loop learning	
Internal commitment to the choice and constant monitoring of its implementation	Task is jointly controlled	Learning-oriented norms	Frequent public testing of theories	
	Protection of self is a joint enterprise and oriented toward growth	High freedom of choice, internal commitment, and risk taking		
	Bilateral protection of others			

or the problem to be solved. They seek to build viable decision-making networks in which the major function of the group is to maximize the contributions of each member so that when a synthesis is developed, it incorporates exploration of the widest possible range of relevant views.

Finally, if new concepts are created under Model II conditions, the meaning given to them by the creator and the inference processes used to develop them are open to scrutiny by those who are expected to use them. Evaluations and attributions are minimized. When they are used, however, they are coupled with the directly observable data and the reasoning that led to their formation. Their creator feels responsible for presenting them in ways that encourage their open and constructive confrontation.

If these Model II governing values and behavioral strategies are used, the degree of defensiveness in individuals, within groups, and among groups will tend to decrease. Free choice will tend to increase as will feelings of internal commitment and essentiality.

The consequence of Model II behavioral strategies and values should be an emphasis on double-loop learning through which individuals confront the basic assumptions behind others' present views and invite confrontation of their own basic assumptions, and through which they seek public tests of their underlying hypotheses so as to make them disconfirmable, not self-sealing. Where individuals function as agents of organizational learning, the consequences of Model II should be an enhancement of the conditions for double-loop learning in organizational inquiry where assumptions and norms central to organizational theory-in-use can be surfaced, publicly confronted, tested, and restructured.

Social Virtues

There is another consequence of using Model II theories-in-use to create O-II behavioral worlds. The meaning of the social virtues taught early in life are altered in important ways. The social virtues in good currency are consistent with Models I and O-I. When applied correctly, they may make individuals feel good or righteous, but they may also exacerbate conditions for error and reduce the likelihood of producing good organizational dialectic and productive organizational inquiry.

We illustrate our position by contrasting the meanings of the social virtues of help and support, respect of others, strength, honesty, and integrity in Model I and Model II.

Model I Social Virtues	*Model II Social Virtues*

Help and Support

Give approval and praise to others. Tell others what you believe will make them feel good about themselves. Reduce their feelings of hurt by telling them how much you care and, if possible, agree with them that the others acted improperly.

Increase the other's capacity to confront their own ideas, to create a window into their own mind, and to face the unsurfaced assumptions, biases, and fears that have informed their actions toward other people.

Respect for Others

Defer to other people; do not confront their reasoning or actions.

Attribute to other people a high capacity for self-reflection and self-examination without becoming so upset that they lose their effectiveness and their sense of self-responsibility and choice. Keep testing this attribution.

Strength

Advocate your position in order to win. Hold your own position in the face of advocacy. Feeling vulnerable is a sign of weakness.

Advocate your position and combine it with inquiry and self-reflection. Feeling vulnerable while encouraging inquiry is a sign of strength.

Honesty

Tell other people no lies, or tell others all you think and feel.

Encourage yourself and other people to make public tests of their ability to say what they know yet fear to say. Minimize what would otherwise be subject to distortion and cover-up of the distortion.

Integrity

Stick to your principles, values, and beliefs.

Advocate your principles, values, and beliefs in a way that invites inquiry into them and encourages other people to do the same.

We now turn to several examples of how Models II and O-II can be used to design and implement conditions for double-loop learning in organizational inquiry.

The first example is a classroom where we are trying to expose a group of senior executives to the strategies and values of Model II reasoning. Our task is first to help them begin to become aware of the degree to which they use Model I theory-in-use and defensive reasoning. At the same time, we seek to help them see how unaware they are of what causes their unawareness. In this example, we show how a classroom situation can become a first test of the hypothesis that the participants use Model I and that this Model I theory-in-use is likely to lead them to create the conditions for a Model O-I behavioral world.

The second example is a more comprehensive intervention in an organization, beginning with the director-owner of a leading consulting firm that was established ten years ago.

6

The Classroom: Intervention for Learning and Research

The purpose of this chapter is to show how interventions can be designed to teach participants features of the theory-of-action perspective and, at the same time, make the learning experience an occasion for testing features of the theory. We will illustrate how this can be done in relatively large group settings of from 30 to 100 participants.

We will present excerpts from transcripts of two classes, each attended by 75 executives of which 19 were female, representing 35 different countries in all. We will attempt to show how the activities of learning about and testing of theory can interpenetrate and enrich each other.

The Focus of the Testing

In this chapter we will illustrate several different types of tests. First, we test the claim that the participants who use Model I in their cases (and all of them did so) will also use it in classroom discussions of cases. This connection should hold for any participant regardless of age, sex, culture, education, and position in their organization. We should observe the participants advocating, evaluating, and attributing in such a way that they do not encourage inquiry into or testing of their actions. Their advocating, evaluating, and attributing should be crafted high on the ladder of inference. The participants should not be aware of the degree to which they rely on high-level abstractions, nor should they be observed connecting their abstractions with actual behavior. (The participants' actions should illustrate Whitehead's famous concept of "misplaced concreteness.")

Second, the participants will be observed in class creating left-hand columns about their classmates, and should be expected to act as if they were not doing so. If they are asked whether they are doing so and they answer yes, we expect them to justify their action strategy as a way of preventing individuals from becoming defensive. If the participants deny they are covering up and if the instructor asks others in the class what attributions they were making, the others should report that they were attributing to the respondents a cover-up of the thoughts and feelings in their left-hand columns and a cover-up of that cover-up. The resulting differences in views can themselves become a subject of dialogue. Such a discussion typically illustrates the self-sealing, limited learning processes that occur when human beings using Model I strive to deal with their differences.

Third, we claim that participants will defend such actions as bypassing conflict and covering up the bypass, as consistent with Model I interpretations of social virtues such as caring and concern. Or they should defend their Model I forthrightness as consistent with Model I social virtues such as honesty and integrity. If the instructor illustrates the use of the Model II social virtues of caring, concern, honesty, and integrity, participants will either reject these as likely to get them in trouble, or state that they find the illustrations helpful. In either case the participants will say that they would not produce such meanings because they are culturally unacceptable. During the early sessions, any attempt by the instructor to recommend that participants consider actions consistent with Model II will be rejected as, at best, romantic and unrealistic.

Fourth, we will test for the degree of skilled unawareness individuals reveal as they design and produce their conversations in class, as well as their openness to learning how to monitor their actions so that they can become more aware of their theories-in-use.

Fifth, we will test for the degree to which participants are aware of the counterproductive features of a Model I and O-I world but deny that they have any personal responsibility for beginning to change that world. In doing so, they will claim that they are helpless victims of that world as it presently exists.

We try to craft such tests as these so that the participants are free to produce alternative interventions of their own. If they do so, we predict that they will remain consistent with Model I (e.g., unilaterally advocating a position or evaluating other persons in ways that do not invite inquiry) or the opposite of Model I (e.g., giving up control to the other or suppressing their own views, also without inquiry). No one whose case was written consistently with Model I should be expected to craft Model II conversations and meanings during the early class sessions, even if they say they will. Their classmates, who may wish the participants to succeed in doing so, will provide data that the participants themselves did not provide.

Often such experiences lead the participants to feel stuck, since nothing they do seems to be effective in the eyes of their fellow students, the instructor, and eventually themselves. How they deal with being stuck turns out to be an indicator of how likely they are to learn Model II. For example, some people become angry at themselves, or accuse others (including their instructor) of not being helpful, and they conclude that change is not possible. So far, we have found that most participants, while they also feel frustrated and angry, tend to invite the instructor and others to help them move toward Model II. The pace at which they move in this direction varies with the individuals.

The Class As A Setting for Relevant Tests

Our experience has shown that the classroom situation provides a more robust test of the features of our theory than the use of questionnaires and interviews. There are several reasons for this. First, the participants in the classroom are able to provide the instructor with behavioral data that can be used to test the theory-of-action perspective. Second, because the participants have left their everyday job pressures and have paid substantial tuition and travel costs to learn new, actionable concepts, they are not bashful about confronting the faculty members' claims to offer concepts that are valid and actionable.

Third, the classroom can provide a robust test for features of our theory because we expose the participants to ideas they are often more disposed to reject than to accept. For example, we show that their theories-in-use are counterproductive to double-loop learning and that they are systematically unaware of their skilled incompetence. We also show that they exhibit a systematic hate-love relationship with organizational defensive routines. On the one hand, they express open dislike for the defensive layering and rigidity produced by the routines. On the other hand, as they come to realize what it takes to produce organization double-loop learning, they begin to defend their skilled use of the routines as realistic and required by everyday pressures and norms.

This leads to the fourth reason why the classroom can become a setting for robust tests of features of our theory. A common experience in the classrooms, as we have noted, is that the participants begin to feel stuck. While they acknowledge the dysfunctional bases of their Model I theory-in-use, they also see that most of their attempts to produce new and productive behaviors are, by the judgment of their fellow participants, counterproductive. Many people report that they have never before experienced this feeling of being stuck, a feeling they cannot blame on others. This challenges their sense of competence and their confidence, which leads them, in turn, to a deeper exploration of issues involved in organizational learning. By deeper, we mean that they not only struggle to learn the new skills, but in so doing, they also explore their core values and the dilemmas created by their adoption of fads and quick fixes, which they often condemn but nevertheless seek out as they experience their feelings of being stuck.

The use of the case method illustrated in this book relies heavily on action research, but it contains some elements familiar to normal social science. Like any other pencil-and-paper instrument used by researchers, the cases and transcripts of classroom dialogue can be scored, and interrater and interobserver reliability tests can be run. But the classroom dialogue stimulated by patterns found in the cases, and the participants' attempts to challenge the instructor's views, can become a rich source of on-the-spot learning and testing. For example, when the participants make what they believe are valid claims, only to find that others reject them, the resulting disagreements provide opportunities for exploring their reasoning processes and theories-in-use for dealing with potentially embarrassing or threatening issues.

We find that the most profound cause of embarrassment or threat is not the class members' disagreements with one another (classes, after all, are supposed to be settings where differences are discussed), but their discovery that their automatic reactions either violate their espoused theories or turn out to be counterproductive. It is the recognition of their skilled incompetence that mainly upsets them.

This consequence becomes the basis for learning about issues that are typically bypassed. This is true for the faculty members as well as for the participants. If the faculty members are unable to provide Model II types of reactions when they are being confronted, it is unlikely that the exercise will be seen as credible and worthy of the emotional investment it appears to require.

Transcript of Class Discussion: Dealing with the Left-hand Column

We now turn to passages taken from the transcript of the first of our classroom dialogues. The excerpts illustrate what has occurred so far in all the class situations that we have led. The data illustrate Model I and O-I limited-learning systems created by the participants in the classroom. There are no episodes in any of the transcripts of Model II behavior; hence, none are included.

We begin by presenting the following list of the unstated thoughts and feelings contained in the left-hand columns of the participants' cases (similar in format to the ones discussed in Part II).

Extracts from Left-hand Columns of Participants' Cases

1. I must be cautious not to break the news too early lest he becomes upset.
2. It is obvious. Why does he not see the same as I?
3. Try to make him comfortable. How could you destroy the morale of your department in such a short period?
4. Relax. Don't get too defensive. (Later) I expected you to be uncomfortable with the discussion, and I can see that I was correct.
5. He will listen but without commitment.
6. Let him feel completely in control.
7. Bad start! Try to get more objectivity without sounding negative.
8. Be concrete and direct. Tell it as it is so that he will hear. Be courageous.
9. Start positively.
10. Keep positive and do not push it too hard. We will not agree otherwise.
11. Start positively. Get down to business as soon as possible.
12. Say "we" so that he feels as if he is part of the decision. (Later) This is the tough part. Don't let him interrupt.
13. You cannot object. This is a fact.
14. You probably think that I am blowing this out of proportion.
15. If we don't, the president will have my head and yours.
16. They think I'm full of s—— They are telling me what they think I want to hear.

The following conversation then took place:

CA (Argyris): What are your reactions to the list of left-hand column statements?

Participant A: It is obvious. Why does he not see the same as I? Why is the (other) so blind? So defensive?

> *CA:* So one thing that you recognize is people giving themselves orders. Be careful, relax, and so on. We appear to be giving ourselves advice such as "don't become too defensive."
>
> *A:* I kind of looked at them all and grouped them as expressions of defensiveness in one manifestation or another. This is life.

Instructor's comment: The response is high on the ladder of inference. It is necessary to get more directly observable data. The intervention could have been crafted more concretely. For example, "I would like to understand what you mean by 'This is life.' Could you be a bit more concrete?"

The responses indicate Model I rules; namely, in order to be in control, do not express emotion or defensiveness. If you feel either, hide it and act as if you are not hiding it.

> *Participant B:* There seem to be three parties here: me, you, and us. "Me and you" are balanced about 50/50 and "us" seems to slack behind. Maybe most people don't understand that there is a unity between the two people present.
>
> *CA:* If I am hearing B, let me just check it out. "B, I think you are saying, 'If I look at most of these, or many of these, they seem to be about me or you, and there isn't much of us. There isn't much unity. How many people in this room do you think make the same inference of a lack of unity?'"
>
> *B:* Ask them. (Laughter)
>
> *CA:* Are you saying to me, "That's an illegitimate question." Or are you saying, "It's a legitimate one." Or "Would you rather not answer?"
>
> *B:* No, I don't mind having a go at answering it, but I think there obviously are views on either side. Let me have a go at answering it. I would say that most people enter into a situation like that trying to define the situation in manageable terms. Many times you want to simplify it and reduce it to the basics. Here the basics seem to be two parties rather than a small complex concept of the unity. Depending on the issue, I suspect there's a situational variable at play here: you are either going to feel defensive about our own position, or, realizing that it's a persuasive situation, you're immediately going to concentrate your energy on the other party and start thinking about the him or the her.

Comment: Instructor makes an attribution about the meaning B was trying to communicate and tests it. B interprets the comments being about the writer (of the cases) or the writer's view about the other person. There is little sense of the writer trying to create a dialogue with the others. The instructor asks the degree to which others in the class would confirm B's diagnosis.

This is the first attempt by the instructor to generate a dialogue by some of the members about other members. Such a request may seem inappropriate, and the instructor tests this attribution.

> *CA:* Let me ask you a question. Is it fair to say you didn't expect me to ask the question I asked of you?
>
> *B:* That's probably a fair road to take.
>
> *CA:* Okay, so your proposition was: I'm now going to put words into your mouth, so you help me if I'm wrong. It's really not a good idea to have "we vs. they"; it ought to be "us," as much as possible. There's a unity.
>
> *B:* Yes.
>
> *CA:* Okay, how much unity were you creating? To what extent were you following your own advice when you were making your comments?
>
> *B:* Not much.
>
> *CA:* When did it occur to you that you weren't?
>
> B: It occurred to me after this discussion.
>
> *CA:* Okay, so it occurred after you did it, right? The things that we're beginning to get at are very important. One thing is that people may, in fact, be, as somebody said, insecure. Another thing is they may be oversimplifying and they miss the possibility of the unity. Let's keep these in mind. Yes, sir?

Comment: The instructor wanted to test more directly the attribution that B found the intervention to be unexpected. The instructor then wanted to show that B's original evaluations were of the "we-they" variety. Therefore, he was creating in the classroom the very condition he criticized.

The instructor asked how aware B was that he was acting in this counterproductive manner, intending to begin to generate data about skilled unawareness. He also wanted to show that there were several other possible explanations that would be discussed later during the classroom session.

> *A:* Reading through this paper (of our left-hand column comments), it seems to me that there is not a central unique point. Some thoughts are related to our behavior. Some are related to what you think that the other people will think about you. Some you don't tell because it seems that it is better not to tell the other person something.
>
> *CA:* Right, so you're saying these conversations have several different levels of meaning, and you described three. Now, let me ask you if it would be fair to say you believe that all three could be relevant and important for learning?

Participant C: I think all three can be important.

CA: What do you think leads people to place these views in the left-hand column instead of talking about them?

C: They think if they talk it's more dangerous.

CA: Right. And how will they ever learn that it's dangerous if the ideas are kept private?

Participant D: I think what it gets around to is experience. You bring all of the history you yourself have accumulated into every discussion or negotiation or learning session that you enter into. And if you had an experience of whatever you called it a while ago and you missed your target and had to go back and do some internal feedback, you bring that with you the next time. You say, well, that's one of the options that I'm not going to pursue; I'm going to try something else.

CA: Yes, and our research would back it up as experience. One of the interesting things is that if you take both groups (in this program), there are almost 150 who come from different countries, different backgrounds, different genders, and so on. One of the interesting things is how come people of different cultures, genders, and ages seem to have the same experiences and deal with them in similar ways. And then, what's the impact of that on organizations?

Comment: This was an opportunity to remind the participants that their left-hand columns contain information that the executives in the classroom consider to be important for learning.

Once the participants confirmed this assertion, it became possible for the instructor to ask the next question; namely, what would lead individuals to designedly not communicate information that they judged to be important for learning.

The answers given were directly consistent with Model I theory-in-use. The instructor then raised the puzzle. The response was instructive in that it confirmed that the respondent has learned not to be candid because of the danger experienced through many years of interactions in organizations.

The instructor takes the opportunity to note that a similar fear could be found in all the cases that were submitted. Moreover, the executives represent many different cultures, backgrounds, organizations, and managerial positions.

CA: Okay, let me, if I may, add a bit to it. I find that there are three categories in the handout (of your comments) that I gave you. One comment is that the person is advocating something, like the one that (name)... mentioned before when he said, "Be careful, don't get defensive"; or, "Be positive; be concrete and direct." These are orders, so to speak, to yourself.

The next set of comments is attributions. Examples are, "They tell me what they think I want to hear," "He will listen without commitment," "Say 'we' so that he feels as if he's part of the decision." Finally there are evaluations such as "He is unable to see what is obvious," "What's wrong with her?" and so on.

To what extent would you say the case writers are testing to see whether their attributions or evaluations are valid? (None)

Right. Does anybody have a different answer? (Silence)

Now the question arises: If we're interested in learning, how facilitative is it to have a left-hand column which in one form or another says not even to test your views? If you make a statement and it's not tested, what do you think is likely to be the receiver's reaction when he or she hears an attribution or an evaluation that is not tested?

Participant E: Rejection.

CA: Rejection. Anybody else?

Participant F: Challenges, opinionated.

CA: Challenges. Opinionated. So we've got rejection, challenge, opinionated. What if the receiver is like us in this room? How would he or she react? I think they'd put their reactions on the left-hand side of their column. Notice what's beginning to surface. Regarding the information that we think we're hiding, somebody else actually begins to make inferences like, "Oh, he's challenging me." or "Oh, he's making evaluations; he's opinionated, or she's opinionated or whatever."

A: Suspicion, what is in his mind.

CA: Right.

Comment: It is interventions like these that permit the instructor to begin to illustrate how Model I action strategies lead to self-reinforcing, limited learning, and how this, in turn, can lead to self-fulfilling prophecies being made about each other. For example, the instructor intervenes to illustrate that the very information purposely kept private by the case writers is often inferred by the others. Thus the information that is assumed to be hidden is often not hidden.

This is an opportunity to show that one reason individuals make inferences such as those illustrated earlier is that they themselves have made such inferences and crafted such cover-ups.

F: Which is very important, by the way, when you draw conclusions. After studying such a large segment, it reminded me of what Jean Paul Sartre used to say, "Hell is in the other." It's an obvious gap between the two. Myself, I start, for instance, with asking, "Is it right what I'm doing with the other guy? Is my message correct?" It has to have a certain homogeneity; it's a common learning when you share something.

When you initiate the process, you should also be careful to read the response. I understand it as a learning process where both sides are supposed to learn to adjust to different processes. This process is very important.

Comment: F's comments indicates a learning orientation in that he asks questions such as, "Is it right? Is my message correct?" and so on. These descriptions are often espoused theories that serve to hide, even from the speaker, the Model I features of the theories-in-use employed when the speaker is faced with a dialogue that is potentially embarrassing or threatening.

In order to test for the likelihood that this is occurring, the instructor proposes a role play where the other participant is evaluating F's ideas as wrong.

CA: Assume for a moment (on any subject you want) that I do not agree with you.

F: Okay.

CA: (Role playing) I think you're wrong, I think the figures are wrong, I think the data are wrong.

F: Then I might indeed be wrong, and I will be trying to adjust to the new reality that you are making obvious to me.

CA: All right, but what if you're not wrong? What if you believe that you are right?

F: I'm trying to clarify my concepts and to share them again with you.

CA: But what would you say?

F: Let us look into the matter together.

CA: (To the class) What's on the left-hand side of your column when you hear, "Let us look at the ideas together?"

A: (someone) Bullshit. (Laughter)

F: Don't forget; I'm leading the process. I will be leading the process; I will see to it that at the end he will come along with me.... (Laughter)

Comment: The instructor then asks the class members to give their reactions. Of the four participants who spoke, none believed F.

Note that when F is evaluated directly in a Model I manner, he responds to assure the class members that he intended to be in unilateral control. (Model I value)

CA: What I'm saying is, under those conditions I doubt if learning is going to occur. Saluting may occur, but not learning, not learning to detect error. What is your view?

F: I'll end up with one sentence. I just wanted to emphasize that I'm eager to learn.

CA: I believe you. I should like to categorize your statement as part of your espoused theory of action. I believe that the role play illustrates that where there is some degree of negative reaction by others, you act in ways that are different from your espoused theory. Your theory-in-use inhibits learning on your part as well as on the part of the other.

Comment: F is asserting that he strives to behave in ways that support the learning process. The faculty member focuses on the possibility that he does not behave in these ways when the context is embarrassing or threatening. (Indeed, if he did, he would be disconfirming our theory, because his written case was consistent with Model I.)

Note that when class members say that they were feeling that F was "bullshitting them," F immediately reminded the group that he would be in control! This illustrates Model I governing values as well as discrepancies between espoused theory and theory-in-use. The faculty member then turns to examining the relationship between the emphasis on "being positive" and the governing value of minimizing the creating and experiencing of negative feelings. He is then able to connect "being positive" to causing limited learning. Later he could connect these responses with Model I social virtues.

CA: The single most frequent order that you people gave yourselves in your private conversation when writing the case was, in one form or another, "Be positive." Now I'm beginning to think that to be positive means to act in ways that do not upset people, even though this may require your withholding the information you just said is important for learning. Why would that be a concept of positiveness?

Participant G: We have learned over time that there are certain things you say and certain things that you don't say. There's good reason why we don't say many of those things.

CA: I agree there's very good reason. And I say that's the human dilemma, that for good reasons you learn to make sure you don't say things that will help people learn and you then say you do it for their good, which is true. Many of you may espouse learning, yet, as we see, this learning is going to be limited at best. So you're in a bit of a double bind.

Participant H: In doing this, I guess, it seems to me that, when you set up these left-hand column comments in your mind, you're setting up an envelope around this discussion. This is what you think is protecting your flank.

CA: Right, yes.

H: But you don't come out and say it. And by your conversation you're looking for the other person to either confirm or change what your perception is, so in a way you are testing by talking to that person. You don't want to come out and say some things that you know will probably hurt yourself, but you are looking for a sign that maybe you're wrong, maybe these comments are not right. And if you feel that, then you're going to move the conversation into a different direction and perhaps start to become more direct in your conversation.

Comment: The class members begin to explain their actions by asserting they learned to act as they do early in life. They begin to make explicit such Model I governing values as minimizing losing (e.g., protect your flank) or minimizing hurting yourself.

The instructor agrees that their explanations are likely to be valid and, at the same time, can be a basis for inconsistency and skilled incompetence.

> *CA:* And what would prevent you from saying that to the other person?
>
> *H:* Which?
>
> *CA:* Let me role-play again. If I'm following your advice, it might go something like this: "So and so, as we have our dialogue, I'm going to be keeping an eye out for the kinds of reactions that you have. From those reactions I'm going to make my inferences about degree of agreement, defensiveness, and whatever." Would you say that?
>
> *H:* No.
>
> *CA:* Right. Now, why not? All you're doing is publicly saying what you're thinking privately. I think of designed cover-up. Anytime you cover up, you have to cover up that you're covering up; that's why you were correct in saying no. And it's a puzzle. I want to listen; I want to learn; I want to test, listen, learn, test. A few sentences later you add, "And I would never say that to the person with whom I'm listening, learning, and testing."
>
> *H:* I see where you're going. It just seems to me that both people in the conversation have to be coming at this from the same direction.
>
> CA: Yes, yes, that's right. And do you think they are?
>
> H: Experience would say no.
>
> *CA:* Right, and I want to emphasize that you're right—experience would say no. I'm here to see if we can alter that experience.

Comment: H is presenting an insightful description of the bypassing, cover-up strategies intended to avoid upsetting others while keeping H in control.

The instructor takes the opportunity to provide another illustration of the cover-up of important information that would be helpful if genuine learning is to occur. H is also acting consistently with the Model I social virtues of caring and helpfulness.

> *Participant J:* Part of what H says is that sometimes it seems as if you wouldn't say that you're going to be observing this body language motion because you may feel that the other person is not acting on the same intellectual level that you're trying to arrive at. You learn something from their body language...you more fully understand how they feel, because they won't tell you—when you communicate that they're not going to be the next vice president. When they sort of just collapse. So, the reason you don't tell them why...would then be because you'd shut off some communications you're trying to get, recognizing the faults in the way communications are handled.

> *CA:* Again, J, I'm in agreement, but to illustrate a point, I'm going to reformulate what you've just said. "Chris, if we're in the world of the kind we're bringing out in this class, then it's important to be careful how you test—looking for the body language, for example—and so we have to do it somewhat covertly."

> I should like to ask how come you have to have that world? I'm not denying the validity of what you're saying. I think you're dead right, but again, I want to focus on the human dilemma that we're creating because it has tremendous impact on all of your organizations.

> You will increasingly find yourself in a situation where you can have data through information technology; years ago a senior executive would not have ever had it. So, having a technology whose fundamental notion is truth is a good idea. The computer people will tell you if you put garbage into a computer, garbage will come out. The only difficulty with human beings is they have a different theory. Their theory is, truth is a good idea when it isn't threatening. And when it is, massage it, distort it, cover it up.

Comment: The instructor begins to raise the idea that the Model I theory-in-use and social virtues should not be taken for granted and accepted as not to be altered. The instructor is trying to open up the idea of a different world, one that would enhance double-loop learning.

> *Participant K:* I think if I learn to have self-discipline in the process, this is the most that I could deliver.

> *CA:* What does that mean, self-discipline?

> *K:* Self-discipline means if what is said makes me angry, I say to myself: stay still, don't speak, listen, try to understand, maybe there is a point. Maybe you are wrong if you are angry. Cover your emotions by having this self-control and self-image, and some perspective will help you understand.

Comment: Note the Model I action strategies to suppress his feelings as well as his thoughts.

> *CA:* That's one hypothesis, and I'm asking you to consider another one. That's what limits learning. You sit there calmly, with discipline, maybe even with a smile on your face to make sure you hide that he has upset you. The other thinks that he or she is doing pretty well here. (Laughter) That's another hypothesis to consider.

Comment: Point out the counterproductive consequences of Model I bypass and cover-ups.

> *Participant L:* I was going to ask this question. Is it to some degree that what is said is in relationship to the context and the risk of saying it? What I mean by that is, if I'm a boss evaluating someone and we decided we're going to go in a certain direction, I will say whatever is on the left-hand side if that's what it takes to get me where I want to go. But what we were talking about here was evaluating the risk and the reaction of someone whom you are trying to get to go your way, where you do not have this total control of getting to that place, and you're trying to make them buy in. And there are cultural as well as other backgrounds that relate to how you put that in context and to how important it is for you to be able to move that person to your way of thinking without creating walls and barriers.
>
> *CA:* Yes, and I'm saying in all the cases that I read, walls and barriers were created. I may be dead wrong; and, needless to say, should anyone want to blow his or her cover, we could look at some of those cases. But I'm saying, you're absolutely right. It depends, I have no problem with that. But the point of this class is to take a look at to what extent we have some causal responsibility for creating the world we wish did not exist.

Comment: The class members now begin to dig deeper into the culturally approved norms of bypass and cover-up. In so doing, they reveal the depth of their Model I strategies and values. They also begin to be more openly critical of the views the faculty member is espousing and recommending.

> *Participant M:* Let's take the issue of truth a little bit further. I think you said that truth is okay unless it's threatening.
>
> *CA:* That's what we find, yes.
>
> *M:* By implication, when it's threatening it's not okay. Now I would dispute that. I think it's the way you deal with truth, not truth per se. And there are times when it's better leaving the truth unsaid but not denied.
>
> *CA:* Yes. That is probably true in the world as it is.

M: If we don't put it out explicitly between us, that doesn't mean that we don't both recognize it. There's always a conversation on multiple levels. And one of the levels, which is often a rather superficial level, is the one where what we say we say explicitly. However, we often understand very clearly what's not being said.

CA: And do you hide that? In your world as you've seen it, do people make that explicit, that second one?

A: It would depend on the context.

CA: All I'm saying is that, in all the cases that were written, they didn't.

M: But that doesn't mean that they're not aware of it, that they don't accept it. The truth is there, but because having it explicit between us is threatening, we deal with it implicitly.

CA: Right, so we can conclude that when the conditions are threatening, you should deal with it implicitly. Does the rule also state that you should make that rule explicit?

M: Well, society doesn't do it. No.

CA: Well, not only society, but neither do the people in this class. You're right, it doesn't. I'm asking you to consider that that's what harms double-loop learning. Now the question arises, what are we going to do about it?

Comment: The instructor could have asked for illustrations. But the issue had already been discussed by others. Hence, he chose to emphasize that M's claim is supported by research describing the world as is and to raise the possibility of changing the world. The instructor raises doubts about M's claim that he might not hide the information, pointing out that such information was hidden by all the writers of the cases. Note that M uses social virtues to make his claim. The instructor can connect these to Model I social virtues.

M: Chris, I think M is saying that underneath the manifest conversation there is an implicit or latent conversation, and he's saying something else. He's saying basically that conversation is a form of learning. He didn't say this, but I think he would say this. There is learning going on in that conversation which is implicit; it's tacit, but it's going on.

CA: That's what I heard; and I'm saying, what would lead people not to make that explicit?

M: I think he's saying, why make it explicit? The learning is going on anyway. He may not agree with that.

Participant N: I don't entirely agree with your thesis that the denial of making things explicit necessarily harms double-loop learning. I agree that it can. But sometimes I believe that double-loop learning will actually be facilitated by dealing with it in another form, on the implicit level.

CA: Could you give an example of what you're saying, where it's a good idea to keep it implicit?

N: Sure, the norms of different societies if a particular society does not encourage explicit communication on a confrontational level, for example. You walk into that society and you become confrontational; you're dead. You can deal with these things on another level, and people understand that you're dealing with standard rules by which you're playing. And over a period of time it works.

Comment: This transcript is from the first session with the class. In a subsequent session the instructor might take the opportunity to use N's analysis and apply it to the class. For example, how free are the members in this class to confront each other constructively? What N is asserting about different cultures may be happening in this class composed of executives representing many cultures.

CA: Well, N, where you claim that it works, you're doing precisely what I try not to do when I make my claims. I try to bring some data. You may be right, but I don't believe you are. And I'll tell you why I don't believe you are right, and I'll ask for your reactions. When we study executives in different cultures, we find Malaysia is different from Tokyo, and Tokyo's different from New York. But we also find in companies within Japan, within Malaysia, and within New York, there's as much variance as there is between countries. So your generalization is true not only about different cultures, it's true about different companies within the same culture. Now if it's true about different companies, it can't be culture then, because you have as much variance within New York as you do between Malaysia and New York.

And so to the second problem. I have no data that you're wrong, but you don't give me data to decide whether you're wrong. Here's how I hear you: "Trust me, Chris, I know there are times in which this works, and I can't..." That's the equivalent of saying, "Chris, if you could just think the way I do, everything would be all right." I don't want to agree with that rule. I do want to agree with being confronted with data, and by data I mean the kind that I'm presenting here or some other kind.

Participant P: I don't understand. Is there is a unique rule or not? In my opinion, reading these cases, can mean that sometimes some thoughts and feelings, if they are disclosed, can help the purpose of the meeting. Sometimes not. Sometimes these feelings could help but not with other people.

CA: The rule that I am recommending is to test that attribution first in a given situation.

P: What do we test? Everything?

CA: Well, when it has to do with making evaluations and attributions about other human beings related to important issues, yes, I would test everything.

Participant Q: I think P is asking, what the ground rules are for knowing when to test or not to test? And I think a second implicit statement is how you test. First of all, I am sure that there is not a unique rule that you have to disclose everything and test everything. I'm sure that my comment didn't help with the conversation in this case; (laughter) sometimes it doesn't help the conversation, I'm sure. And it also depends on the people because some people can better accept your thought; somebody else cannot accept your thought in the same way. You also have to be clever enough to understand what is in front of you.

CA: I hear you, Q, and I'm asking you to consider the possibility…what I'm asking you to learn here, in addition to those skills that you appear to have, is to know when and when not to do it. Let's explore that when you decide to do it, *how* do you decide to do it? And so that it might, in fact, lead to less defensiveness, other than by withholding.

Comment: N raises the idea that double-loop learning can be produced through implicit conversation. The instructor asks for an illustration. The instructor then focuses on two features of N's response. First is the claim that there are important cultural differences. Second, he focuses on the self-referential logic used by N. Both of these responses illustrate Model I. They also begin to provide the participants with some insight into the challenge of moving from Model I toward Model II. Bringing up the issue of testing helps the instructor begin to define some Model II rules such as "test attributions." This, in turn, leads to a dialogue about when and how to test. Again both issues are crucial to moving from Model I to Model II.

A: Perhaps it's just me, but there's a quality of abstractness that I'm not grasping here. Let's take the example that you just gave (of a mixed message). Be creative, but be careful. How would you have stated that differently so I can learn from what you're trying to convey here?

CA: Let me try it. You picked the middle part. I'd want to start from the first part and ask the question, "Why would I even have to say that?"

A: Say what?

CA: Be careful; be creative, but be careful. I don't want to be in a world in which I have to say that, but if I had to be in that world, I think I'd say to M, "M, I'm going to give you a message that is admittedly mixed. The mix is, on the one hand, to be creative, on the other hand, to be careful. The reason I'm giving you this mixed message is that I have the following concern." Then I would ask if the other shares those concerns or do you think they're real or unreal and so on? What's on the left-hand side of your column right now?

Participant R: Well, on the left-hand side of my column is the presumption that she's going to be confused by what you just told her. (laughter)

CA: How confusing did you find that, M?

M: When you first stated that, I found it confusing; the information afterwards was better.

CA: Notice what happened? I asked her, "What is your reaction?" She gave what I thought was a very helpful and appropriate response: "Chris, your first couple of sentences weren't helpful; the others were helpful." I've learned that's a good thing for me to learn.

Comment: Crafting Model II responses, even if done well (and this was not done as well as it could have been), is often bewildering to those operating with a Model I theory-in-use for most of their lives. When R claims that the instructor's comments are confusing, the instructor then points out that M's answer is helpful because it permits the instructor to make a more informed change.

Participant S: My left-side .... (laughter) If you said, "Be creative and be careful," it is broadcast to me, as a recipient of that message, that there's something here I need to be worried about.

CA: Oh, I think maybe I misunderstood. You're right, that's exactly what I think a mixed message does. I don't like mixed messages. I'm not in favor of them, but they're all over the organizations that I've studied, so maybe I misunderstood you. I do not think mixed messages are a good idea; that's why when you asked me.... .

S: I understood that; I wasn't troubled by that.

CA: Let me put it another way. Often when a person gives a mixed message, in fact, let me role play. Here's what we often find. We ask, "Are you clear?" "Oh, yes, Chris, very clear, thank you very much." The person who thinks there is a mixed message, even the way I gave it, bypasses that and says, "Oh, yes, I understand that. I'll get back to you." And so now they begin to withhold information that is important for me to know, information which Annette did give me, that the first part was unclear and the second part was clear.

Intervening for Testing and Learning: Class II

This first session began with a dialogue similar to the one above. It illustrated that the participants were acting so as to be in unilateral control, but acting as if they were not doing so, making attributions about others' feelings and views and refraining from testing them (illustrative of Model I).

In this class we were able to dig deeper, earlier than is typically the case, into the issues of moving from Model I to Model II. We began by examining the left-hand column comment that "the writers appear to stack the deck positively." The faculty member identified several puzzles in this phrase. To combine it with the meaning of being positive illustrates that the executives see unilateral control as positive. Yet, in their written cases they complained about the counterproductivity of others acting unilaterally toward them.

The second puzzle is that the executives say that in order to implement this strategy effectively, they would have to keep it secret from the other. Why, asks the faculty member, is it necessary to keep secret a strategy that is intended to be positive for all concerned?

Comment: The instructor could have taken a different tack. He could have asked members of the class to define the meaning of "positive" by asking them to give concrete illustrations. This usually leads to illustrations whose "positiveness" other members question. The instructor took the approach he did because of its potential for learning. For example, the group could examine in more concrete detail the contradictions (for effectiveness in learning) that arise when individuals craft their attempts at double-loop conversation in the form of unilateral actions. The instructor introduced the second puzzle in order to begin a dialogue that will eventually surface the costs of such a strategy.

> *A:* They want to feel completely in control. They strive to make him feel that he is in control, even though they don't want him to be in control.
>
> *CA:* Please note the rule: "Let him feel that he is in control although I don't want him to be in control." Do you have any hunch as to what led him or her to place that on the left-hand side of the column?
>
> *A:* Maybe because he had something bad to say, he didn't really want to come out and say it.

Comment: The diagnosis made by A is consistent with Model I action strategies.

B: It seems to me that these people who wrote the cases seek to be in control. They do not want to allow others to interrupt. They want to control the situation, to project it as being positive.

I don't see these individuals as being risk-takers. They use a fairly conservative, consensus-making kind of strategy to build a consensus, to stay positive; but they don't allow others to interrupt. That is the strategy I see.

CA: How do others feel or react?

A: It seems that in these cases we are trying to guess the other person's feelings instead of just trying to get them out into the open. We are kind of guessing at them and maybe setting our strategies by what we try to guess.

CA: To use my language, we make attributions about the other person, but we do not, if I hear you correctly, appear to test them.

D: It seems people are bringing preconceived notions about what will occur, and I must say they are probably appropriate. Given the circumstances, this is a dialogue with people who know and work with each other. I think it's sort of a good decision to sort of try to stack the decks positively in terms of the outcome you are trying to create.

CA: Help me to understand how you know it's stacking the deck positively?

D: I wouldn't attach pejorative attributes to that, but you are trying everything that you can to communicate or portray a set of circumstances favorable to the goals that you are trying to reach. Stacking the deck, I guess, would be conveying the idea or the issue I suppose as accurately or at least as favorably [as possible] to his point of view.

CA: If you were stacking the deck in order to be positive, would you say that you were doing that to the other?

D: Of course not.

CA: This is a puzzle which I hope we explore. Why is it appropriate to keep secret a strategy whose intentions are intended to be positive?

D: I would suggest this is not a first-time thing. This is also based on experience and what has succeeded in the past—either with this particular individual or with other individuals—because there has been a history of negotiations of putting these things forward before.

(later)

CA: If I can summarize for a moment: people are inferring a need for control, a need to act as if not trying to be in control. Secondly, from your experiences there is a sense of appearing—and I don't think this word was used, but if you think it's unfair, tell me—opinionated, and they do not try to test. Finally, as _____ said, this may be realistic.

E: I sort of characterize this as a lack of openness and honesty between them.

CA: How could you put that statement together with the position that this is realistic?

E: I think it fits, in a sense, because what they were saying is a continuation of practices and the defenses that have been built up. The words that are used would imply there is a lack of honesty, and the kind of wall that is put between the two of them is demonstrated by these statements which can be broken down only by more honest approaches between the two of them.

F: I don't think all of these comments indicate dishonesty, maybe just one or two.

CA: Show me one that suggests honesty?

F: "Start positive" suggests honesty.

CA: If it is positive, why should "start positive" be hidden? (It is in the left-hand column.)

F: I hadn't thought it was hidden. I think that word would be a prompt to oneself to make sure one did keep on coming on positively. It's just a prompt, but it's a silent prompt. You don't go in and say, "I'm going to be positive about this."

CA: Hold on; what's funny about saying that? Several of you laughed. The most frequent statement I received in the cases is "Be positive." Yet, as we are seeing, the most frequent consequence is negative. May I ask what this says about ourselves.

G: I think it's the common practice. On the one hand, you know you are going to go into this discussion, and the end result of the discussion is not going to be positive to the other party. On the other hand, you don't want to treat the other party with dishonesty or lack of dignity. You want to start the conversation, as F said, "I need to be positive. I don't need to go around the bush." Yet, as human beings, we know in the end we are going to hurt the person on the other side. So I agree with F; this is sort of a silent prompt for one to say, "I don't mean to demean this person." I'm going to go down to the very fact positively, and I am going to have to face the consequences which are not pleasant.

Comment: G's comments illustrate Model I reasoning processes that are defensive, yet the executives see them as humane. G states, in effect:

1. It is common practice to go into a discussion that we know is not going to be positive to another individual;
2. We seek to treat the individual with dignity;
3. Although we prefer not "to go around the bush," we must in order not to hurt the other;

4. Keep prompting yourself not to forget to be positive. He points out that this perspective is taken for granted. All of this illustrates the Model I social virtues of caring and support.

H: It sounds as if this is a lack of honesty, and actually it's just so natural that you don't say that. When I start talking to someone, I don't have to start positively. This is inside what I am going to say; it's going to be positive. And if you start having this back thought and you don't tell the other person, it's because you are acting. So when you start positively, in here it sounds more of an acting role than real life.

CA: So there is a kind of deliberateness as you see it?

H: Yes, it's false.

(later)

J: So why can't I walk in and say you probably have a real need to control this or actually let loose with that?

CA: It may well be that if we were free to be more honest, we would actually be quite destructive. For example, many of you describe the left-hand column as containing upsetting information. If we were honest and said those views, we are likely to upset others.

K: I'm not sure I am following the point exactly. Civilized behavior requires a certain convention of going about doing things. I don't see any of these things here as necessarily being wrong. If you are having negotiations with another person, you need to set the scene. What's happening here is you are setting a scene. Otherwise, you just get in trouble. If you say straight out, you are wrong, I want this, or we are going to do this or you're fired, you don't exactly win friends that way.

CA: It depends what it means to be civilized. If civilized means face saving, for example, I don't know how you could ever be civilized (as I think you mean it) without lying. Let me illustrate that point I just made. If I say to you, "K, I'm about to save your face," I have blown it. The only way I can be skillfully civilized is to act as if I am not trying to be skillfully civilized. So maybe, K, this is going on in our world all the time. It may be time that we interrupt that practice. That is the part I'm asking you. We have examples of civilized strategies in this group which, as far as I can see, get uncivilized consequences; but it's unlikely the other person is going to say that, especially if you are his boss.

Comment: In the previous class, the faculty member used these comments to illustrate a dilemma faced by the Model I executives. On the one hand, they craft private conversations that contain evaluations and attributions in ways that would be difficult to test. On the other hand, making these comments public would simply move the untestable and defensive features into the public domain. It makes little sense to define honesty or openness or candidness as making public one's left-hand thoughts and feelings, because they are crafted in ways that would produce defensiveness. *The underlying problem is why the executives think the way they do when dealing with such issues.*

In addition to these points, the faculty member noted that the above dilemma is caused by skills that the executives have and use. Their skillful actions, intended to show concern and caring, may lead to counterproductive consequences. The faculty member was able to use the classroom dialogue to illustrate one such unintended consequence.

CA: Let me ask you something. You began by saying, "I'm not sure I follow this conversation," or something like that. Then you said things that said to me you were following the conversation very clearly. Now, are you being civilized? Let me ask the group, "Did anybody else say privately, 'like blazes he didn't understand it!'?"

M: Sure.

CA: Did anybody say that to him?

M: No, we are civilized.

CA: Is it fair to say that the question I asked to see that you were playing out your point of being civilized was not in your awareness while you were doing it? You didn't say, "I'm about to illustrate to this class," and so on and so on. Is that fair?

K: I did not have a conscious thought.

CA: We have to take a look at this as we go along because I don't think, at least if our data are right, K is handing us a line. His behavior is so skillful that it is taken for granted. This leads to us becoming unaware. So unawareness is caused by skill. I should like to return to this issue later. When something is taken for granted, it becomes automatic.

N: I agree with K. Quite frankly, what K was saying was not the message I was hearing from around the room. I would not have used the word "civilized" necessarily, but you need a stable base to start from when you go into a difficult discussion. The point is you can come back to where there was no confrontation, in case things get carried away farther down the line. But around the room I heard words like "dishonesty." K was saying it's not dishonest. You need that for a reference point to come back to, so I think the meaning was different than what I heard around the room.

CA: How would you explain those who had a different view than yours?

N: I think you would have to ask them.

CA: Could I cut you off for a moment, N, because I want to give you the reasoning why I asked you that question. What if you and K are correct and the others are not, how would you help them to learn? With that in mind, that was what was going on in my head. I then said, "N, how would you account for...?"

O: I think perhaps that what some of the people are doing is saying that the intention of the discussion is actually to put this guy down or correct him or whatever. Perhaps they don't realize that in some of the words that have been expressed here, people are saying that in order to get to the end of the road, they had to go in different directions; they're not just going right to the end. I think people are saying that they are dishonest and they are too cautious or whatever, assuming that you actually have to go right to the end point. We walk in, you sit down, you are fired.

CA: Let's check that out, M. Is that your view? So far, she is saying no; she does not agree. Go ahead.

O: The way I perceive it is that in most of the cases you should explain what you really think or believe. When I read this, I perceive that if some of the issues here were spoken, there would be a much quicker understanding and agreement than just not saying anything. Honesty in this case does not necessarily mean a judgment, a moral judgment, because it's not something very wrong being hidden.

CA: It may be a worldwide skill. So far, O, is it fair for me to say that you would still disagree with what M is saying?

A: Not necessarily. It depends on the case; it depends on the actual details of the discussion you were having, the nature of the conversation and, in fact, your assessment of the character and the behavior of the person you talked to.

CA: O, if you listened to the tape recording of your behavior when you first began, I think you will hear that you began with, "There was no 'it depends' or anything." Now you are getting to the stage where it depends on what situation you are in. Notice what's happening to your reasoning. At one point you appear relatively clear as to what might be an explanation. You weren't saying it was the explanation. M then said, "I don't think so." You now get conditional. So far, can I trust that conditionalism, or is it part of being civilized?

O: I think it's an element of being civilized.

P: Chris, I'm not sure I understand. If I adopt a set of behaviors I can work with, why would I want to change them?

Comment: This is a crucial question. Typically this question begins to be asked openly by several different individuals. After a trend develops, the instructor illustrates the trend and asks the class members to what extent they feel that once they adopt a set of behaviors that appear to work, they are not likely to want to change them.

CA: The reason I would want you to consider changing them is that you, at the upper levels, ought to behave in ways that encourage double-loop learning. The way to encourage double-loop learning is for you to model it.

O: Chris, can I give you a hypothetical case? You have clearly been lecturing for a long time, and I'm sure you have come across situations in which a student has said something that was absolutely ridiculous and stupid, and you thought, "God, that was stupid!" Are you being dishonest by not saying, "What you just said is really stupid"?

CA: First of all, you are making attribution about what I think. Let me tell you what I think is in my mind, because it illustrates the way I would like to ask you to consider going. If this student says something that's way out, it wouldn't even have to be way out, I think I would say to the student, "I'd like to understand the reasoning behind the conclusion you just stated." In fact, I would do to the student what I did with others here.

The point that I am asking you to consider is that to evaluate automatically and privately an idea as stupid, you create the context where, in the name of caring, you have to be dishonest. I'm asking you to consider developing an automatic reaction of understanding and testing your evaluations.

So I would dig into their reasoning. I think the notion that we automatically evaluate actions as stupid and so on is itself the basis or the beginning of poor communication. Now if somebody is holding a gun or if there is a terrorist, I'm not likely to be inquiring; but I don't attribute what we are doing here as living and working with terrorists. We are really trying to create double-loop learning. Keep in mind that this is what this is about.

Comment: The conversation took a different direction with O's comments. He picked up on the instructor's metaphor of terrorists to say that many of them have worked and continue to work in a setting that has some powerful features of win/do-not-lose, of competitiveness, which, in his opinion, leads to selling behavior if they are to succeed.

Q: What I am about to say is totally honest; it's not a challenge. It's really an observation. Let's stick with the terrorist challenge. Many of us work in hierarchical organizations. We may work, we are men or women, we are at the ends of the career, we have different objectives in our positions than they do in theirs. Frequently as middle managers, I think most of us at one point in our careers were very rapidly on the rise. I think this is true, and we weren't motivated only by money; we were motivated by achievement, by seeing things done well. And because those were our motivations, we tended to be agents of change. Those kinds of change agents, unless they are in an environment that's very receptive, constantly find themselves in a selling kind of situation, situations which they hope will be win-win. Win for the organization, but also a feeling of fulfillment that they have done the right thing.

CA: Absolutely.

Q: Let's get back to the terrorist situation. In hierarchical organizations it's not unusual to find at the root, without being true "terrorists," that these kinds of executives clearly have been present in IBM and Sears and General Motors. They are not listeners. As a consequence, when we read through these left-hand, right-hand kinds of conversations, these seem to be selling situations where agents of change are trying to get something constructive done for the organization, and the listening is not there. The "terrorist" part of what is not here is the implication that this and this are part of the conversation we can't see, that this is the other side, that this is the senior individual, that if you keep pushing me for this change, your career is at risk. That is not a situation that is exactly conducive to honesty any more than the terrorist with a gun to your head is.

CA: Right on.

Q: It's conducive to dishonesty. I think that is the issue that really needs to be probed here, because we are kind of skirting it.

Conclusions

The chapter illustrates the use of the left-hand, right-hand case method as a research and teaching device.

It is possible to analyze these transcripts in order to identify the following:

1. The frequency of Model I action strategies such as making attributions and not testing them.

2. The frequency (and the nature) of defensive reasoning such as self-referential logic.

3. The frequency with which the left-hand column is filled with comments that the respective writers believe are true and important for learning yet are kept hidden and underground. Moreover, the act of making them hidden and underground is also hidden and kept underground.

4. The frequency with which individuals use abstractions as if they are obviously concrete, for example, "be positive."

5. The frequency with which inconsistencies are created by the students. The frequency with which others see the

inconsistencies and the frequency with which the creators of the inconsistencies are unaware of what they are creating. The frequency with which the inconsistencies are blamed on acculturation to one's culture.

6. The frequency with which individuals make assertions about cultural differences yet do not test them in a class where nearly 45 percent of the executives represent different cultures.

7. The frequency with which the executives in the class behave consistently with behavior that they criticize and the degree to which they were unaware of this incongruity.

Second- and third-order analyses are also possible. For example:

1. The frequency of self-fueling processes and the degree of their complexity and the degree to which they close off the individuals to learning.

2. The degree to which the individuals are willing to explore puzzles and paradoxes in order to learn.

3. The processes that first have to be surfaced and then altered in order for individuals to admit to their feeling of being stuck. To begin to learn how to make themselves vulnerable without feeling weak.

4. An example of third-order analyses would be the development of organizational defensive routines in the class. This would require that the class be held for a period of time (at least the equivalent of six hours). If the participants are from one organization, they could develop a map of their classroom defenses and compare these defenses with a map that they develop of their own home organization.

Turning to the classroom as a context for learning, especially of double-loop learning, every one of the dimensions described earlier can be used as a basis for such learning. For example, the first step toward double-loop learning at the interpersonal level is to become aware of one's Model I action strategies such as

1. making attributions and evaluations in ways that discourage learning,

2. using defensive reasoning,

3. resisting accepting personal responsibility when it is operating, and

4. creating antilearning self-fueling processes.

As the participants become aware of their errors, they can confront and question the validity of the instructor's position, or they can challenge him to present concrete, useful alternatives. The dialogue involved in both of these activities is full of opportunities for learning how to begin to generate Model II inquiry. The classroom can also be used as a setting to practice the new skills and to reflect on the requirements of moving from Model I to Model II.

Finally, the classroom can be used as a setting in which to alert the participants to the difficulties that they are likely to face when they attempt to try out their newly-learned skills. The classroom can be used to generate ideas about organizational arrangements that will encourage and reinforce double-loop learning among the participants.

7

A Comprehensive Model II Intervention

In the previous chapter we illustrated features of a process of teaching and research in which groups of individuals were helped to explore the transition from Model I to Model II. In this chapter we will focus on a **comprehensive intervention**—an intervention aimed at helping a whole organization move from an O-I to an O-II learning system. This intervention, conducted by Argyris, was in its sixth year when it was first published in 1993. The intervention not only continues but its scope is being enlarged.

The study began because the directors, who were also the founders and owners of a management consulting firm, concluded that their firm could develop the negative internal characteristics they had so much disliked in the consulting firms they had left. They also concluded that these very characteristics could limit the quality of consulting they gave to clients, especially around issues that involved double-loop learning. The directors believed that double-loop learning would be increasingly important if they were to produce added value for their clients in the future. They also concluded that they were unlikely to provide such assistance if they did not manifest these learning competencies in managing their own internal activities, as well as those that bridged toward the client organization.

Argyris began by holding a series of meetings with the directors in order to set the terms and chart the directions of the intervention. In this process the directors displayed an extremely strong internal commitment to learning. They made no attempts to place sole responsibility upon the intervenor, water down their aspirations for change, or set direct or indirect constraints on what would be studied. The directors expressed support for eventual publication of the research, believing that a publication requirement would assist in producing a high-quality intervention.

Design of the Research/Intervention Activities

The design of the comprehensive intervention was derived from our theoretical framework. There were five initial goals:

1. Discover the degree to which the directors' theories-in-use are consistent with Model I.

2. Discover the degree to which the directors use defensive reasoning whenever they deal with embarrassing or threatening issues.

3. Discover the designs (rules) the directors have in their heads to keep them unaware of the discrepancies among their espoused values, their actions, and their theories-in-use.

4. Discover the degree to which the directors discourage valid reflection on their actions while they are acting. To put this another way, discover how the directors create designs for action that they do not follow but believe they follow, while they remain systematically unaware of this discrepancy and behave in ways that prevent them from discovering it or the causes of their unawareness of it.

5. Discover the defensive routines that exist in the organization and that inhibit double-loop learning. Develop maps of these organizational defensive routines, specifying the actions that lead to limited-learning consequences and cause them to persist even though the directors wish to be free of them.

In order to reach these goals, it would be necessary to conduct programs not only of diagnosis, but of reeducation and change. These would have to:

- Produce relatively directly observable data about the directors' reasoning and actions. The directors would have to accept responsibility for creating these data in a form (for example, a recorded conversation) from which the directors' theories-in-use could be inferred.

- Encourage the directors to examine inconsistencies and gaps in the reasoning that underlie their actions.

- Surface and make explicit the rules that "must" be in the directors' heads if they maintain there is a connection between their designs for action and the actions themselves.

- View any resistance, bewilderment, or frustration resulting from the intervention as further directly observable data that could be used to test the validity of what is being learned.
- Produce opportunities to practice Model II ways of crafting actions that would reduce counterproductive consequences.

Framing the Problem

The seven directors of the organization in this case study framed their initial problem in various ways. They said they wanted to create an organization capable of persistent double-loop learning, both within the organization and between itself and its clients. They also wanted to know how to reduce the existing "politics" they thought inhibited their objective of building a genuine "learning organization." And they wanted to discover how to build an organization where double-loop learning not only occurred persistently, but did so under conditions of stress, embarrassment, or threat.

During his first interviews, the intervenor tried to determine the extent to which the directors believed that counterproductive activities were occurring and their view of the organizational consequences of these activities. He also tried to discover the directors' causal explanations of these phenomena. As we shall see, most of their explanations were high on the ladder of inference—at several levels removed from directly observable data. And their explanations were not testable because they were not rigorously connected to such data. For example, the directors' explanations included unillustrated attributions that "people are not candid," "group decision making at the top is poor," and "coalitions exist that create rivalries."

The interventionist faced two major tasks. One was to provide a causal explanation that gave a coherent, holistic, testable account of the directors' many multileveled, disconnected explanations. This holistic explanation also had to be usable for designing and executing the intervention program. In turn the intervention program and its consequences could provide opportunities for further tests of the explanation.

The second task was to develop generalizations about how to interrupt and reduce organizational defensive routines and skilled incompetence and then to help the directors (and later, consultants at all levels of the organization) acquire the skills necessary to spread the learning throughout the organization in such a way that it not only persevered but also enlarged and deepened.

Using the theoretical framework described in Part II, Argyris interviewed the directors to learn their respective causal explanations of the problems they considered important. These explanations were mainly representative of the directors' espoused theories. These theories and observations of actual behavior were then translated into descriptions of individual and organizational theories of action, at the levels of both espoused theory and theory-in-use. Next, an organizational map was developed to illustrate the organization's theory-in-use for dealing with the issue of organizational politics. This map makes explicit the organizational defensive pattern on this issue, a pattern that partially explains the existence of activities counterproductive to learning.

The map was fed back to the directors. One purpose of the feedback was to assess the degree to which the directors confirmed or disconfirmed features of the map or, indeed, the map as a whole. The intervenor placed a heavy emphasis on encouraging attempts to disconfirm the map for two reasons. As a researcher, he wanted to encourage the toughest possible tests of his ideas; as an intervenor, he knew that the design and implementation of the change program would greatly depend on the explanatory map. If the map was faulty, he wanted to know early so that he could correct it, and he did not want the directors to withhold their doubts only to raise them after the change activities began.

Purposes of the Feedback Session
The first feedback session had six purposes:

1. to describe to the directors what had been learned from the interviews and the early observations of their meetings,
2. to encourage any disconfirmation or confirmation of the findings,
3. to start building an incremental relationship of trust among the directors and between the directors and the intervenor,
4. to plan actions that would correct whichever counterproductive activities the directors chose to correct,
5. to plan the intervention steps required to implement these corrections, and
6. to conduct planning in ways that would facilitate the directors' internal commitment to further steps in the intervention. This internal commitment would mean that the directors would be motivated to implement the changes, because doing so would be intrinsically rewarding.

The Feedback Process

Whatever methods are used to diagnose an organizational situation and whatever data are collected, four features are important to an effective feedback process:

1. The material should be organized to describe the variables that cause the functional and dysfunctional activities of the group being studied. The basic criterion for separating functional from dysfunctional activities is the degree to which each activity facilitates or inhibits the detection and correction of important errors or the production of innovations within the group.

2. The variables should be organized into a pattern that shows explicitly how the variables evolved and how their mutual reinforcement leads to the persevering of the pattern. The description of the pattern should enable the prediction of its consequences.

3. The pattern should make explicit the likely personal responsibility of each director in causing and maintaining the pattern.

4. The pattern should be presented in the form of an action map, and that map should present the data in ways that allow the participants to derive the inferences that permit comprehensive understanding as well as those that illuminate each unique, individual case. The data must also be conducive to generalizing about the present and the future. In addition to providing the information for all of these analyses, the map ought to be generalizable (by reflective transfer) beyond the group to include other parts of the organization as well as to other individuals in other organizations.

The feedback process should help to provide a more holistic and systemic picture of organizational reality. This picture should be holistic in the sense that it covers a bigger slice of reality than the existing views of individuals or subgroups do. It should be more systemic in the sense that it makes explicit the interdependencies that result in a self-maintaining pattern.

Tests of Validity

An action map constructed for a feedback session is primarily a representation of actions, strategies, consequences, governing conditions, and the feedback and feedthrough mechanisms that relate these phenomena to one another in a persistent pattern. Action maps are, in effect, hypotheses about what drives learning and antilearning activities within the organization. Therefore, all action maps have to be tested as frequently and as completely as possible.

There are several strategies that may be used to test a map's validity. The first is to show it to the participants to see what features they confirm or disconfirm. However, the researcher should be aware that certain conditions predispose individuals to provide too easy confirmation. We have found that participants are too easily willing to confirm a map if they believe the end result is only research knowledge. They are unwilling to put themselves, their peers, and their organization on the line for the sake of producing maps for scholars to publish in professional journals. This is not to say that they would confirm glaring errors; if the error is glaring, it is unlikely that they risk much by disconfirming it. But in our experience, they are reluctant to disconfirm when opinions vary widely, when topics are "hot," and when topics are encased in long-standing organizational defensive routines—precisely the conditions under which researchers would seek a healthy debate.

Conversely, if the participants have agreed at the outset that the research will include intervening in order to change the status quo and open up the Pandora's box they have feared, as well as the defenses they have created to protect themselves, then they are more likely to surface their doubts about the map.

A second strategy to test the validity of a map is to make predictions based on it. An especially robust test will occur when the researcher's predictions are made known to the participants, the participants disagree with the predictions, and yet the researcher turns out to be correct. For example, the map presented to the directors (which is reproduced later in this chapter) described how organizational politics were created and maintained. The directors discussed the map in a lively session; some felt the session was so productive that they would be able to change their actions immediately. The intervenor and his coresearchers predicted that they would not be able to do so. They were able to test this prediction because they observed and recorded several board meetings that took place after the feedback session but before the first two-day change sessions. An analysis of the tape recordings confirmed that the defensive routines described in the map were alive and well.

Such experiences raise questions about the commonly made assertion that any intervention, including asking people to fill out instruments or to be observed, leads to changes. In our experience this assertion is likely to be true only when the changes are changes in action strategies, rather than in values, that is, when they are related only to single-loop learning. It is possible, for example, to help an authoritarian, aggressive leader behave less aggressively, but that behavior often vanishes when the individual is exposed to embarrassing or threatening conditions. The moment the individual experiences moderate to high stress, he or she reverts to Model I theory-in-use and the defensive reasoning, which the individual has never abandoned. Managerial gimmicks and fads are often based on behavioral changes that are not accompanied by changes in governing values.

A third testing strategy is to predict the likely consequences of attempts to change the status quo. These tests will be even more robust if the change requires altering what is taken for granted. The more one can specify ahead of time the conditions of change, the sequences of actions that do and do not lead to change, the individuals or groups that will learn faster, and the conditions under which this learning will occur, the more robust the test will be.

These specifications can be produced by designing reeducational experiences directly from the knowledge embedded in the map. For example, the intervenor and his coresearchers could predict that the map they had created for the directors was not going to change unless the directors changed their Model I theories-in-use to approximate features of Model II. In moving toward Model II, individuals would have to unfreeze Model I. The researchers could assess the degree to which each director (and later, others) would unfreeze Model I and practice Model II. They could also make predictions about the likelihood that the directors would be able to effect nontrivial changes in organizational politics. Note that this does not mean that individuals in this situation have to get rid of their Model I skills. Such skills may still be relevant for routine issues requiring only single-loop learning. Nor does it mean that all the new behavior produced will be a pure example of Model II. There will be many instances of hybrids of Models I and II as well as instances of pure Model I behavior. What the researchers will observe, if there is genuine movement toward Model II, is that individuals will recognize and reflect on their Model I actions or will express discomfort about such actions without inhibiting their learning.

Constructing the Action Map

The first step in constructing an action map is to identify its components. The second is to order each component according to the role it plays in the learning system described by the map. What contribution does each component make to the values served by the pattern as a whole, to the functioning of other components, and to its own functioning?

These criteria come from an operational definition of **interdependence of components**: the degree to which each component gets sustenance from and gives aid to the others and the degree to which each component facilitates or inhibits the values served by the pattern as a whole.

To identify the components of a map and to decide their likely consequences, we depend on our theory. Model I and Model II alert us to examine action strategies and their consequences as well as governing values. Each model also specifies characteristics of action strategies. Model I action strategies include evaluating actions or making attributions in ways that do not encourage inquiry or public testing. Model II action strategies for evaluating and attributing require that they be crafted in ways that encourage inquiry and public testing.

Our theory specifies that behavior consistent with Model I will lead to defensive consequences (for example, self-fulfilling and self-sealing processes and escalating error). The theory also specifies the nature of defensive and productive reasoning. Researchers can be taught to score transcripts and observations by using these concepts (Argyris, 1985a).

Causal Reasoning

It is our assumption that all individuals create designs for action, and they act in order to maintain the world within which they live. Effective actions in this context are those that persistently produce intended consequences. Embedded in this requirement is the following type of causal reasoning: "If I act in such and such manner, the following will occur and the following will not occur." The causal patterns so predicted will persist under specified conditions. However, Model I theory-in-use will always require a categorically different result from causal reasoning than will Model II. Because Model I requires protective results, it will also require defensive reasoning, while Model II will require productive reasoning to create productive learning outcomes.

If actions are explained by actors' causal reasoning and if our map is a pattern of actions, consequences, and values, then it should contain identifiable causal reasoning. We should be able, for example, to identify the degree to which defensive or productive reasoning has been used in creating and maintaining the pattern revealed by the map.

Governing Conditions

As we have already shown, effective human action, individual or organizational, requires some order within which on-line acting in a specific situation is possible. Crucial variables in that order are the master values that are not to be violated. Master values act as criteria for assessing the effectiveness of action. They also define the intention of action. For example, in this case study, one governing value for organizational action held by the directors was "produce high 'value added' for clients." Therefore, every concept the directors used and every recommendation they made could be evaluated legitimately in terms of their concept of value added. Moreover, the same concept could be used to define what was not acceptable, such as analyses and recommendations crafted in ways that hid significant portions of what was learned.

The Directors' Action Map

An action map was developed from interviews with the directors and from observations of several directors' meetings (see the figure on pages 160 and 161). The map depicts a pattern of interdependence among governing conditions, generic action strategies, and several orders of counterproductive consequences. It also depicts the feedback and feedthrough processes by which the pattern is maintained.

Directors' Governing Conditions

All the directors agreed that the governing values described in the first column existed. These values governed actions in the sense that whatever actions were designed would always take them into account. The actions would not violate the values; if they did so, further actions would be designed to deal with the violations. For example, the violations would be covered up, unless there was an intention to change one or more of them.

The second governing value, low respect and trust on interpersonal issues, requires an explanatory word. The map depicts governing variables of the directors' theory-in-use. In the case of the other five governing values, there was high congruence between the values the directors espoused and the ones they used to guide their actions. But there was a relatively large gap between the values the directors espoused about trust and the values that guided their actual behavior. Thus it was *low* respect and trust that was the theory-in-use variable.

The next column asked how the directors dealt with "wicked problems," those that are embarrassing or threatening, as opposed to tame problems.[1] How did they deal with "hot" situations?

Directors' Generic Action Strategies

The seven generic action strategies listed in the map describe typical ways of handling wicked problems that were seen to be used by the directors. To take one instance, the directors made attributions about one another's intentions and motives. For example, they might say, "So-and-so is control-oriented," "So-and-so's thinking and actions are dominated by money," or "So-and-so manipulates in order to get what he wants."

The directors also attributed to each other a low capacity to deal effectively with wicked problems. Moreover, they shaped their attributions to fit predictions in which change would be unlikely, saying, for example, "I know so-and-so; he'll not change," or "Trust me, believe me, that is ingrained in so-and-so. He'll never change." This reasoning was crafted so as to make the predictions difficult to test. The directors were maintaining that they knew the others would not change, that this prediction was valid, and that it required no further testing.

When they were asked if they had ever tested their claims publicly, the answer was that they had not done so. When they were asked why they had not tested them, their answers were that they did not want to upset the other person, open up a Pandora's box, or create bad feelings. In effect, they stated (design causality) that their reason for not testing their attributions publicly was that they cared for the others and the group.

In these ways, the directors made their attributions and the reasoning behind them undiscussable. They also made the undiscussability undiscussable. The latter action strategy was necessary because, if they openly admitted this instance of undiscussability, they would have to make public all their other attributions and cover-ups.

---

[1] Our use of "wicked problems" differs from, although it overlaps with, the original use of that term to refer to ill-defined and open-ended problems, by Rittel and Webber (see Rittel, Hurst and Webber, Melvin, in "Dilemmas in a General Theory of Planning," *Policy Sciences* 4: 155–169.

The Director's Action Map: An Organizational Defensive Pattern

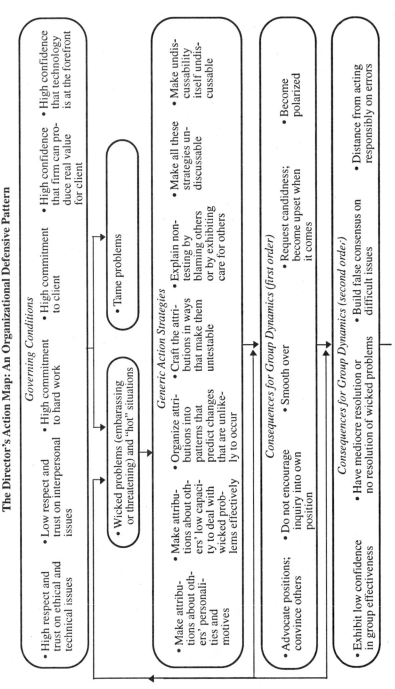

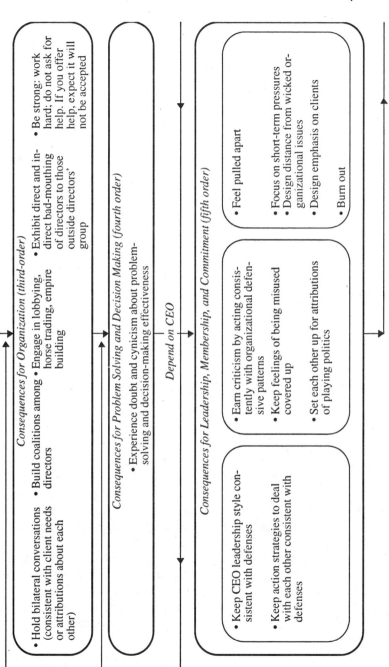

Consequences for Organization (third-order)

- Hold bilateral conversations (consistent with client needs or attributions about each other)
- Build coalitions among directors
- Engage in lobbying, horse trading, empire building
- Exhibit direct and indirect bad-mouthing of directors to those outside directors' group
- Be strong: work hard; do not ask for help. If you offer help, expect it will not be accepted

Consequences for Problem Solving and Decision Making (fourth order)

- Experience doubt and cynicism about problem-solving and decision-making effectiveness

Depend on CEO

Consequences for Leadership, Membership, and Commitment (fifth order)

- Keep CEO leadership style consistent with defenses
- Keep action strategies to deal with each other consistent with defenses

- Earn criticism by acting consistently with organizational defensive patterns
- Keep feelings of being misused covered up
- Set each other up for attributions of playing politics

- Feel pulled apart

- Focus on short-term pressures
- Design distance from wicked organizational issues
- Design emphasis on clients

- Burn out

These seven generic action strategies were likely to inhibit the detection, as well as the correction, of errors. In addition, the strategies reinforced each other and thereby contributed to constructing a social reality that was antilearning and overprotective. This meant that the concepts of antilearning and overprotectiveness were also protected.

Consequences for Group Dynamics (first order)

Whenever the directors met to discuss wicked problems, they advocated their positions as persuasively as possible, intending to convince the others of their views. Because they crafted and defended their views on the basis of undiscussable and untestable generic action strategies, they gave little encouragement to others to inquire into the positions they advocated.

They acted this way because they believed that as directors they were responsible for expressing their views. And as the data in the map show, the directors knew that their organizational norms supported antilearning and overprotective actions and cover-ups of those actions. Under these conditions, directors who opened their ideas to inquiry ran the risk of losing and of being dominated by others. Hence, the directors bypassed these issues and covered up the bypass. The bypass and cover-up were inferred from the smoothing-over actions that were reported during the interviews and observed during the meetings. For example, the directors reported that whenever they had invited others to be candid, they had experienced either "being bloodied" or an awkward silence. Both reactions were upsetting; neither invited further discussion.

Consequences for Group Dynamics (second order)

The directors' generic action strategies, combined with the first-order group dynamics, led to at least four second-order consequences.

First, the directors went into meetings with a low sense of confidence that their group would deal effectively with the wicked issues. They did not discuss their low confidence because that was itself a wicked problem.

Second, they evaluated the meetings' resolution of issues as mediocre at best. Again this evaluation was not discussed during meetings because it, too, was a wicked problem. After meetings, the directors might meet privately in dyads to discuss their evaluations and attributions with those colleagues whom they expected to hold similar views.

Third, a false consensus was created. For example, the CEO might ask, "Are we all in agreement?" Or he might say, "I think we have discussed this well and have reached the following decision," or "It's time for action steps. Who will do what?" Individuals would sign up or be appointed to take certain actions. The CEO would express pleasure for the team effort, and they would all go on to the next problem. Weeks later, most of the commitments had not been implemented.

Fourth, in the interviews everyone reported scenarios such as those just described. Everyone reported feeling that the group members were distancing themselves from detecting, discussing, and correcting wicked problems.

Again all the consequences were not discussable and their undiscussability was not discussed; the consequences reinforced themselves as well as the previous values, actions, and consequences.

Consequences for the Organization (third order)

In this column of the action map were the organizational consequences of the features in the previous columns, ones that could also be observed in settings beyond the directors' group.

The directors developed coalitions among themselves based on their personal attributions about each other. They reported on, or could be observed in bilateral conversations about, the wicked problems they saw in clients or in their own organization. The directors used these coalitions to lobby for controversial views, to trade favors ("I owe you one"), and to build whatever empires they believed were just. The intervenor did not observe, nor was he given reports of, one director trying to take over another's turf. The empire building was more akin to building protective walls against penetration by others than to increasing span of control. One especially troublesome issue for some directors was how the CEO distributed leads for new clients. Some felt that the CEO had favorites. The CEO felt that he allocated leads according to his honest judgment of who would best serve the client.

Directors reported and could be observed bad-mouthing other directors within their coalition groups. They acted similarly toward senior consultants if the latter were being pressed by other directors to work with those directors.

Finally, a norm existed as to what it meant to be strong. A strong director did not ask for help (the protective walls might then be breached). Moreover, if one director decided to offer help to another, the expectation was that it would not be accepted.

Consequences for Problem Solving and Decision Making (fourth order)

The action strategies, the group dynamics, and the organizational consequences combined in the mind of each director to create a strong doubt about the group's problem-solving and decision-making effectiveness for wicked problems. Moreover, there was a good deal of cynicism about any suggestion that changes could occur without outside help.

The doubt and cynicism seemed sensible. Every action and every consequence created and reinforced bypass and cover-up activities. These resulted in the overprotection of the directors and reduced the likelihood that they could detect and correct important errors or create new policies that required discussing difficult issues.

Consequences for Leadership, Membership, and Commitment (fifth order)

There is a fifth-order set of consequences that arises from the values, actions, and consequences described so far. First, a dependence upon the CEO is created. If a group is not a reliable problem-solving and decision-making body, then the members may turn to one person for leadership. That leader is expected to behave in ways that do not violate the group's defensive pattern as described in the action map. This creates a double bind for leaders. If their acts are consistent with the defensive pattern, they will encourage overprotectiveness and limited learning. The leader's direct reports can then make attributions that the leader prefers their dependence because he or she can unilaterally manage the group. On the other hand, if the leader's acts are inconsistent with the pattern, he or she will create disruptive consequences. For example, if the CEO in our case decided to make discussable what was not discussable, he would have done it in the context of a group where mutual trust on the issues was low. Moreover, the skills the directors had developed were those that served bypass and cover-up. If the directors were required to be candid, it would likely have led to disruptive actions because they would not have had the skills to discuss wicked problems candidly without creating further wicked conditions.

The same would have been true for each director. If anyone had tried to discuss the undiscussable, he would have run similar risks of creating counterproductive consequences and of being accused of harming the status quo. If he acted consistently with the defensive patterns, he could be accused of protecting his turf and himself.

Under these conditions, the directors felt misused, and the misuse was covered up because it was a wicked problem. The CEO and the directors appeared to be setting themselves up for attributions that they were behaving politically.

These nested double binds, in turn, led the directors to feel pulled apart. They were damned if they did and damned if they did not. It was rational, under these conditions, to distance themselves from the wicked organizational issues and to pay attention to short-term pressures instead. It was also rational to focus heavily on clients, not only because high-quality value added was a governing value but because a client emphasis legitimized the distancing from internal organizational problems.

The ultimate double bind for the directors was that they knew that every defensive action they took discouraged development of the kind of "learning organization" that would reinforce their espoused governing values.

Discussions During the Feedback Session

The intervenor began the session by describing the governing values that appeared in the first column of the map. The directors did not have much difficulty in agreeing that these were their values. When asked if they could think of other governing values, several responded that they could not. They reserved the right, however, to question or add to the list later.

Next came a series of questions about the causes of nontesting and blaming others. The intervenor focused on the coerciveness of the system as well as on the directors' skillful behavior in bypassing and covering up. He did so because he wanted to make the point that the directors' actions were predictable from these factors and not from the untested attributions that they had made, such as saying that someone was power-oriented or competitive. Their attributions might have been valid, but the data did not directly support them at this time.

In acting this way, the intervenor was illustrating actions and rules that he wanted the directors to learn. For example, whenever there are competing causal explanations, one should select those that are closest to the directly observable data. Also, one should strive to select causal explanations that require the fewest number of inferences from the available relatively directly observable data. Inferences about bypass and cover-up, for instance, can be tested by reference to tape recordings of actual behavior as well as by directors' reports of such incidents. However, inferences about being power hungry or competitive require inference processes that are much more complicated and difficult to test publicly on the basis of recordings.

This does not mean that the latter inferences are not valid. It means that it is more desirable if explanations can be constructed, predictions tested, interventions designed, and changes made with the use of a simple inference structure. It is more desirable in the sense that the simpler the valid explanations, the more likely it is that tests can be crafted to be rigorous, intervention strategies can be reliable and complete, and the learning required for change can be produced with relative ease.

These rules have a further practical value. The shorter the chain of inferences from the directly observable data, the easier it will be for practitioners to test their hypotheses under conditions of everyday life. They can use the ladder of inference, focusing first on the actual behavior, then on the meaning of that behavior, and finally on their explanation of it. For example, focusing either on testing attributions or on determining whether they are testable is less likely to create the communication difficulties that arise when attributions of being power hungry or having low self-esteem or a big ego are publicly defined and explained.

Inferences connected to what was said and done make it easier for the intervenor to educate the clients. For example, when questions arise regarding alternative explanations, the intervenor can make his or her views known and illustrate them while modeling the reasoning and the skills that he or she hopes to get the clients to consider. The intervenor is not simply feeding back data but is beginning to create the conditions where the clients can choose, if they wish, to learn how to develop new causal framings of familiar issues.

Looking back, we can identify a trend that occurs in most groups where the members are genuinely interested in learning, a trend that occurred in this case as well. The conversations began with the directors' concerns about ideas and issues related to the intervenor's theoretical positions. These centered on how skills can trap people, how it is possible to intend to be caring yet come across as uncaring, how untestable attributions lead to self-sealing consequences, and how these consequences become functional in the systems where the directors work.

The intervenor emphasized that the directors were causally responsible for creating their defensive, limited-learning system and that this occurred even though they did not intend to hurt others or the organization as a whole.

Then the conversation shifted to an attempt by the directors to define causes of their counterproductive actions, causes that were external, lying beyond their control. If they could find such causes, they seemed to think, they might be able to resolve their problematic situation without having to focus on such internal factors as their theories-in-use and personal causal responsibility. When the intervenor suggested that these internal factors were crucial, he provoked a genuine confrontation of his views. Maybe what he assumed to be desirable was not? Maybe his argument was self-sealing? Who said that his normative position was correct? Maybe the directors were unable to change the factors that the intervenor suggested should be changed? Could not the fault lie in the weaknesses of their technical knowledge? How about the siege mentality that developed because of client pressures?

The third phase of the conversation occurred when the directors returned to examining their personal causality. This led to the episode we look at next in which the directors deal with their own internal politics.

The episode begins with the CEO's candid reflections on how he builds coalitions and how he reacts to certain actions by the directors. This leads to a deeper analysis of what he and the other directors are doing to each other. The CEO describes the double bind he experiences. If he heeds many of the directors' complaints, he could conclude that the firm is in serious trouble and that he is responsible for solving the problem. If he does not heed the directors, he can be accused of being indifferent toward them or rejecting them. This leads other directors to explore their feelings about the CEO.

The conversation then turns to problems that plague most consulting organizations, including how to evaluate consultants' performance and how to allocate business leads fairly.

This part of the conversation encourages the CEO to talk about what the directors do that leads him to feel victimized. The intervenor adds that the directors might also feel victimized by the system they and the CEO have created. If the map is correct and the system is both self-sealing and antilearning, then it could eventually lead everybody in the organization to feel victimized. The directors support this view.

> *CEO:* I, too, want to discuss [internal politics and coalition building]. I plead guilty to coalition building for a substantive result in

some cases. There is also coalition building where you truly want help and discussion. But I have found that some people are inefficient participants. Even though I want genuine participation, I have learned to bias myself in favor of some of you more than others. Those that I choose do not give me a ten-hour answer, nor do I get the feeling that they are working out personal problems.

Jim: But isn't that making attributions?

CEO: I agree. I would like to see all this changed. All I am doing is adding more data and asking that we put it on our agenda. ...The whole currency is debased because whenever someone is thanked, he goes around and makes speeches about how he saved someone's rear. Remember the motto we created for ourselves, "Shut up and get back to work?" This could be interpreted as, "Don't bother me with your problems; fix them yourselves."

David: One reason that we are profitable is that we work hard. A work ethic driven out of fear is wrong. A work ethic driven out of a sense of teamwork, that you're achieving something, that's worth investing your life in, that's positive.

CEO: From my perspective, people working hard is not a problem because people love what they are doing. If we shut up and can't help or learn from each other, that would be a problem. How can we become the learning organization we say we want to become? How do we help clients become the learning organization that we say we can help them become?

Summary of the First Seminar

The topics discussed in the feedback session can be grouped into two broad categories. The first concerns the characteristics of the defensive, limited-learning organizational pattern and their interrelationships. It includes the following:

Undiscussable Attributions:
Feeling plain ordinary fear of confrontation
Thinking it is okay to have limited-learning systems and the politics that go with them
Using a siege mentality to protect oneself
Putting down clients
Using technical knowledge to overpower
Examining what it means to be a director
Building coalitions, distancing by the CEO, and covering up both actions
Describing the reciprocal distancing

Haggling over who gets the credit

Perceiving client leads to be allocated in accordance with secret rules and friendships

Needing to be strong by never asking for help

Self-fulfilling and Self-sealing Consequences:

The CEO feels double binds, bypasses, covers up and becomes upset, all of which leads him to act like a "blast furnace." The other directors cover up their feelings; hence, these processes become undiscussable.

Directors create discussions that are not helpful and then assign responsibility to the CEO to take action. They condemn him for taking unilateral action.

Directors engage in distancing, which leads to more distancing and an increased likelihood that distancing is not discussable and hence is self-sealing.

Directors all feel victimized by a system they created.

System Paradoxes:

Bypassing and covering up are functional to the pattern that the directors have created and dysfunctional to their vision of the firm.

Participation can lead to wasting a lot of time and can reduce the value of participation.

The second category includes topics that show the directors reflecting on the total pattern as well as on its implications.

Multiple Causality and Circularity:

Individuals cover up, and the pattern rewards such actions. There is a circular relationship between individuals' responsibility for dysfunctional behavior and the pattern's rewarding such behavior.

The tension is caused by wicked problems *and* by failure to deal with fear, embarrassment, or the sense of being threatened in the presence of these problems.

High-level Inferences:

Directors make attributions about having nasty motives and about being power-oriented, competitive, and money-crazy.

Questions that Test Hypotheses:

To what extent are dysfunctional consequences true for all organizations?

To what extent are directors able to change their theories-in-use and the ways they reason? To what extent do they wish to do so?

To what extent can directors assess their effectiveness as individuals and as a group?

To what extent can directors assess the intervenor's normative views and values?

The directors provided many illustrations of the functioning of the whole pattern, along with its component parts and its possible impact on the organization's lower levels. The illustrations were, in many cases, enriched by explanatory comments. For example, a major portion of the time was spent talking about the impact of the CEO's actions upon individual directors and the group.

The feedback discussion also led members to describe how they felt victimized by the pattern. All of them, especially the CEO, reported continual double binds and explained how they came about.

As the members discussed the pattern, several things began to occur that provided important foundations for change. First, the directors confirmed that they made negative attributions about each other and that they did not test or encourage others to test them. The apparent ease and candor with which they admitted their attributions provided evidence that the directors' intentions were not as nasty as the directors themselves evaluated them to be. Moreover, the directors appeared more capable of discussing the undiscussable topics than they had originally thought they would be.

The very act of a thoughtful, spirited inquiry about the action map, in the context of a feedback session managed by an intervenor, provided initial evidence that the overprotective features described in the map were valid but alterable. As a result the directors became optimistic about changing what they had feared was unchangeable. These changes in aspirations, we believe, came from the fact that the directors owned up to faults that were attributed them in such a way as to disconfirm the further attribution that such faults were undiscussable. Moreover, when each director gave reasons for acting as he did, those reasons made sense to the others.

At the end of the session, all the directors expressed an enthusiasm for the discussion that had occurred and a cautiously optimistic prognosis for change. There were at least two reasons why the optimism was cautious. First, many directors wondered what would happen after they left the room and especially what would happen when they returned to the pressures of everyday life.

Second, as the intervenor pointed out, in order for the optimism to become credible, new actions would have to develop and persist. In his opinion, the directors did not have the skills to produce the new actions even though they wanted to do so.

The intervenor recommended a second seminar to examine the generic action strategies and the theories-in-use that produced them, to learn theories of action that could lead to more productive actions, to practice enacting these espoused theories so that they became a new theory-in-use, and to explore the organizational changes that the new theory-in-use could create. The directors agreed to hold this seminar.

The Second Seminar

Each director completed a left-hand/right-hand case as described in Chapter 4. Each case was discussed by the directors as a group. They acted as consultants to each other. All the cases illustrated features of Model I that we have described in several previous chapters. We will summarize how the cases and their discussion confirmed features of the action map presented earlier.

Action Strategies

The action strategies in the cases were consistent with Model I. For example, whenever the writers attempted to explain another person's intentions, the following actions were apparent:

> Negative attributions were made about the other's intentions and defensiveness.
>
> Attributions were not tested publicly.
>
> Negative evaluations were made about the other's performance.
>
> Evaluations were not tested publicly.
>
> The stated reason for avoiding testing was that the writer was showing concern for the other.

Cover-ups

The cases' left-hand columns contained the writers' attributions and evaluations of the CEO, other directors, and clients. They were not communicated to the other person in the conversation, yet these thoughts and feelings were crucial to the way each writer developed his strategies and produced his conversation.

Limited Learning

There was no reflection on or discussion of the critical issues that were being covered up. Moreover, each case showed that the writer protected himself, that the writer believed the CEO protected himself, and that underlying issues in the resource allocation system were never discussed.

Self-fulfilling and Self-sealing Processes

The case writers found serious faults with the allocation system and with the CEO's behavior. They entered into the dialogue with doubts that the basic problems would be resolved. The way they crafted their conversations and censored them in order to cover up their thoughts and feelings made it likely that the problems identified in the cases would not be resolved by those conversations. Moreover, given the undiscussability of the left-hand columns and the Model I crafting of the conversation, it was unlikely that the parties would see that they were responsible for creating self-fulfilling processes as well as conditions under which these processes would not be discussed. Hence, their action strategies led to processes that sealed the dysfunctional processes, and these self-sealing processes were not discussed.

Analysis of the Discussion of the Cases

All the dysfunctions apparent in the cases should be expected to lead to the sense of helplessness and the distancing identified in the map. Indeed these consequences were actually produced during the discussion of the cases in the two-day change seminar. Here are some telling episodes from that discussion:

> *Larry:* My attitude in this conversation and in the thirty-five times that I have had it in the last two years is not that the CEO obstructs the solution. It is that there is literally no solution.
>
> *CEO:* Yes, I agree with the conversation in the case. My thoughts and feelings were something along the lines of "Why are we bothering to have a conversation about something there is no decent answer to? We can solve 50 percent of this problem, but I wonder if we are going to talk about the 50 percent for which there is no answer."

Several directors openly confirmed their sense of hopelessness. They also admitted that the only strategy left for them was to deal with the CEO individually and to hold him responsible for solving the problem. They said they ask for more resources than they expect to get and they act as if this were not the case. The CEO, on the other hand, sensed this but covered up his views.

> *CEO:* My left-hand column is that I will probably be asked to give each of you the eighteen people whose names you've written down.
>
>   (Later) I feel our discussions are useless because there is no flexibility on your part.
>
>   (Later) Everyone tends to use overly dramatic statements; therefore, I have to discount what you say and, of course, act as if I am not doing so.
>
> *David:* (Tells the CEO that he does not realize how he causes the very problems that he wants to solve.)

CEO: (disagrees that he causes the problems) If you all agree that we have too few people, then the majority of the problems are created by you fellows. Why can't you guys manage yourselves?

David: The problem is that each of us has different views of the rules.

CEO: I don't believe that. I have resisted exerting coercive power over you. You are allegedly both adults and my partners. I will never order you to do these things. If you want me [to become coercive], then you can have my letter of resignation.

Larry: What is the nature of the compensation scheme? On what basis are we rewarded?

CEO: I do run the compensation scheme as a political process in order to keep the coalition together. I have had the belief that some of these undiscussable issues would cause so much upheaval that I have deliberately made things vague. The alternative would be collective discussability, which I have always thought would be too disruptive.

Jim: Compensation that is dollars is a minority issue. The issue is self-worth and relative worth. We shouldn't kid ourselves.

Several directors: (They discuss Jim, who brings more business to the firm than the others do. Some see him as arrogant and self-centered; others are annoyed because they believe he is getting most of the human resources, as well as keeping the best clients. The discussion is candid on all sides.)

Jim: (says he feels he is in a bind) If I get the business, I am damned; if I did not get it, I would be damned. I work my butt off for the firm [and I am not appreciated].

John: I suspect that all of us envy you, and those feelings get in the way.

Signs of Learning

As the two-day seminar progressed, apparently inconsistent actions were observed. While most of the actions were guided by Model I theory-in-use, others, often little ones, suggested that Model II theory-in-use was being learned. (This imbalance of Model I over Model II is typical of most sessions during the early stages of intervention.)

The context of the episode, from which the comments reproduced above were taken, was the discussion of a case in which the problem concerned a director evaluating a senior consultant. Some directors felt the case was not one from which they could learn. They made attributions that the writer chose the case in order to bypass difficult issues about his performance and to look good. The conversation is scored to show which actions are characteristic of Model I.

What Was Said

Jim: I find this case interesting but not very useful for our learning.
Bill: Well, I checked it out with Chris [the intervenor].
Jim: My left-hand side (that is, his uncensored thought) in reading the case is that you picked a bunny.
Ted: I had the identical reaction. I thought it was the ultimate safe topic.
David: I strongly disagree.

Jim: Another left-hand attribution is that you resent being described as mushy or soft or chicken, and you wrote the case to prove you are none of these.
David: It does not surprise me at all that he wrote this case because it is a tough one, politically speaking, in the firm and the guy he wrote about is his friend.
Larry: I think that Bill is trying to learn not to be mushy.
Bill: What do you think would have been a more appropriate case for me to write?
Jim: (Answers with an example.)
Bill: I didn't remember that incident.
Jim: My attribution is that [when you raise these issues] it takes the form of "Doctor, I have a friend who has a problem." My read of your tone is that [you are saying to the individual in the case] "I have a problem with your behavior. I have a lot of anxiety about you." As I read it, my left- had column was screaming, "This is a cop-out."
Bill: I agree with the first part but not with the second. I believe you are wrong.
Larry: My impression of this discussion is that we are exorcising ghosts again. It's not the reality today. We are focusing on ancient concerns.

Scoring the Conversation

Advocacy: no illustration, no inquiry, no testing

Evaluation: no illustration, no testing

Evaluation: no inquiry, no illustration, no testing
Advocacy: no illustration, no inquiry, no testing
Attribution: no illustration, no inquiry, no testing

Attribution: no inquiry, partial illustration, no testing

Attribution and evaluation: no inquiry, no illustration, no testing

Evaluation: no illustration, no inquiry, no testing

Evaluation: no illustration, no inquiry, no testing

Evaluation: no illustration, no inquiry, no testing

Evaluation: no illustration, no inquiry, no testing

Embedded in this primarily Model I dialogue were signs of learning. For example, Jim raised doubts about the value the case had for learning, and several directors decried the use of "bunny" cases because a norm was developing that such cases did not provide much food for learning.

Individuals were beginning to make public their uncensored or left-hand-column thoughts, noting that before this seminar the thoughts would have remained censored. Bill appeared to look for an example of an attribution when he asked the others what case they thought would have been appropriate. Later Jim began to use the concept of attribution, and he also revealed his feelings about Bill's tone in the case and his anxiety that Bill was copping out.

Finally, Larry stated that the discussion was focused on "ancient concerns." This eventually led to a discussion of how the case might represent current issues. The session concluded with the directors evaluating it positively. They acknowledged that they had a long way to go to develop the competency that they desired. Indeed, several said that they now realized that this program was truly continuous and probably never ending. They concluded by committing energy, time, and resources to continue the program.

Conducting Learning Experiments

In the next phase each director planned his own follow-up sessions. Each selected a problem that not only was important to him but that called for skills that, if he could develop them, would be applicable to many future problems. These sessions were also tape recorded for research and educational purposes. The recordings were used to analyze the degree of progress the directors were making or the lack thereof. The directors used the recordings to reflect on their learning and to further develop their skills.

The problems the directors selected represented crucial challenges to their skills and continued their learning. For example, two directors examined their mistrust of each other. A director questioned the underlying commitment of the CEO to his role in the firm. The directors examined the meaning of being an owner, and the CEO developed a new ownership plan that the directors approved. The directors then held a group evaluation of the CEO's performance. Two directors resolved the problem that each believed he was being undermined by the other.

An analysis of the tape recordings of these experiments indicates that the directors have continued to expand their range of competence to produce Model II conversations, although Model I has by no means disappeared.

The intervention is now being expanded in several directions. First, sessions similar to the first ones in which the directors participated are being offered throughout the organization. Second, concepts of Model II inquiry and learning are being integrated into the education of senior consultants and case team managers. Third, a group of consultants who can become the internal change agents and educators for the firm is being developed. Finally, there has been an expansion of the intervention into the firm's client relationships. For example, the firm is using action maps to describe important features of the behavioral worlds of the client organizations. The firm is also developing ways to produce maps that genuinely integrate behavioral features with technical features. Several directors have designed and implemented with senior clients change programs similar to the one they experienced.

Part IV

Strengths and Weaknesses of Consultation and Research in the Field of Organizational Learning

Prologue

In Part IV, we will approach key issues of organizational learning within the larger context of the field. In chapter 8 we describe how the field's two branches have evolved since the publication of our 1978 book, what controversial issues have arisen, and what debates have unfolded around them.

In Chapter 9 we consider what our theory-of-action perspective has to say to certain key issues: explaining the phenomena of limited organizational learning; clarifying the nature of "productive" learning; assessing the capability of real-world organizations to learn productively in the face of threats to organizational coherence, cognitive adequacy, and effective action; and evaluating interventions that seek to enhance organizational learning capability. We consider these issues through a critical analysis of the writings of some well-known researchers and interventionists.

In Chapter 10 Wim Overmeer extends these analyses to questions of organizational learning and strategy.

8

The Evolving Field of Organizational Learning

We divide the literature that pays serious attention to organizational learning into two main categories: the practice-oriented, prescriptive literature of "the learning organization," promulgated mainly by consultants and practitioners, and the predominantly skeptical scholarly literature of "organizational learning," produced by academics. The two literatures have different thrusts, appeal to different audiences, and employ different forms of language. Nevertheless, they intersect at key points: their conceptions of what makes organizational learning "desirable," or "productive;" their views of the nature of the threats to productive organizational learning; and their attitudes toward whether—and if so, how—such threats may be overcome.

In the following sections, we describe the main currents of thought at work in the two branches of the organizational learning literature, and identify some of the controversial issues to be explored in Chapter 9.

The Literature of "The Learning Organization"

Although this literature takes many forms, its underlying conception of a central ideal is broadly shared. This ideal includes notions of organizational adaptability, flexibility, avoidance of stability traps, propensity to experiment, readiness to rethink means and ends, inquiry-orientation, realization of human potential for learning in the service of organizational purposes, and creation of organizational settings as contexts for human development. Different authors articulate the ideal in different ways and single out different issues as central to its realization.

For example, David Garvin's review of literature on the learning organization (1993) pays special attention to ideas of systematic experimentation, movement from "superficial knowledge to deep understanding," "comprehensive frameworks" for the evaluation of progress, and the "opening up of boundaries [to] stimulate the exchange of ideas." In their review article, Ulrich, Jick, and Von Glinow (1993) also emphasize, in contrast to demonstration projects that too often become "sequestered showcases," the importance of the "ability to move lessons learned from experience and experiments across boundaries"—including boundaries of time and geography, levels of hierarchy, functional units, and links in the supplier-firm-customer value chain. These authors focus on continuous improvement, competence acquisition, experimentation, and boundary spanning. They stress the need for managers to make a visible commitment to the generation and the generalization of organizational learning by incorporating it in strategic intent, measuring it, monitoring it, investing in it, talking about it in public, and giving it symbolic expression.

Within such a broadly shared background of assumptions and values, views of the learning organization differ according to the organizational functions to which the authors give primary attention. In each subfield, authors tend to stress different features of the ideal and to concentrate on different enabling prescriptions for its achievement.

Sociotechnical Systems

Sociotechnical systems—also known as the Quality of Work Life, or Industrial Democracy Movement—grew out of the postwar activities of the Tavistock Institute in England. It was extended in the 1960s and 1970s by the work of Einar Thorsrud, David Philip Herbst, and their colleagues in Norway along with Fred Emery in Australia and many others. Gradually, the status of sociotechnical systems has shifted from fringe movement to established profession.

Its conception of a learning organization focuses on the idea of collective participation by teams of individuals, especially workers, in developing new patterns of work, career paths, and arrangements for combining family and work lives. According to this view, individuals, workers and their supervisors, can and must learn to redesign their work, and upper-level managers must learn to create the contexts within which they can do so.

Organizational Strategy

This field, some twenty-five years old, created by management consultants and academics in schools of business and management, takes its root metaphor from the military: organizations, like nations, engage in warlike games of competition for markets. Organizational strategy was originally conceived as a kind of planning aimed at formulating broad policies based on appreciation of a firm's position in relation to its markets, competitors, technologies, materials, and skills. As the field matured and the idea of strategy penetrated governmental and nonprofit sectors, concepts of the strategic game have become dynamic. Effective strategy tends now to be seen as requiring continual development of new understandings, models, and practices. Attention has shifted from planning to implementation of plans and then to the interaction of planning and implementing in a process explicitly described as organizational learning.

In a recent review of the literature on corporate strategy, Edward Bowman (1994) traces the intellectual development of the field, asking "how people in organizations...can understand and/or prescribe decision processes." Bowman makes a broad distinction between "rational" and "natural" approaches to the analysis of strategic decision making (a distinction that Overmeer also takes as central to his discussion of strategy and learning in Chapter 10). For Bowman, the rational approach, which he associates mainly with economists and management scientists, adopts a "Cooks-tour" view of planning where all is calculated in advance. The "natural" approach uses the narrative, case-based methods of behavioral theory to describe a "Lewis-and-Clark" view of planning that follows the "habitual, unfolding, trial-and-error, learned, isomorphic pattern of decision processes." Bowman argues for an integration of the natural and the rational through a synthesis of economic and behavioral theory.

Production

In the 1970s and 1980s, as the United States slowly and painfully became aware of the competetive challenge posed by Japan, Germany, Korea, and other nations, and as attention focused on the the need for continual improvement in the quality of products and production processes, authors in this field began to speak of learning.

For example, *Dynamic Manufacturing* (1988) by Hayes, Wheelwright and Clark, carries the subtitle "Creating the Learning Organization," which the authors apply not only to the production process but to the performance of the organization as a whole. The authors claim that

> companies that are quick both to learn new things and to perfect familiar things, that adapt imaginatively and effectively to change, and that are looked up to by their competitors because of their ability to lead the way into new fields, tend to have certain attributes in common. Moreover, companies with these attributes tend to be excellent throughout. (p.25)

Economic Development

After World War II, the field of economic development, in close connection with the rise of international development agencies like the World Bank, emerged. This field has been dominated by economists, especially macroeconomists, but a few of its influential practitioners have emphasized the development of institutions on which national economic development depends.

Albert Hirschman's *Exit, Voice and Loyalty* (1970) is subtitled "Responses to Decline in Firms, Organizations and States." Hirschman sees all such institutions as inherently subject to deterioration in the form of "lapses from efficient, rational, law-abiding, virtuous or otherwise functional behavior" (p.1). He is concerned with two principal mechanisms of recuperation: the "exit" option, through which "some customers stop buying the firm's products or some members leave the organization," and the "voice" option, through which

> the firm's customers or the organization's members express their dissatisfaction directly to management or to some other authority to which management is subordinate or through general protest addressed to anyone who cares to listen.

In both cases, the basic schema is that of signal and response: customers or organization members signal their dissatisfaction by exit or voice and managers respond.

The recuperative processes with which Hirschman is concerned have many of the attributes of the organizational learning processes described above: they affect the organization as a whole, they operate continually throughout the life of the organization, and they involve the detection and correction of decline, deterioration or dysfunction. Hirschman's view of development—of organizations, regions, or societies—contains an elusive theory of social learning, one that evinces itself most clearly in the three books that grew out of his experience as an economic development consultant (see Rodwin and Schon, eds., 1995). In Hirschman's normative, practice-oriented theory of development, his diagnoses and prescriptions hinge on what would now be called "structural enablers"—institutional structures of incentives that compel or attract individuals to learn to produce behavior conducive to development.

Systems Dynamics

The systems modeling discipline first developed by Jay Forrester in the 1960s on the basis of servomechanism and control theory—and applied in grand sequence first to industry then to cities and finally to the world—has turned in recent years to organizational learning. Peter Senge, one of Forrester's best-known followers, has published *The Fifth Discipline* (1993), subtitled "The Art and Practice of Organizational Learning." Senge's treatment of the subject unites systems thinking with organizational adaptation and with the realization of human potential in a mixture that has a distinctly Utopian flavor. On the one hand, he asserts that "the rate at which organizations learn may become the only sustainable source of competitive advantage." (p. 3). On the other hand, he envisages learning organizations where

> people continually expand their capacity to create the results they truly desire, where new and expansive patterns of thinking are nurtured, where collective aspiration is set free, and where people are continually learning how to learn together. (p. 2)

Senge's prescriptive approach combines the methodology of systems dynamics with certain ideas adapted from our theory-of-action perspective, notably an awareness of the importance of the "mental models" held by organizational practitioners, including those that constrain or facilitate reliable inquiry into organizational processes.

Human Resources

In recent years writers in the field of human resources have picked up the language of the learning organization, stressing the development of human capability for questioning, experimenting, adapting, and innovating on the organization's behalf. Characteristically, writings in this subfield emphasize the mutually reinforcing interactions between enhanced opportunity for individual development within organizations and enhanced organizational capability for competitive performance.

For example, Jones and Hendry (1992), researchers at Warwick University in England, base their review of the literature on a pivotal distinction between "an incremental approach" to training and development and a "fundamental mind shift." They envisage a stage of "transformation" toward the latter where "learning focuses on managing personal change and self-assessment," management structures flatten, managers become more like coaches, thinkers and doers come together, everyone learns to go after the root causes of problems rather than assigning blame, and "the whole organization becomes committed via personal involvement." Beyond this stage the authors describe an as-yet-unrealized ideal of "transfiguration" in which people give priority to a concern for society's general welfare and betterment. They question why organizations exist in their present forms and treat their organizations as representing "a way of life to be cherished because of its values."

Organizational Culture

Organizational culture is a term whose currency among practitioners in present-day organizations rivals that of *organizational learning*. Managers have learned to speak of "our culture" as familiarly and with as little sense of the problematic as they speak of "our kind of people." Edgar Schein's *Organizational Culture and Leadership* (1985) offers the most careful attempt to provide a clear analysis of the meaning of organizational culture, and its second edition (1992) links organizational culture to the ideal of a learning organization. Schein argues that in a world of turbulent change, organizations have to learn ever faster, which calls for a learning culture that functions as "a perpetual learning system" (p. 372). The primary task of a leader in contemporary organizations is to create and sustain such a culture, which then, especially in mature organizations, feeds back to shape the leader's own assumptions.

Schein defines leadership as "the attitude and motivation to examine and manage culture." (p. 374) He regards the organization as the group, and analyzes organizational culture as a pattern of basic assumptions shared by the group, acquired by solving problems of adaptation and integration, working "well enough to be considered valid and, therefore, to be taught to new members as the correct way to perceive, think, and feel in relation to those problems." In organizational learning, basic assumptions shift in the heads of the group members. The job of a learning leader is to promote such shifts by helping the organization's members to "achieve some degree of insight and develop motivation to change." (p. 390)

A learning leader must assess the adequacy of his organization's culture, detect its dysfunctionality, and promote its transformation, first by making his own basic assumptions into "learning assumptions" and then by fostering such assumptions in the culture of his organization. Among the most important learning assumptions: people want to contribute and can be trusted to do so; one should advocate one's own not-knowing, becoming a learner and trying to get others to do likewise, thereby diffusing responsibility for learning; and "the process of learning must ultimately be made part of the culture." Leaders can foster a learning culture by envisioning it and communicating the vision, by rewarding those pockets in an organization that represent the desired assumptions, and by fostering their creation through cultural diversity.

Acting in these ways is a large part of what Schein means by "managing the culture." He believes cultural change *can* be managed, although he is aware that it also depends on changed assumptions found to work in effectively adapting to the external environment and producing "comfort" in the internal one. Schein does not address the possible conflict of these managerial strategies (for example, promulgating a vision vs. accepting one's own not-knowing) nor what happens when changed assumptions fail to work.

Schein seems to be aware that managing a culture contains a hint of internal inconsistency (cultures are usually seen as growing up and evolving, rather than as objects of direct control), and he tries to argue simultaneously that the culture of an organization can be shaped by its leader, evolves in response to selective pressures exerted by external and internal environments, and can persist in the face of its not working. To some extent, Schein tries to reconcile these propositions by reference to different stages in an organization's life cycle. Specifically he recognizes that the culture of a mature organization may contain dysfunctional, taken-for-granted assumptions, products of past successes that "operate as silent filters on what is perceived and thought about." (p. 382) He observes, for example, that

> the overt and espoused values that are stated for [organizational] solutions (e.g., TQM) often hide assumptions that are not, in fact, favorable to the kind of learning I have described.

When a culture becomes dysfunctional, learning leaders must be careful to "look inside themselves to locate their own mental models and assumptions before they leap into action." (p. 373) In order to avoid "unwittingly undermining [their] own creations," leaders must cultivate insight into their unconscious conflicts as well as into their conscious intentions. Consultants, in turn, can foster such insight, by "helping the leader make his own sense of what is going on in himself and his organization," functioning as "cultural therapists" who help the leader figure out "what the culture is and what parts of it are more or less adaptive." (p. 387)

But Schein does not grasp the full burden of paradox inherent in the idea of managing a culture toward the ideal of a learning organization. He focuses on the danger that organizational cultures are inherently stability-seeking. He does not focus, directly and critically, on the issue of the *controllability* of a culture—the degree to which it may be subject to design causality—nor does he specify how learning assumptions such as not-knowing, trust in others, and "Theory Y assumptions about human nature" can actually be imparted to human beings. He addresses the limits of culture management mainly through his notion of "cultural humility," i.e. the recognition that culture is partly affected by powerful forces which may lie beyond a leader's direct control.

Some writings on the learning organization—like those of Schein, Senge, and the sociotechnical theorists—make significant contributions. They describe a range of types of organizational learning. They offer prescriptions that are useful at least as guides to the kinds of organizational structures, processes, and conditions that may function as enablers of productive organizational learning—for example,

- flat, decentralized organizational structures;
- information systems that provide fast, public feedback on the performance of the organization as a whole and of its various components;
- mechanisms for surfacing and criticizing implicit organizational theories of action, cultivating systematic programs of experimental inquiry;
- measures of organizational performance;
- systems of incentives aimed at promoting organizational learning; and
- ideologies associated with such measures, such as total quality, continuous learning, excellence, openness, and boundary-crossing.

On the other hand, the literature on the learning organization is inattentive to the gaps emphasized in the arguments of the learning-skeptics. It ignores the analytic difficulties posed by the very idea of organizational learning. It treats the beneficence of organizational learning as an axiom. It does not give serious consideration to processes that threaten the validity or utility of organizational learning. And it gives short shrift to the difficulties of implementation, the phenomena that undermine attempts to achieve the ideal or cause such attempts to be short-lived.

These gaps and difficulties are fundamentally dependent on the behavioral worlds of organizations that make for limited learning systems. Writers on the learning organization tend to focus on first-order errors, due to mistaken or incomplete action strategies and assumptions of the sort that practitioners ordinarily detect and try to correct. They tend to be selectively inattentive to second-order errors, which are due to the organizational designs that make people systematically unaware of the behavioral phenomena that underlie the production and reproduction of first-order errors. We refer here, for example, to defensive routines, mixed messages, taboos on the discussability of key issues, games of control and deception, and organizational camouflage. As we have argued throughout this book, reflection on such phenomena and the theories-in-use that underlie them, is essential both to the task of explaining the limitations of organizational learning and to the design of interventions that can overcome those limitations.

The Scholarly Literature of Organizational Learning

This literature—intentionally distant from practice, nonprescriptive, and value-neutral—focuses on just those questions the first branch ignores: What does "organizational learning" mean? How is organizational learning at all feasible? What kinds of organizational learning are desirable, and for whom and with what chance of actual occurrence? The scholars of organizational learning generally adopt a skeptical stance toward these questions. Their skepticism tends to revolve around three main challenges.

1. There are those who argue that the very idea of organizational learning is contradictory, paradoxical, or quite simply devoid of meaning.
2. A second challenge to the idea of organizational learning accepts it as a meaningful notion. What it denies is that organizational learning is always or ever beneficent.
3. A third kind of skepticism about organizational learning questions whether real-world organizations do learn productively, and whether, in principle and in actuality, they are capable of coming to do so.

Organizational Learning Is Contradictory

As we stated in Chapter 1, when we begin by assuming that individuals are the only proper subjects of learning and that we know what we mean when we say that individuals learn, then we are likely to be puzzled and disturbed by the notion that learning may also be attributed to organizations. Indeed, some researchers have argued, as

Geoffrey Vickers did, that if the term, "organizational learning," means anything, it means learning on the part of individuals who happen to function in an organizational setting. From this perspective, to say that an organization learns is to commit what the philosopher, Gilbert Ryle, called a "category mistake."

Yet even a cursory reading of the recent literature suggests that the disposition to regard organizational learning as a paradoxical idea was far more vigorous twenty years ago than it is now. Economists such as Marin (1993), Herrnstein (1991), and Holland and Miller (1991) have begun to introduce learning into economic discourse, making explicit the references to learning that have long been implicit in such branches of economics as the theory of the firm, which treats the firm as a decision maker optimizing to a utility function, and theories of free-market competition, which give an essential place to gains in efficiency and productivity stimulated by market forces. Contemporary researchers in the fields of organization theory and strategy concern themselves with high-level, intraorganizational entities, such as management or R&D and seem relatively untroubled by sentences in which "organization" is the subject and "learning," the predicate. For example, Fiol and Lyles (1985) define learning, whether undertaken by individual or organizational agents, as "the process of improving actions through better knowledge and understanding." (p. 803) Organizations learn, in the sense proposed by Leavitt and March (1988), when they "encode inferences from history into routines that guide behavior." (p.319) Huber (1989) suggests that

> an organization has learned if *any of its components* have acquired information and have this information available for use, either by other components or by itself, on behalf of the organization. (p. 3)

One increasingly influential research tradition, derived from the work of Campbell (1969) and Nelson and Winter (1982), draws on the Darwinian language of evolution, adaptation, and natural selection. Researchers in this tradition see organizational learning as a process in which whole organizations or their components adapt to changing environments by generating and selectively adopting organizational routines. For example, Robert Burgelman (1994), whose work we will discuss at greater length in the following chapter, describes business firms as "ecologies of strategic initiatives,"

> ...which emerge in patterned ways and compete for limited organizational resources so as to increase their relative importance within the organization. Strategy results, in part, from selection and retention operating on internal variation associated with strategic initiatives. (p. 240)

In Burgelman's description, the agents that generate and select internal variations are collective entities labeled managers, departments, or top management.

It matters greatly, of course, in Burgelman's theory as in the theories of others mentioned above, whether entities defined at relatively high levels of social aggregation are taken to be uniquely appropriate or at least sufficient for the study of organizational adaptation and learning, or whether they are seen as needing to be complemented by a view that reveals how individuals enter into these processes. Many sociologically oriented researchers who see organizational learning as an intraorganizational phenomenon avoid the difficulties of bridging between individual and organizational phenomena by consistently treating agents and processes of learning at a relatively high level of social aggregation.

We insist, on the contrary, that a theory of organizational learning must take account of the interplay between the actions and interactions of individuals and the actions and interactions of higher-level organizational entities such as departments, divisions, or groups of managers. Unless a theory of organizational learning satisfies this criterion, it cannot contribute to knowledge useful to practitioners of organizational learning; nor can it explain the phenomena that underlie observed limitations to organizational learning. A few researchers share our view. For example, Daniel Kim (1993) has observed:

> Although the meaning of the term "learning" remains essentially the same as in the individual case, the learning process is fundamentally different at the organizational level. A model of organizational learning has to resolve somehow the dilemma of imparting intelligence and learning capabilities to a nonhuman entity without anthropomorphizing it. (p. 12)

Anyone who adopts such a position faces the rather daunting task of explaining how the "fundamentally different" processes carried out by individual and by higher-level entities can interact to yield the phenomena we are prepared to recognize as organizational learning. Clearly, although organizational learning has long since become an idea in good currency, it is no less problematic for organization theorists than when it languished at the margins of the field. Indeed, it holds a special interest for us just because it stretches the boundaries of our ordinary understandings of individual and organization.

What, then, are the possible modes of explaining the interplay between individuals and higher-level entities that constitutes organizational learning? Should we imagine that individuals who play certain organizational roles (perhaps those who exercise greatest authority or control over action) can learn from their experiences and that when enough of them do so, the organization as a whole can be said to learn? Should we think of organizations as groups of individuals, recognizing that groups are real entities irreducible to the individuals who make them up? Should we then attribute to such groups a capacity for thinking, inquiring, experimenting, and learning? Should we think of organizations as cultures that consist of systems of beliefs, values, technologies, languages, common patterns of behavior, shared representations of reality; and should we then use learning to designate certain processes of cultural change? Should we think of organizations as cognitive constructs—perhaps theories in their own right—so that organizations may be said to learn when their members contribute to the cumulative accretion or modification of these constructs?

We presented our own approach to the paradox of organizational learning in Chapter 1. A key concept for us is that of inquiry, the intertwining of thought and action carried out by individuals in interaction with one another on behalf of the organization to which they belong in ways that change the organization's theories of action and become embedded in organizational artifacts such as maps, memories, and programs. A key question for us, then, is the meaning of the phrase, "on behalf of the organization." We argue that it is possible for individuals to think and act on behalf of an organization because organizations are political entities, in a fundamental sense of that term. Collectivities become organizational when they meet three constitutional capabilities: to make collective decisions (so that groups of individuals can say "we" about themselves), to delegate authority for action to an individual in the name of the collectivity, and to say who is and who is not a member of the collectivity. Under these conditions, it makes conceptual sense to say that individuals can act on behalf of an organization. It also makes conceptual sense to say that on behalf of an organization individuals can undertake learning processes (organizational inquiry) that can, in turn, yield learning outcomes as reflected in changes in organizational theories of action and the artifacts that encode them.

But our emphasis on organizational inquiry as linking interpersonal and organizational phenomena in organizational learning and our insistence on the importance of the behavioral worlds that constrain or facilitate organizational inquiry, have led some critics of the views we first expressed in our 1978 book to dismiss our approach as one that deals exclusively with the interpersonal or social-psychological dimension of organizational life. For some critics, indeed, our approach to organizational learning is about individuals and not about organizations at all.

Clearly, the issue underlying the controversy over our approach to organizational learning or over any attempt to treat organizational learning in terms of the interaction between individuals and organizations hinges, first, on what level or levels of aggregation one chooses to treat as distinctively organizational and, second, on the features one selects as critically important to learning at the level of aggregation in question. As we have noted, some researchers focus on clusters of organizations grouped together in larger systems, such as markets or ecologies within which learning is predicated of whole organizations (the firm or the state) or even the larger clusters to which they belong. For other observers, such as Nelson and Winter, and Burgelman, attention focuses on the interactions of larger entities (departments, divisions, top management) within organizations. For some organization theorists, such as Crozier (1963), or theorists of policy implementation (Pressman and Wildavsky, 1973; Bardach, 1974), the key focus is on games of freedoms, interests, and powers that unfold among groups of individuals who occupy kinds of roles within organizations. For other theorists, such as Hirschman, the focus is on structures of incentives, created in part through the operation of the mechanisms of exit and voice, that drive changes in organizational performance.

For theorists of a social-psychological bent, such as Schein (1992), attention focuses on individuals in interaction with one another within the settings organizations provide. Some researchers, following the directions set out in Marvin Minsky's *Society of Mind* (1991), treat individuals themselves as organizations whose thought and action must be conceived in terms of the interplay of intrapsychic microagents in direct analogy with the operation of complex computer programs.

The issue of choice of level(s) of aggregation, and the closely related issue of selective attention to features at any given level, seem to occupy in the realm of organizational phenomena a place analogous to the one they occupy in the realm of theories of material objects. Physicists, mechanical engineers, materials scientists, and physical chemists focus on strikingly different levels of aggregation (for example, galaxies, bridges, composite materials, molecules) and give privileged status to different descriptions of phenomena discovered at these levels. In part, their different foci of attention reflect what they happen to be interested in and, in part, the purposes to which their respective inquiries are addressed. At certain key points, however, their research interests intersect, especially when the researchers are concerned with questions about the prospective guidance of technological practice. For example, civil engineers who are interested in the behavior of large-scale structures may consult materials scientists or even physical chemists, when their research leads them to think about metal fatigue or about the sources of the propagation of cracks in concrete. It remains controversial and intellectually fruitful whether descriptions of the behavior of higher-level entities, such as machines, can be reduced to descriptions of the behavior of lower-level entities, such as materials or molecules (Polanyi, 1967), or whether or in what particular ways it is both feasible and useful to develop theories of the behavior of higher-level entities without worrying much about the lower-level phenomena that might be adduced to account for that behavior.

In the broad and varied field of research on organizational learning, different interests and purposes also lead researchers to focus on different levels of aggregation and on different features of the phenomena discovered at any given level. We have argued that intersections among individual, interpersonal, and higher levels of aggregation become critically important if we wish to understand and, all the more so, if we wish to redesign the practices of organizational life, as carried out by individuals who inhabit organizations and bear responsibility for contributing to organizational performance, including especially the performance of organizational learning. But researchers on organizational learning are far from agreement on this point. There is disagreement not only about the nature of the kinds of interactions among individual, interpersonal, and higher-level entities that may be involved in organizational learning, but also whether an adequate theory of organizational learning demands an account of such interactions.

Organizational Learning Is A Meaningful Notion But Not Always Beneficent

Once organizational learning is taken as a neutral term rather than as a normative ideal, it is obvious to us, and others, that it need not be for the good, given some view of the good. In the Nazi period, Eichman's bureaucracy clearly became more efficient at carrying out its evil mission and may be said, with some plausibility, to have "learned" to do so. But the ethical critique of organizational learning varies with the kinds of evil to which the critic believes organizations are particularly disposed.

Some authors treat the ideal of the learning organization as an instance of contemporary rhetorics of "high-performance organizations," (see Kunda, 1992; who refers, in term, to Bendix, 1956; Van Maanen, 1988; and Goffman, 1959.) They claim that organizational power elites use the ideal of the learning organization as they use other rhetorical ideals as cunning vehicles of normative control to gain the compliance, indeed, the commitment, of subordinates, and in ways that may be good for those in control but bad for those who are subordinated to them. As Kunda puts it:

> Normative control is the attempt to elicit and direct the required efforts of members by controlling the underlying experiences, thoughts, and feelings that guide their actions. Under normative control, members act in the best interests of the company...[because] they are driven by internal commitment, strong identification with company goals, intrinsic satisfaction from work...elicited by a variety of managerial appeals, exhortations, and actions... .In short, under normative control it is the employee's self...that is claimed in the name of corporate interest. (p. 11)

Finally, some authors criticize organizational learning because they claim that much of it, perhaps even the greater part, is in the service of stability rather than change. On this view, organizations learn to preserve the status quo, and learning of this sort is the enemy of organizational change and reform (Fiol and Lyles, 1989; Leavitt and March, 1989).

All such criticisms rest on the idea that organizational learning is not a value-neutral activity but proceeds from values, has implications for values, and is subject to critique in terms of a conception of what is good or right, and for whom. These implications, which seem obvious once they are stated, come to light only when organizational learning is stripped of its normative aura and considered as subject to evaluation in particular contexts on the basis of particular criteria of goodness or rightness. In short, we cannot escape the need to declare what kinds of organizational learning we will take to be desirable or undesirable and why.

Do Real-World Organizations Learn Productively

In order to speak of an organization learning, we must see it as a more or less coherent agent. And we must also see it as capable of acting rationally, at least in the sense of being able to remember past events, analyze alternatives, conduct experiments, and evaluate the results of action. But some authors claim that these attributions have little or no validity for organizations as we find them in the world. We categorize their doubts in terms of threats to coherent action, valid inference, and efficacy.

Threats to Coherent Action. Some theorists have argued that organizations are actually pluralistic systems, little more than stage settings for performances by agents such as professions, disciplines, or social groupings that by their very nature cut across organizational boundaries. Some authors see organizations as political systems, made up of subgroups, each with its own interests, freedoms, and powers, crucially engaged in battles for control or avoidance of control and incapable of functioning holistically as agents of learning (Crozier, 1963; Bardach, 1974). In his middle period, March, along with various coauthors (Cohen and March, 1974; March and Olsen, 1976), proposed that organizations are inherently chaotic, at best organized anarchies. His "theory of the garbage can" presents decision making in terms of ideas, interests, images, and values in search of problems, rather than in terms of problem solvers actively searching for ideas, images, and values. Where the garbage can is in operation, it is hard to see how organizations can be considered capable of coherent action or inquiry.

Again, these lines of argument appear to have had more weight twenty years ago in the full flush of the reaction against unreflective theories of organizational rationality (e.g., Perrow, 1979) than they do at present. Although attributions of organizational incoherence still present themselves as sources of doubt about claims made in the name of organizational learning, they tend no longer to be taken a priori as reasons for outright rejection of the idea. Rather, it seems, there is a growing sentiment that the degree of coherence manifested in organizational action or inquiry is an empirical matter to be ascertained at particular places and times. A case in point is March's transition from viewing organizations as "organized anarchies" to the far more modulated position he has expressed in his more recent writings, where he suggests that there are periods in which institutional reform can be pursued through "integrative processes...that treat conflict of interest as the basis for deliberation and authoritative decision rather than bargaining." (March, 1989, p. 142)

Threats to Valid Inference. Across the wide-ranging descriptions of organizational learning processes presented in scholarly literature, there is a consistent emphasis on rational inference, inference in the form of lesson drawing from observations of past experience, inference about the causal connections between actions and outcomes, and inference from cycles of trial and error. A number of authors, including some of those noted above, base their skepticism on "threats to valid inference" which seem to them to make real-world organizational learning a dubious proposition.

March, who defines organizational learning as "encoding inferences from history into routines that guide behavior" (Leavitt and March, 1988, p. 319), has been prolific in identifying threats to the validity of such inferences. For example (1988, pp. 322–23), he underlines the importance of "competence traps," wherein organizations falsely project into the future the strategies of action that have worked for them in the past. He calls attention to various sources of ambiguity that undermine organizational judgments of success or failure:

> The lessons of experience are drawn from a relatively small number of observations in a complex, changing ecology of learning organizations. What has happened is not always obvious, and the causality of events is difficult to untangle. What an organization should expect to achieve, and thus the difference between success and failure, is not always clear. (p. 323)

He describes instances of "superstitious learning" that "occur when the subjective experience of learning is compelling, but the connections between actions and outcomes are misspecified." (p. 325)

March also identifies a "dilemma of learning" that constitutes a family of threats to valid inference. When learning proceeds gradually through "small, frequent changes and inferences formed from experience with them," then a likely outcome is the reinforcement or marginal change of existing routines. Such behavior "is likely to lead to random drift rather than improvement" (Lounamaa and March, 1987). On the other hand, when organizations learn from "low probability, high consequence events," then inferences about them are often "muddied with conflict over formal responsiblity, accountability, and liability" (Leavitt and March, 1989, p. 334). The upshot is that

> ...learning does not always lead to intelligent behavior. The same processes that yield experiential wisdom produce superstitious learning, competence traps, and erroneous inferences. (p. 335)

In this line of argument, March treats learning in the narrow sense of drawing lessons from history as an alternative to other models of decision making, such as rational choice, bargaining, and selection of variations. He argues that under some circumstances learning may prove inferior to its alternatives; although he adds the caveat that the alternatives may also make mistakes, and it is, therefore, "possible to see a role for routine-based, history-dependent, target-oriented organizational learning." (p. 336) (From our point of view, all of March's alternate strategies may enter into the processes of *inquiry* around which we build our broader approach to organizational learning. The relative vulnerabilties of lesson drawing from history would be relevant, not to the general question of the cognitive capability for learning in real-world organizations, but to the problem of choosing, in any given context, what strategy of inquiry to pursue.)

A very different kind of threat to the validity of inference in organizational inquiry stems from the observation that organizational learning depends on the interpretation of events, which depends, in turn, on frames, the major story lines through which organizational inquirers set problems and make sense of experience. Framing is essential to interpretive judgments, but because frames themselves are unfalsifiable, organizational inquirers may be trapped within self-referential frames. Padgett (1992) writes that "the collectively constructed frame or 'membrane' through which information and rewards are assembled and received" is an "axiomatic construction of the world" that is "reciprocally tied to the constitution of the observer." Communication across divergent, self-referential frames is bound to be problematic.

However, Schön and Rein (1994) explore the frame conflicts that underlie persistent policy disputes, for example, those that revolve around welfare, homelessness, or the costs and benefits of advanced technology. They argue that in actual policy practice inquirers may be capable of reflective inquiry into the frames that underlie their divergent positions and can sometimes hammer out, in particular situations, a pragmatic resolution of their conflicting frames.

Threats to Effective Action. Even if organizational inquirers are sometimes able to draw valid inferences from historical experience or current observation, their inferences may not be converted to effective action. A number of contemporary researchers (Fiol and Lyles, 1985; Kim, 1993) call attention to the fact that learning outcomes may be fragmented or situational and may never enter into the organizational mainstream. In earlier research, proponents of the "behavioral theory of the firm" (Cyert and March, 1963; March, 1963; Simon, 1976) described dysfunctional patterns of organizational behavior that undermine productive organizational learning. They noted that organizations depend on control systems which set up conflicts between rule setters and rule followers, which leads to cheating and that in such an organizational world, "everyone is rational and no one can be trusted."

"Fragmented" learning outcomes are closely related to the "conditions for error" that we described in Part II. And the dysfunctional, defensive patterns of behavior described by Simon, Cyert, and the early March are closely related to the patterns we have ascribed to limited learning systems. The question is how we should view such phenomena. Should we consider them along the lines of the behavioral theory of the firm, as pervasive and inherent features of organizational life which it is the business of organizational researchers to "discover" rather than to change? Or should we treat them as critically important impediments to productive learning that call for and may be malleable in response to, double-loop inquiry?

Conclusion

Our review of the two-pronged literature of organizational learning leaves us with challenges to the beneficence, the feasibility, and the meaningfulness of organizational learning. Proponents of the learning organization are not worried about the meaningfulness of organizational learning and take its desirability to be axiomatic. They prescribe a variety of enablers through which they claim that organizations can enhance their capability for productive learning, but they do not inquire into the gaps that separate reasonable prescription from effective implementation.

Skeptical researchers into organizational learning present, from a variety of perspectives, important reasons for doubt. Some of them have raised questions about the paradox inherent in the claim that organizations learn, which hinges on assumptions about relationships among individual, interpersonal, and higher levels of social aggregation. Other writers have challenged the desirability of organizational learning, arguing that organizations may learn in ways that foster evil ends or reinforce the status quo, or arguing that the ideal of the learning organization may be used to support a subtler and darker form of managerial control. Still other researchers observe and categorize phenomena that function as impediments to valid inference and effective action.

The problems raised by the two branches of the literature are largely complementary: what one branch treats as centrally important, the other tends to ignore. Both branches do concern themselves with the capability of real-world organizations to draw valid and useful inferences from experience and observation and to convert such inferences to effective action. But authors of prescriptive bent tend to assume, uncritically, that such capabilities can be activated through the appropriate enablers, and learning skeptics tend to treat observed impediments as unalterable facts of organizational life.

In the next chapter we consider these challenges in the light of the theory-of-action perspective.

9

Making Sense
of Limited Learning

Controversial Issues of Organizational Learning

From our review of the organizational learning literatures, we draw the following issues which seem to us crystallize the most important current debates in the field.

The first issue centers on the problem of *levels of aggregation*. At what levels of aggregation—individual, interpersonal, group, intergroup, or whole-organization—does it make sense to speak of productive organizational learning? More specifically, how should we think about the role of interpersonal interaction and its relationship to patterns of activity at higher levels of aggregation? As we noted in Chapter 1 and again in Chapter 8, some of the most prominent researchers in the scholarly branch of the field of organizational learning refer mainly to the actions or interactions of departments or groups within the world of an organization or of whole organizations within larger ecologies. In contrast, we emphasize the importance of interpersonal inquiry carried out within the constraining or enabling context of an organizational learning system, focusing on how such inquiry interacts with processes described as occurring at higher levels of aggregation. We adopt this emphasis in order to provide both knowledge useful to practitioners and robust explanations of the phenomena of organizational learning and nonlearning.

A second issue relates to *the meaning of "productive learning."* Our treatment of this issue centers on the distinction between single- and double-loop learning, a distinction that has been rather widely adopted, in one form or another, by authors in both branches of the organizational learning literature. Some authors, especially economists and proponents of the learning organization, focus on the importance of instrumental, single-loop learning. Other authors, mainly among the scholarly skeptics, question the values served by initiatives taken in the name of the learning organization. Still other authors speak of the importance of double-loop learning but without serious attention to the behavioral conditions for its achievement. In addressing the issue of the meaning of productive organizational learning, we underline the importance of distinguishing between two kinds of organizational double-loop learning. The first kind involves change in organizational outcomes, especially in the values contained in an organization's instrumental theory of action. The second involves change in the values of an organization's theory-in-use for the process of organizational inquiry. How are these two kinds of double-loop learning related? Is it possible for an organization to achieve the first without achieving the second?

A third issue has to do with the nature of *the impediments to productive organizational learning that arise in real-world organizations.* Learning skeptics have discussed cognitive limitations, the pull of past success, and the subversive effects of organizational politics. What is the likelihood that, in the face of such impediments, real-world organizations can achieve productive organizational learning, especially of the double-loop variety?

A fourth and final issue has to do with *the kinds of interventions that are likely to be effective* in enhancing organizational capability for productive learning. What can we expect from interventions based on the introduction of various sorts of **organizational enablers**: formal role- and authority-structures (e.g., decentralization), information systems (e.g., activity-based costing), systems of incentives (e.g., high-performance organizations), procedures and systems for organizational inquiry (e.g., TQM and Reengineering)? What can we expect from attempts to introduce new cultures, with their associated beliefs and assumptions? Each of these types of enablers has been advocated, at one time or another, by some proponents of the learning organization.

The four issues are distinct, but as they arise in particular cases, they are logically and empirically interconnected. In this chapter, we consider them through the lens of two groups of studies. We begin with two studies of naturally occurring innovation or adaptation: Van de Ven and Polley's study of technological innovation in the medical field, and Burgelman's study of the processes that led to Intel's "strategic exit" from the DRAM business. In these cases, we focus mainly on interactions between interpersonal inquiry within a limited learning system and processes of learning or nonlearning at higher levels of aggregation. We turn next to studies of attempts to promote productive organizational learning through the introduction of organizational enablers: a review of Cordiner's decentralization of the General Electric Company; a study by Argyris and Kaplan of the introduction of Activity-Based Costing; two retrospective analyses, by Schneiderman and Mallinger, of programs of Total Quality Management (TQM); George Roth's study of two cases of Business Process Reengineering; and Michael Beer's analysis of his Strategic Human Resource Management (SHRM) intervention.

Research Studies of Organizational Adaptation and Learning

Van de Ven and Polley: "Learning While Innovating"

In a noteworthy study of technological innovation in the medical field, Van de Ven and Polley (1992) set out to test the familiar adaptive model of trial-and-error learning. In its simplest form, this model says that we persist in a prior course of action if we perceive its results as positive and deviate from that course if we perceive its results as negative. The authors propose to apply this model which had previously been explored in "unrealistic laboratory or simulation studies" to the "highly uncertain organizational field setting" of entrepreneurs in an innovation unit. (p. 113) In certain respects, they attempt to make a rigorous test of the model; but in other respects, at least as important, we find their treatment of organizational innovation and learning to be limited and unrigorous.

The authors tell two complementary stories of technological innovation. The first, articulated at a relatively high level of aggregation and couched in the language of statistical analysis, tests hypotheses derived from the adaptive learning model against the behavior of two organizational units, the "innovation's internal management team" and the "external resource controllers." The second story, presented in a running narrative (but not illustrated by actual dialogue), tells how individuals behaved at key points in the innovation's trajectory. But while the authors suggest some possible causes of the behavior that resulted in limited organizational learning, they offer no coherent theory to account for it, nor do their concluding prescriptions offer much of a basis for improving it. Their article demonstrates the limits of both a high-level analysis of organizational learning and a reliance on quantitative, statistical methodology. One has the impression that, although the authors intuit the importance of their behavioral story, they have no way of explaining or getting underneath it.

Testing the Adaptive Learning Model. The subject of Van de Ven and Polley's longitudinal study is

> a joint venture by three corporations to create a business by developing a new medical technology called therapeutic apheresis ...which treats disease by removal of pathogenic blood components. (p. 98)

Apheresis had been around for some time, but it had not gained widespread usage because of its limited ability to remove specific components of blood. The Therapeutic Apheresis Program (TAP) centered on a device consisting of filters, pumps, and computer controls that was designed to make more specific separations possible. The joint venture partners sought to combine their respective competencies in separation techniques, pump technology, and marketing. They planned a three-phase development process:

1. a product to compete with existing apheresis technology;
2. an advanced product to treat specific diseases using advanced filtration modules;
3. the development of future apheresis technologies.

Van de Ven and Polley conducted a "real-time field study of TAP's development from October 1983 to July 1988."(p. 99) They divided the innovation's eight-year trajectory into three stages:

1. an initial three-year gestation period, culminating in a formal decision to initiate and fund the TAP innovation as a joint interorganizational venture,
2. a three-year expansion period aimed at producing a commercial TAP device, expanding the development program and meeting FDA requirements, and
3. a two-year contraction period when the TAP device entered the market, experienced product difficulties, and was terminated.

As the authors test their model of adaptive learning against the data of the TAP story, their findings vary with the three phases of development. In the gestation period they find actions and outcomes unrelated; in the expansion period, they find them negatively related; and in the contraction period, positively related.[1]

In the expansion period, the authors find "little or no learning by trial and error." Rather, negative outcomes "led directly to continuing with the prior course of actions" which had "no effects on subsequent assessments of positive or negative outcomes nor on changes in goals or criteria."(p. 104) The authors interpret this "direct negative relationship" between outcomes and subsequent actions as suggesting that "TAP's early development may have largely consisted of escalating commitments to failing courses of action (as observed by Argyris and Schön, 1978, and by Ross and Staw, 1986)."

In the contraction period, the authors do see evidence of adaptive, trial-and-error learning. They observe that entrepreneurs showed a propensity "to select the course of action that was rewarded," whereas negative outcomes "triggered interventions by resource controllers, which resulted in changes in the innovation unit's course of action."(p. 104) These changes led, in turn, to shifts in outcome criteria, suggesting to the authors that "outcome criteria may have shifted largely to justify changes" in the course of action.

The authors' findings lead them to pose three puzzling questions:

1. Why did trial-and-error learning not occur during TAP's expansion period?
2. What explains the dramatic shift from little or no learning during the expansion period to trial-and-error learning during TAP's contraction period?
3. When learning occurred, it appeared too late. Why was TAP's development terminated? (p. 106)

---

[1] In order to test their hypotheses, the authors decompose their case into "events," which they define as "critical incidents when changes were observed to occur in the innovation idea and activities, personnel appointments and roles, innovation unit relationships with others, environmental and organizational context, and outcomes."(p. 99) They adopt a monthly interval for the aggregation of events, collecting some 325 of them over a five-year period. They code outcomes of events as positive or negative or mixed, depending on their embodying good news or successful accomplishments, bad news or instances of failures or mistakes, or combinations of these. They seek to test their hypotheses by ascertaining correlations or lack of them, between positive, negative, and mixed events, on the one hand, and, on the other hand, continuation or change in a prior action course, resource controllers' interventions, shifts in outcome criteria, or events (judged significant) in the external context.

The Behavioral Story. It is in their exploration of these puzzles that the authors turn to the phenomena they call "behavioral." They observe that during the expansion phase the innovation entrepreneurs were held accountable for achieving the overly optimistic plans they had presented in order to secure funding. This, in turn, triggered "'sugar-coated' administrative reviews."(p. 106) None of managers of the innovation team interviewed by the authors showed a willingness to "document uncertainties or to propose a more extended timetable for start-up, because they feared that would decrease their chances of obtaining startup funding." The top managers of the parent companies that funded TAP accepted the overoptimistic planning targets presented by the entrepreneurs, although they admitted privately that "they discounted certain projections as 'fluff' and expected the plan to change." Nevertheless, they held publicly to the conviction that TAP managers should be kept accountable to their plans. This, in turn, "precipitated [our emphasis] *the onset of a vicious cycle of impression management* between innovation managers and resource controllers."(p. 106)

While development efforts were largely successful in this period, they did encounter critical difficulties—for example, manufacturing defects and problems in scaling up production of the filtration module—which resulted in slipped schedules for market introduction, deferred sales revenues, and delayed development of the Phase II device.(p. 106) During the administrative review sessions that were held every six months or so, the TAP managers reported information about these problems to the resource controllers, but they did so in ways that were calculated to discourage problem solving and learning. Van de Ven and Polley report that before each review session the TAP managers spent a day

> ...rehearsing their presentations, developing tactics and scripts on how they would respond to possible questions of top managers, ...preparing "slick" visuals...and [reconstructing] negative information in a positive frame, with assurances that they were in control of problems and presented action plans for addressing [them].... The resource controllers...relied on this indirect information to assess TAP's progress...and tended to mimic the TAP success criteria and concerns they were told by innovation managers. (p. 107)

In the expansion phase, setbacks occurred frequently, and red flags were raised with increasing frequency concerning TAP's development, schedule, directions, or financing. Nevertheless, the authors observed relatively few attempts to "detect these warnings as errors and correct the detected errors." Some warnings provoked discussion and debate, but most "were simply aired without response or were dismissed as irrelevant ." At no time in the expansion period did TAP managers "seriously question the assumptions or validity of the technological paths they were pursuing."(p. 108)

The authors account for these remarkable (though classic) findings by reference to two main factors, in addition to vicious cycles of impression management. First, they state that a high level of discontinuity in the TAP personnel, due to normal job mobility and promotion in the parent companies, disrupted the continuity of attention necessary for adaptive learning. Secondly, they observe that the proliferation of "parallel and independent streams of research activities" appeared to have the effect of "[masking] attention to the core innovation idea: the viability of producing a single reliable filtration device."(p. 107) They suggest that this noise, which went far beyond the information processing capacity of individuals, makes it easy to understand "why so few messages were detected as errors," and "why few attempts were observed to correct detected errors."(p. 110)

In the contraction phase, things changed. First of all, TAP got into serious trouble when its managers tried to introduce the Phase I devices into the European market and use them to conduct clinical trials of the Phase II filtration module. Even so, the authors report, the negative assessment of TAP's performance did not begin to grow until it was revealed at an administrative review session that development targets for the Phase II device had slipped by over a year and that sales revenues from the Phase I device were at ten percent of projections. Only then did resource controllers begin to raise serious questions about TAP's development and intervene to break the pattern of persevering in failing courses of action. At this point the resource controllers put new TAP managers in charge of manufacturing. These managers suspended all shipments of Phase I devices and conducted an extensive internal review and audit of the scaleup and manufacturing problems; as a result several TAP people were laid off. As one member of the TAP unit observed at the time, "The honeymoon is over!"(p. 112)

These events produced what the authors regard as a further cause of increased adaptive learning, that is, a concentration of attention on pressing operational problems which had the effect of "reducing complexity and focusing attention on a single issue," which, in turn, "facilitated trial-and-error learning."(p. 110) Sophisticated technological and engineering trials and adaptations were made, and long-standing manufacturing defects were finally corrected. As a result, the TAP device was found to achieve "a reliability rate comparable to competing apheresis devices in the market."(p. 112)

Nevertheless, the troubles experienced in this phase shook the resource controllers' confidence. They began to pay serious attention to the mounting development costs that were draining resources from alternative investments. In contrast, the innovation managers saw the recent setbacks as temporary and maintained their long-term commitment to the program. (p. 112) The two parties developed "alternative stories that interpreted the same experience quite differently." Meanwhile, in the external environment, "latent forces" were gathering. In the parent companies, budgets were being reduced in the face of negative corporate earnings. A CEO, who had been one of TAP's principal supporters, died unexpectedly. There was news of technological advances by TAP's Japanese competitors and rumors that a new drug might do away with the need for apheresis hardware. Then, when it became evident that development targets had slipped by over a year and that market trials had revealed serious manufacturing defects, these latent forces were unleashed. In November of 1988, TAP was terminated.

In actuality, the authors point out, there were fewer threatening events during the contraction period than in the expansion period, but TAP had lost its credibility. The resource controllers launched a search for a new corporate investor, and, finding none, they declared TAP a failure. Was it a failure? The authors end their story by quoting a senior executive in one of TAP's parent organizations: had the program been allowed to continue, he thought, it might have succeeded.

The TAP Analysis Analyzed. As an account of a technological innovation, the TAP story has a familiar ring (see, for example, Schön, 1967). Throughout the early stages of the process, researchers and general managers pursue a game of reciprocal deception and attempted unilateral control: researchers smooth over negative information, and general managers delay in attending to negative signals. This goes on until a crisis occurs, at which point the researchers can no longer mask the negative information, managers can no longer avoid paying attention to it, and they overreact.

At the very end of their version of this classic story, the authors suggest some things organizations can do to increase the odds of adaptive learning.

1. separate the planning from the funding of a new venture, so as to avoid optimistic estimates aimed mainly at securing funding (p. 114),
2. find ways to decrease the bull index, i.e., the high amount of impression management that goes on between innovation teams and investors...and distorts information needed for trial-and-error learning,
3. keep the core innovation team intact during innovation development,
4. keep innovation development and business creation separate, so as to reduce information overload (p. 114), and
5. "alter the agendas and formats of...administrative review sessions in order to increase the amount of candid information exchange and learning"(p. 115).

What is striking about Van de Ven and Polley's treatment of the TAP story is that they are so rigorous in their testing of the adaptive learning model, yet they make so little explanatory use of their behavioral data. The mixed results of their test of the adaptive learning model lead to important puzzles:

- Why was adaptive learning so long delayed?
- Why was there a dramatic shift to adaptive learning in the contraction phase?
- Why, when adaptive learning finally occurred, did controllers pull the plug?

In their use of the behavioral story to explain these puzzles, the authors note the ambiguous information, the shifting objectives, the uncertainties surrounding the development, complexity and noise in the information environment, and the discontinuities of personnel. They treat these explanations as partial causes of the lack of adaptive learning in the expansion phase.

But such phenomena are the givens of research and development programs. All such programs encounter them in greater or lesser degree. The key question is how and through what kinds of interpersonal inquiry participants in a development deal with such phenomena. Given the uncertainties inherent in a development project, do the participants seek to make public their doubts as well as their beliefs? Do they invite challenges to their positions or surface the dilemmas with which they themselves are struggling? Given endemic noise, ambiguity, and uncertainty, do they seek out and invite public testing of assumptions that underlie the core innovation idea? Or do they enter into a vicious cycle of impression management, as in the TAP story, with innovation managers suppressing uncertainties and smoothing over negative information in order to keep the controllers from taking setbacks seriously and with controllers colluding with the researchers by holding them publicly to overoptimistic targets whose fluff they privately acknowledge?

The authors note these features of organizational inquiry, which they express at relatively high levels on the ladder of inference ("sugar coating," "impression management"), but they offer no coherent theory to explain them. From our point of view, the participants' vicious cycles of impression management are predictable variants of primary inhibitory loops, triggered by the threat or embarrassment associated with situations of uncertainty and ambiguity. In these collusive processes, both parties employ a Model I strategy of mystery and mastery. They keep mysterious what they know to be true (the fluffy estimates, the likelihood that plans will change), while outwardly they try to master the responses of the other party. Under these conditions, errors and setbacks in the development's trajectory and uncertainties about its future cannot be made public; to do so would reveal both parties' deceptions. So the crucially important errors and uncertainties along with their undiscussability are kept undiscussable, until a critical event (the flawed entry into the European market, for example) makes error unavoidably visible, provoking a crisis that triggers the resource managers' precipitous termination of the project.

In our view, such a vicious cycle is explainable, indeed, predictable, on the basis of Model I theories-in-use, which shape interpersonal inquiry under conditions of threat or embarrassment. These theories-in-use reinforce and are, in turn, reinforced by O-I learning systems. As we see it, this is the systematic explanation of the patterns of unreliable organizational inquiry through which the actors' in the TAP story respond to uncertainty, complexity, ambiguity, and discontinuity—the givens of technological entrepreneurship. From this viewpoint, one sees the flimsiness of the authors' prescriptions for enhancing adaptive learning. How will the separation of planning from funding decisions encourage adaptive learning if, once the funds are granted, the innovation team persists in its strategies of control through deception, and the resource controllers collude in appearing to swallow such deceptions in order to control the researchers by holding them publicly accountable for their formal targets? How will the participants reduce the "bull index" when their theories-in-use lead them to produce and accept the bull? How will altering agendas and formats lead to an increase in candid information exchange and learning when such candidness would threaten to surface data that both parties actively work at keeping undiscussable?

The patterns of behavior implicit in the vicious cycle of impression management are unlikely to change unless the participants invite an intervention that creates the conditions for the kind of "open, fact-based conversation" that Van de Ven and Polley recommend, or unless the participants learn to develop Model II theories-in-use, as we have illustrated earlier, so as to create such conditions for themselves. Model II action strategies—for example, the public testing of privately held assumptions and attributions—do not require a prior removal of conditions of ambiguity and uncertainty. On the contrary, it is precisely under profound uncertainty and ambiguity, when one cannot know what truth is, that Model II inquiry is most needed and most likely to create the conditions for good dialectic.

Whether or not readers accept our approach to the analysis of the behavioral phenomena described in the TAP story, we hope it is now clear why such phenomena must be considered characteristically organizational and crucially linked to organizational learning. Consider the following propositions arrayed in descending order on a ladder of aggregation:

1. In the expansion phase of the TAP project, there was an organizational failure of adaptive learning.
2. In their administrative reviews during this phase, innovation managers and resource controllers engaged in a vicious cycle of impression management.
3. In any given instance of such a review, an innovation manager, A, gave a 'sugar-coated' account of progress, knowing that he was doing so, but keeping that knowledge to himself; and a resource controller, B, privately discounted that statement as 'fluff,' but kept that knowledge to himself.

If, following Van de Ven and Polley, we treat item 1 as a proposition about organizational phenomena and item 2 as a partial explanation of item 1, then how can we not also treat item 2 as about organizational phenomena? And if we treat item 3 as a specification and partial explanation of item 2, then how are we justified in excluding it from the set of propositions that refer to organizational phenomena? We cannot validly exclude from the class of propositions about organizations those that offer explanations of phenomena that we already treat as organizational. More specifically, we cannot validly exclude from the class of propositions about organizational learning those propositions about interpersonal inquiry in organizations that are adduced to explain observed patterns of organizational learning.

If this argument holds for the explanation of organizational learning, it holds all the more so for prescriptions aimed at enhancing it. Practitioners will be unable to act on such prescriptions unless they already have the skills required to carry out the actions prescribed. They will not be able to enact a prescription such as "Cut the bull index," or "Hold candid, fact-based conversations," unless the prescription is formulated in terms that enable them to envisage actions required for its implementation.

Burgelman: "Fading Memories"

In this article, Robert Burgelman (1994) reports on his study of Intel's responses, roughly between 1971 and 1991, to the changing competetive environment of its dynamic random access memory (DRAM) business and details the processes that led to Intel's eventual exit from that business. Like Van de Ven and Polley, Burgelman tells a story of mixed success and failure in organizational learning and stresses the "inertial" lag of formal corporate strategy in relation to shifting conditions in the competetive environment. He differs from Van de Ven and Polley, however, in his conceptual framework, which is not adaptive learning but a theory about the role of strategy in firm evolution. Burgelman sets out to provide

> insight into how the internal selection environment mediates the co-evolution of industry-level sources of competetive advantage and firm-level sources of distinctive competence and into the link between corporate strategy and strategic action. (p. 24)

Burgelman tells the story of a twenty-year transformation in Intel's strategic practice, tracking its passage through three stages:

1. an equilibrium state, harmony of dominant beliefs and strategic context, in which Intel thought of itself as a "memory company" (and more specifically, a DRAM company),

2. a transitional period of disharmony in which the basis for competetive advantage in the memory business changed, while Intel's formal strategy remained inert and momentum developed internally toward the opening up of new business opportunities, and

3. a later harmonious state in which Intel came to think of itself as a microprocessor company.

Ultimately, as Burgelman reveals, Intel learns. It learns to recognize that, through its incremental responses to challenges, mainly from Japanese competitors, it has dealt itself out of the DRAM business and should not try by massive capital investment to reestablish its position in that business. It learns to exploit the technological opportunities that came about as byproducts of its experience in the DRAM business (the EPROMS development pioneered by Dov Frohman, which came through exploring reliability problems with Intel's MOS technology; and the new chip architecture, which grew out of a customer's request for a new chip set). These opportunities, initially recognized or tolerated by top management, were, according to Burgelman, internal variations. They were eventually selected by Intel's internal environment, and they eventually contributed to the technological basis for its microprocessor business. Intel also learns to shift its scarce manufacturing capacity from DRAM to microprocessor technology, and Intel's top management eventually learns to redefine Intel as a microprocessor company.

But, as Burgelman tells it, the Intel story is also one of failure to learn or of inertial delays in learning. Burgelman frames this side of the story in terms of six puzzling questions around which he structures his analysis. We focus on four of these:

1. Why did Intel, the first successful mover in DRAMS, fail to capitalize on and defend its early lead?
2. How did it happen that the bulk of Intel's business had shifted away from DRAMS, and DRAM market share was allowed to dwindle, while top management, even in 1984, was still thinking of DRAMs as a strategic business for the company?
3. How was it possible that middle-level managers could take actions that were not in line with the official corporate strategy?
4. Why did it take Intel's top management almost a year to complete the exit from DRAMs after the November 1984 decision not to market 1 Meg DRAMs? (pp. 29–30)

These questions point to a series of strategic mistakes that Intel seemingly made and to inertial delays in its attempts to reconcile its formal strategy to changing competitive conditions and to convert its new strategic intent into action. Such mistakes and delays are to be understood as failures in the timely detection and correction of significant errors (surprises or mismatch of outcomes to expectations). However, there is some ambiguity and perhaps ambivalence in Burgleman's treatment of his puzzles. He certainly does frame them in terms of Intel's apparent failure to take effective, timely action or to match its thought to a changing reality. But he also suggests that in certain respects Intel's delayed responses were functional. He speculates, for example, that Intel

> would probably have done worse if it had simply divested the DRAM business and entered the new business through acquisition...[because it would have thereby] failed to capitalize on the full potential of its distinctive competencies in DRAMs, [some of which] could be effectively deployed in the microprocessor business... (p. 52)

This ambiguity plays an important role in the discussion that follows.

Burgelman's approach to his puzzles has both an historical and a systems dimension. He argues that Intel secured a strong competitive advantage in the early days of the DRAM business on the basis of its distinctive technical competence in designing, building, and manufacturing the DRAM technology. He argues further that the early successes of DRAM caused Intel's corporate strategy to be dominated by its DRAM technology. He postulates a microtheory of success and failure along the lines of March's **competence trap**: When a pattern of factors is clearly related to a firm's understanding of its success, this pattern tends to be reinforced and thus to persevere, even after it ceases to be effective in the competitive business environment.

Burgelman describes several phenomena that reinforced established patterns associated with Intel's earlier success:

- the self-interest of business unit heads who had considerable latitude for decision making yet had no interest in putting themselves out of business,
- the "bounded rationality" that kept top or middle managers from anticipating the competitive market dynamics of product and manufacturing technology that would squeeze out Intel's share of the DRAM market, and
- top management's "emotional attachment" to the DRAM business, which made it reluctant to get out of that business, just as Ford would be reluctant to "decide that it should get out of the car business."(p. 41)

In contrast to the factors that kept Intel's top management from letting go of its attachment to the DRAM business and its image of Intel as a "memory company," Burgelman postulates an "internal selective environment" made up of "structural and strategic contexts shaping strategic actions" on the part of middle managers. In the Intel case, middle managers used their discretionary freedoms to take actions that had the effect of opening up new business opportunities. For example, they pursued the development of technological offshoots of the DRAM business that would lay the groundwork for microprocessors. And they allocated scarce manufacturing capacity to favor microprocessors over DRAMs, making use of the established corporate rule that manufacturing capacity should be allocated so as to "maximize margin-per-wafer-start"(p. 43), even while top management continued to support the view that Intel should remain in the DRAM business. In these and related ways, middle managers gradually undermined the position of the existing DRAM business and helped "dissolve," as Burgelman puts it, the earlier strategic context of the firm.

Burgelman calls his perspective "inside-out." He tells how Intel's external business environment created conditions—changes in the market and DRAMs becoming a commodity—to which Intel responded with decreasing effectiveness. But he treats the "inside" as crucial. Unlike other writers, especially economists, who relegate inside activities largely to a black box, Burgelman opens up the box. He sees that as Intel sought to maintain its competitive advantage by acting in ways that were consistent with its perception of its distinctive competence, it did and failed to do things that actually led to its competitive disadvantage. For example, although Intel's top managers did realize that DRAM had gone from a premium-priced to a commodity product (the price signals were rather clear), they persisted in believing that they could regain the lead by applying their traditional strengths in process technology to come up with innovative products that would be premium-priced niche products at first but would have to be adopted eventually by the entire market. The moment DRAMs became a commodity, Intel's strategy of being the first to introduce premium-priced products into the market became outmoded. Yet top management acted as if this were not the case.

In addition, Burgelman suggests that middle managers believed top management was closed to constructive confrontation about their emotional attachment to the DRAM business. From our perspective, the middle managers were making attributions about top management's openness to learning. From the data in the case, we infer that they never tested these attributions. In a discussion with Argyris, Burgelman confirmed this inference. He said, in effect,

> Given the status and power of the process development people, anyone who went into a meeting to propose a view different from theirs

would be unlikely to carry the day. Furthermore, top managers were seen by middle managers as believing that Intel could not make changes away from DRAMs. Top management was seen as unsure.

This behavior provides a partial explanation of top management's "blindness": they were never confronted with data that would help them realize the impact of their behavior. Burgelman's explanation focuses on the top management's uncertainty and, in the face of that uncertainty, its resistance to change. We would focus, in addition, on middle managers' actions that helped to keep top management from realizing the full implications of the shift in the DRAM business, which, in turn, let top managers act in ways middle managers explained as resistance to change. Burgelman focuses on the self-sealing processes of the top managers, not on those created by the middle managers. If an intervention were designed to interrupt the limited learning processes revealed by the Intel case, it would fail if it were one-sided.

Burgelman reports that Intel's top management encouraged constructive confrontation. Andy Grove (then COO, now CEO) told managers at all levels that decisions should be data-driven and that power and emotional biases should play no role in decision making. We hypothesize, nevertheless, that middle managers' attributions to the top were not openly discussed and analyzed in ways that would test their validity and allow them to be corrected if they proved mistaken.

Burgelman describes an additional domain of undiscussables. He notes that when DRAMs became a commodity, manufacturing capability became the dominant success factor. Yet process development (TD) people continued to downgrade manufacturing and distance themselves from it. TD people continued to frame problems in mainly scientific terms, treating manufacturing people as "tweakers." The manufacturing people reacted by developing a "not invented here" (NIH) syndrome. Gordon Moore, then CEO, reacted to this interdepartmental rivalry by placing both groups in geographical proximity in order to foster greater cooperation between them. Moore had experienced similar problems at Fairchild and wanted to avoid them now at Intel, an attempt to learn from his earlier experience. Burgelman reports that this strategy was at first effective but became much less effective when competitive pressures made the differences between TD and manufacturing much more salient.

Burgelman also observes organizational defenses at work in the relationship between upper-level middle managers and the Board.

By 1980, when the company's total market share in DRAMs was less than three percent, these managers saw the handwriting on the wall. Yet they would learn of board meetings where Moore, then CEO, and Gelbach, the head of marketing, would defend continued expenditures on DRAM—Moore, because he saw DRAMs as the company's "technology driver" and Gelbach, because he believed Intel had to offer its customers a one-stop semiconductor shopping list. Andy Grove (then COO) remained silent. As a result of such board-level interactions, middle managers were frustrated.

These multileveled undiscussables reinforced by organizational defensive routines would make Grove's advocacy of "constructive confrontation" sound more like espoused theory than theory-in-use, namely, his view that "one of the toughest challenges is to make people see that their 'self-evident truths' are no longer true," or "organizations should practice creative destruction of routines that are no longer effective."

Burgelman told Argyris that top management recognized the organizational defensiveness which they saw as existing primarily at the level of some middle managers. As far as we can tell, top management did not examine this defensiveness directly and forthrightly with the middle managers. If so, we have top managers acting to reinforce middle managers' unawareness of their impact on those at the top.

Top management attempted to deal with interdepartmental conflicts by bringing departments into geographic proximity, defining rules to reduce the conflicts, and providing incentive systems that would do so. Over the long haul, none of these strategies worked, although some of them were effective in the first instance.

Burgelman's Analysis Analyzed. We would say that there is only partial truth in Burgelman's hypothesis that top management persisted in its commitment to the DRAM business because of emotional attachment to it and uncertainty about its importance. What is needed is an explanation of how subordinates colluded with their superiors to create domains of undiscussables that would inhibit learning around these issues.

Like Burgelman, we also try to understand how it comes about that organizations do not detect and correct significant errors, but we seek to go further. We want to understand how it comes about that Intel or other organizations are unaware that they are unable to detect and correct significant errors. The inability to detect and correct error is skilled because we can connect it to a theory-in-use; hence, it is

skilled incompetence. The existence of skilled incompetence means the unawareness of the inability, and unawareness is also connected to a theory-in-use—hence, it is **skilled unawareness.**

We would ask, for example, what is included in this concept of "emotional attachment"? What is the theory-in-use that produces such behavior? Is Burgelman using the concept to mean that emotional attachment always causes blindness? If not, what would be the difference between the two types of emotional attachment?

We would add an additional puzzle to those queries with which Burgelman begins his paper: How could the conditions named in his four puzzles hold when top management espoused a theory of management intended to prevent them from occurring?

To solve this puzzle would require much more directly observable data about what was actually said when people at Intel discussed these issues. For example, how did the middle-level managers craft their conversations? Did they ease in so much that their points were obscured? Or did they become so confrontational that the others could discount their views because they were obviously emotional?

Did the middle managers engage top managers in a dialogue about the attributions they were making about them? Did they explore their attributions that these issues were undiscussable, and their undiscussability also undiscussable? Did they explore their attributions that even if these issues were discussed, top management would be uninfluenced? Did they ever explore whether the top managers were unaware of the "blindness" that middle managers attributed to them?

Burgelman states that Grove did not at first believe that the lag time was as long or the inertia as deep as Burgelman concludes they were. To his credit, however, Grove conducted his own investigation and found that Burgelman's estimate was better than his own. We might ask, then, what Grove actually did. He questioned the relevant players and, months after the decision to exit the DRAM business, they gave him information they had not told him or that he had not listened to before.

Burgelman's explanations of the puzzling phenomena of delayed or failed organizational learning do not account for such phenomena developing in an organization in which cultural context, top management support, and the sheer brightness of the Intel managers would seem to militate against their occurring.

If Intel failed to capitalize on and defend its early lead in the DRAM business, for example, what actually produced the failure? To say that it was top management's emotional attachment to DRAMs is to pinpoint a small group within an abstract explanation. How did top management actually behave? How did the middle-level managers confront top management's emotional attachment, if they actually did? How did they attempt to change it? In other words, we hypothesize that the puzzling phenomena of delay and inertia were caused both by top management's emotionality and blindness and by middle managers' ways of dealing with them, that is, by bypassing these issues and acting as if they were not doing so.

We would also suggest that an operational definition of a more complete explanation of the puzzles could be used to design actions to change the causes of inertia. The causes Burgelman identifies—such as top management's emotional attachment to DRAMs, interdepartmental rivalries between TD and manufacturing, self-reinforcing processes that maintained outmoded strategic frames—are stated at a level of abstraction that cannot be used to change the organization or to enable the organization to learn to detect and correct its errors.

In our view, the fifth puzzle we introduced, how it came about that Intel's management was unaware of its inability to detect and correct its errors, underlies the other four.

Burgelman concludes his analysis by advancing a set of propositions, some of which, in the light of our own analysis, we find misleading. His first proposition states,

> The stronger a firm's distinctive technological competence, the stronger the firm's tendency to continue to rely on it in the face of industry-level changes in the basis of competitive advantage. (p. 48)

We would add, however, that this proposition holds or holds more strongly whenever organizational defensive routines at top- or middle-mangement levels or between departments reinforce the failure to face up to industry-level changes and to legitimize the bypassing and cover-up of such reinforcement.

Burgelman's third proposition states,

> Firms whose internal selection criteria accurately reflect external selection pressures are more likely to strategically exit from some businesses than firms whose internal selection criteria do not accurately reflect external selection pressures. (p. 50)

We would add,

> Firms whose internal selection criteria reflect and deal with external selection pressure should be observed to have minimal defensive routines (of the sort we have described earlier).

Burgelman's sixth proposition states,

> Firms that have strategically exited from a business are likely to have a better understanding of the links between their distinctive competences and the basis of competition in the industries in which they remain active than firms that have not strategically exited from a business.

We believe this proposition is valid under the condition that organizational defensive routines dominate the examination of errors that are embarrassing and threatening to key players. It should not hold for firms that are not dominated by such defensive routines; these firms should have a better understanding before, rather than after, exit.

In sum, Burgelman's analysis of the Intel case focuses on puzzles rooted mainly in the organization's failures to detect and correct error:

- its failure to follow up its early lead in the DRAM business,
- its delay in matching its strategic ideas and self-image to the changing business reality, and
- its inertia in completing its exit from the DRAM business once it had decided to do so.

Burgelman's explanations of these puzzles hinge on the phenomena of top management's emotional attachment to the DRAM business, its bounded rationality and blindness concerning the mismatch of its strategic context to the changing business reality, the power and self-interest of business-unit managers associated with the DRAM business, and the rivalry between technological development and manufacturing departments. But each of these causes raises questions related to another puzzle: How did it happen that Intel's managers were unaware of their inability to detect and correct their errors? This question points, in turn, to the layer of organizational phenomena that we regard as critically important both to the explanation of existing patterns of organizational learning and to the design of interventions aimed at changing those patterns, that is, the organizational defensive routines, and the O-I processes that constrained interpersonal inquiry between top- and middle-level managers, and between departments, thereby reinforcing a lack of awareness of the gap between Intel's strategic context and its changing business reality.

In a private communication to the authors in which he responds to an earlier version of our discussion of his article, Burgelman stresses the uncertainty with which Intel's top managers were dealing at the time they were grappling with the possibility of exiting from the DRAM business. He argues that their inertial delays and the defensive routines that reinforced those delays were actually functional since they enabled Intel to exploit in their microprocessors certain technological advances made by the DRAM process developers and also to prevent TD/DRAM people from leaving the company. He observes, in part,

> I like to emphasize that one of the key points of my study is that it is very difficult for top and middle managers to examine at length what the strategic situation is [that is] faced by an organization in very dynamic environments. So much is going on simultaneously that the kind of exhaustive "airing out" of the strategic situation is probably unachievable. So, while I believe your hypothesis is a plausible one and that perhaps more effort should be spent on airing out strategic situations, I also believe (1) that we do not know enough yet about how "defensive routines" come about(perhaps my study contributes to precisely that!) and (2) that it is improbable that there is no cost at all associated with removing defensive routines. I submit that trying to remove defensive routines altogether might very well paralyze organizations operating in dynamic environments.

In this passage, Burgelman argues, as he further notes, that in dynamic and uncertain environments there may be considerable value in "strategic neglect."

The weakness we find in this argument is the following: We agree that inertial delays in a firm's response to a mismatch between its formal strategy and its actual strategic situation may be retrospectively discovered, on occasion, to be functional. But these delays may just as easily prove to be dysfunctional. How are managers to distinguish between functional and dysfunctional strategic neglect so long as they keep themselves unaware of their discordant beliefs and keep the crucial and threatening issues undiscussable?

Why, moreover, should we assume that the opening up of defensive routines would make it impossible to achieve deliberately the same benefits as those that were inadvertently achieved (through lack of awareness)? For example, Intel's top management could have chosen to keep its TD/DRAM capability on the very grounds of its uncertainty about its possible future utility, even in the face of a clear decision to exit the DRAM business.

Why then should we assume that the airing out of the strategic situation would have to be exhaustive (certainly, a recipe for paralysis!) when it could be limited to just those dilemmas that constituted the main bone of contention between top- and upper-level middle managers? One need not know just how defensive routines come about (although we believe our theory offers some insight into that question) in order to see how they constrain productive inquiry into critically important strategic issues.[2]

Main Points Drawn from Our Analysis of the First Two Studies

Reviewing our discussion of these two retrospective studies of "naturally occurring" organizational learning, we find:

1. Both studies show mixed results. There are some examples of productive organizational learning and some striking limits to productive organizational learning, both of which need to be explained.

2. Both studies illustrate **dynamic conservatism**, that is, an organization's persistence in adhering to past patterns of practice in the face of information that should have caused them to change.

3. The researchers interpret their findings of limited productive organizational learning in two main ways:

    a. the cognitive limitations due to "finite information processing capacity" experienced by organizational actors in the face of complexity, noise, ambiguity, and uncertainty, and

    b. the intraorganizational games of interests and powers that evolve around an organization's dominant action strategy and task system.

4. Our criticism of these explanations is that they only partly account for the first-order errors the researchers set out to explain and do not at all deal with the additional puzzle we find in second-order error: the members' being unaware of their inability to detect and correct first-order error, or their limited ability to act on what they knew.

---

[2] Burgelman's argument here is reminiscent of Hirschman's famous "principle of the Hiding Hand." Hirschman proposed (1967) that ignorance of dangers to come can actually foster the success of a development project because those who underestimate the dangers also tend to underestimate the creativity that may be brought to their resolution. However, in his later writings, Hirschman also recognized the difficulty of distinguishing instances in which the Hiding Hand proves to be beneficent from those instances in which it does not prove to be beneficent!

5. We reinterpret the researchers' findings in terms of organizational defensive routines based on Model I theories-in-use and O-I learning systems which shape and constrain prevailing patterns of organizational inquiry.

6. Our analysis of the researchers' studies addresses the "ladder of aggregation" problem: The dimension of interpersonal inquiry to which the researchers give only slight or ambivalent importance is critical to an adequate explanation of both the first-order errors the researchers identify in their cases and the second-order errors that we have identified in them.

Studies of Interventions Aimed At Promoting Productive Organizational Learning

We turn now to studies of a different sort: analyses of attempts to introduce *organizational enablers* of several different kinds with the aim of enhancing organizational capability for productive learning.

Revisiting Cordiner's Decentralization of GE

The purpose of decentralization is to reduce the inefficiencies and rigidities caused by centralization. Alfred Sloan decided in the 1920s that General Motors was not likely to grow or to be managed effectively if it took, as he found out, nearly a year to get replies to many of his memos. Ralph Cordiner arrived at similar conclusions about GE in the 1950s when he learned during the antitrust proceedings on light bulbs that many of his senior executives were withholding information from him and covering up that they were doing so.

Sloan, Cordiner and many other executives throughout the world attempted to correct this situation by asking what kinds of power and reporting relationships and what kinds of incentive schemes would encourage executives to be more candid with each other and with their superiors. Sloan and Cordiner, as well as many other executives, looked for the answer in new organizational structures and in reward-and-penalty processes. The fundamental assumption they held in common, and one held by many prominent scholars of organization, was that changes in structures and rules (structural "enablers") can cause desired changes in behavior to occur.

Consistent with this assumption is the rule: Place responsibility for action and authority to take action as close as possible to the players who have the relevant information. It is these individuals who should be given the opportunity to make informed decisions and choices. It is they who should be held responsible for implementing their choices and monitoring their effectiveness.

At GE in the 1950s, Cordiner and his colleagues espoused a theory of organizational decentralization based on rules that incorporated Model II values of valid information, informed choice, and personal responsibility for implementing choices and monitoring their effectiveness by detecting and correcting errors. We will demonstrate that GE was able to achieve limited double-loop learning outcomes, but their achievements were undermined over time as defensive routines intervened. The GE case clarifies the relationship between double-loop learning at the level of outcomes in organizational theory of action and at the level of processes of organizational inquiry, as it shows how persistence of O-I organizational inquiry undermined and limited double-loop organizational learning over time.

Cordiner realized that decentralization would require a change in culture and a change in the mental maps executives held about effective leadership. Accordingly he created one of the first executive development universities at Crotonville, New York. The first participants in the Crotonville program were individuals who were general managers of a business unit. Later, individuals who reported to these managers attended. The divisional heads to whom the general managers reported and the group heads to whom the divisional heads reported attended a short version of the month-long course. We will focus on the general managers and their superiors. However, we claim that the strengths and difficulties that emerged in the relations between these two levels were replicated at all the other managerial levels.

Cordiner's senior vice president, Harold Schmiddy, wrote a set of volumes that served as foundation for the Crotonville curriculum. The overwhelming emphasis of these volumes was to define the organizational features of decentralization. First there was an emphasis on defining correct reporting relationships. Then there was the emphasis on defining rewards and penalites to make the reporting relationship, in Cordiner's words, "come alive." Cordiner and Schmiddy, as well as the faculty, realized that "coming alive" meant that the managers' theories-in-use had to be changed. However, the fundamental assumption was that if the structure is defined correctly and correct rewards and penalty processes are in place, then the desired changes in managers' thought and action would occur.

What follows represents the recollections of one of the authors (Argyris) who helped to design the first program for general managers, taught in the programs, and was given the opportunity to observe some of the general managers when they returned to their organizations. Both Agyris and coauthor claim that what follows is not limited to GE but is true of most executive programs in which they and many of their academic colleagues have participated.

The theory of instruction at Crotonville was centralized in that the faculty was expected to teach and the general managers were expected to listen and to confront the faculty whenever they wished to do so. The material the general managers received represented the faculty's best efforts at defining the desired pattern of decentralization and the new controls that would make it happen. The fundamental intention was to specify decentralization and its many features as precisely as possible and to illustrate how these features should be implemented in the back-home situation. The faculty told the general managers that these plans were not likely to be correct or complete and invited vigilant on-line learning.

For the sake of illustration, let us begin with those general managers who learned the new concepts, policies, and skills. We refer to those who made the new espoused theory of action part of their theory-in-use for action within the organization. Argyris did find a few managers who hesitated, either because they did not believe top management truly believed in decentralization or because they did not feel competent and confident in the exercise of their new skills (Baker and Wruck, 1989). But most general managers did make a serious effort to implement decentralization as it was taught to them. For example, if they could now sign checks for $200,000, they did so. If they could decide whether to build or rent within some broad dollar limits, they did so. If they were free to hire new functional managers, they did so. Argyris observed many general managers who acted in ways that were consistent with the delegation of decision rights and exercised their newly given autonomy and responsibility.

These represent double-loop outcomes, although the managers were given no education that helped them to develop Model II skills. Note, however, the conditions for success. The general managers had the skills to sign checks, they had been educated in the new purchasing procedures, and they knew how to hire functional managers. In other words, where there was a relatively high degree of seamlessness between the concept of decentralization and the general managers' ability to produce it, the Model II governing values built into

GE's theory of decentralization were translated from espoused theory to theory-in-use. In our opinion, this does represent double-loop change at the level of organizational theory-in-use without double-loop change at the level of interpersonal inquiry.

Our theory would predict that this success should persist as long as there were no major constraints or errors. As time passed by, however, limitations and errors did come to the surface. For example, no managerial policy for purchasing or for anything else could be so complete that it covered all contingencies. If the gaps between abstract policies and actual behavior did not require changes that were embarrassing or threatening, they were successfully bridged. If the gaps or their solutions proved embarrassing or threatening, they were handled by Model I action strategies. These strategies led to the general managers taking unilateral action, subordinates going under cover, and both groups acting as if this were not the case. For example, the subordinates argued that their newly given autonomy was insufficient, while their superiors often held the view that the subordinates were failing to take advantage of what freedoms they had. The embarrassment or threat involved in engaging these issues was bypassed, and the bypass was covered up.

Argyris observed general managers leading many meetings at their home sites. Whenever embarrassing or threatening issues surfaced, Model I theories-in-use, as well as predictable organizational defensive routines, were activitated. General managers were observed dealing with the "difficult concerns" of their immediate reports with such comments as, "Look, let's give it a try" or "I know we can make this work if you folks would have a more positive attitude." The subordinates saw such actions as discrepancies between the organization's managerial theory of decentralization, which was consistent with Model II governing variables, and the actions of superiors, especially when managers were facing embarrassing or threatening situations.

The general managers were concerned about certain important cases in which they were getting mixed messages from their superiors. In a situation of ambiguity and tension about authority, the superior might say, "Of course you have the authority, but on this one it would be a good idea to check with me because policy questions are involved." Typically, faculty would respond to such examples by saying things such as, "Be positive and be patient" or "Show your superiors that the new rules do give you the authority to decide." This kind of advice bypassed both the mixed messages general managers were getting and the underlying ambiguities that frustrated them.

The consequence frequently observed was that such advice led to the violation of the concept of decentralization precisely when it was most needed, namely, when there were ambiguities and conflicts that made the dialogue embarrassing or threatening. Then consequences were bypassed by advice to be positive and patient. Indeed, such advice required that the bypass be covered up. The bypass strategy employed by the faculty at Crotonville was similar to the one used by the general managers in their back-home setting. This, we suggest, is why the Crotonville program and many other similar programs were dubbed "charm schools."

There was another problem that spurred the advice to "show your superiors that the new rules do give you the authority you want." There were general managers who took this advice seriously and pushed back against their superiors. Their superiors, in turn, tended to see such behavior as problematic. If the general managers met their goals for financial performance, their problematic behavior was discounted; they were seen as "diamonds in the rough." But those general managers who pushed back and did not meet their performance goals were eventually transferred, demoted, or fired.

From the experiences described earlier, we suggest the following conclusion: Whenever double-loop changes in organizational theories-in-use are coupled with reasoning and interpersonal theories-in-use for organizational inquiry that remain consistent with Model I, self-fueling defenses that limit learning, along with such accompanying consequences as distancing and cynicism, will be activated whenever issues are embarrassing or threatening.

Under such conditions, it makes sense for managers to operationalize the social virtue of trust as "Just leave me alone, and monitor my results." Indeed, superiors were often proud to say to their subordinates that since they trusted them, they would leave them alone and simply monitor their results. Subordinates held a complementary concept of trust, that is, to distance themselves from their superiors. This eventually led to superiors being excluded from dialogue over business issues, even when they had the relevant knowledge and skills. Similarly, superiors excluded those subordinates with whose performance they were increasingly disappointed, thereby undermining their chances of promotion to the upper echelons of management.

Interestingly, there were some occasions when superiors and subordinates violated this concept of trust. These occasions were related to the possible activation of organizational defensive routines. Meetings about how to get around these routines would be held.

Almost no meetings were held on how to eliminate or reduce them. One reason was that this possibility had never been legitimized during the early processes of implementation and education. Such a topic was treated as undiscussable, and its undiscussability was also undiscussable. A second reason was that no skills that might lead to double-loop changes in these phenomena were taught. A third was that organizational defensive routines were often seen as unfortunate but predictable features of all organizations.

Under these conditions, autonomy and authority could develop for issues that did not activate organizational defensive routines. When the defensive routines were activated, individuals often used their delegated authority to cover up their bypass activities. For example, in one large business unit, the senior executives approved spending two million dollars a month because they felt a certain project was close to the CEO's heart and he could not be influenced about the project. As several of these executives reported, it made little sense to waste precious "chits" on this issue.

As a consequence of bypassing situations of tension and ambiguity in the delegation of authority and of the hands-off attitude that resulted, it took a while before upper levels of management at GE discovered that profit center managers were attempting to meet bottom-line targets by dubious methods. Expected sales might be treated as actual, or reports of losses might be delayed until the next quarter. Upper management responded to such discoveries by introducing tighter controls and information systems.

These consequences are more general. Whenever bypasses and cover-ups are discovered, the usual remedial action is to tighten controls, usually by including more detailed specifications. The difficulty with this strategy is that as the specifications mount,

1. they violate the idea of profit center autonomy and responsibility and
2. they become so cumbersome that they tend to fall of their own weight.

We conclude, then, that as organizations move from centralized to decentralized policies and practices, a characteristic sequence develops over time:

1. Superiors and subordinates tend to report satisfaction and enhanced performance because of their newly delegated decision rights. A minority may resist taking charge

because they are doubtful that top management "really means it" and/or because they are not yet confident of their own abilities.

2. As time goes by, issues surface over which strong differences in views come into play and cause conflicts. These consequences activate the participants' Model I theories-in-use and the organizational defensive routines that accompany them. They lead to superiors taking charge, thereby appearing, in the view of subordinates, to violate the concept of decentralization. The subordinates, in turn, may distance themselves and cover up. This, in the eyes of superiors, violates the responsibility they must assume if decentralization is to be effective. How often have we heard superiors warn subordinates that there must be "no surprises"? This warning applies not only to performance results but also to the use of organizational defensive routines.

3. Model I social virtues become strengthened. This, in turn, strengthens the defensive routines at all levels of the organization. For example, managers help and support by telling others what they believe will be positive and, therefore, reduce their hurt feelings. Managers show respect by not confronting the reasoning processes other managers use.

    Individuals who strive to be strong (advocating their positions in order to win), to be honest (not to lie), and to show integrity ("stick to one's principles"), will likely do so around issues that are relatively objective or where the control procedures make such action transparent. Whenever issues go underground and become undiscussable, Model I views of strength, honesty, and integrity lead to polarized positions that inhibit double-loop learning at the interpersonal level.

4. A perverse sense of trust—namely, trust coupled with mutual distancing—develops, making that distancing undiscussable.

5. This produces a space of free movement that allows behavior that violates organizational norms to emerge—specifically, ways of achieving results that meet the letter but violate the spirit of the policy.

6. When upper-level managers become aware of these consequences, they tighten controls, in turn violating the concept of decentralization.

Since Cordiner's time, advances in information technology have made it possible to develop tighter and more efficient controls and bring to the surface actions that would otherwise remain underground. As the rigidities of the self-fueling, antilearning processes become increasingly difficult to hide, upper-level managers are beginning to realize that managerial practices, if they are to succeed, require reeducation that includes a focus on individuals' Model I theories-in-use. It is at this point that organizational theories-in-use and interpersonal theories-in-use become interdependent.

It is ironic to note that when the connection between the organizational and interpersonal theories-in-use was not made, the reeducational programs became known as "charm schools." Now, when the connection is seen as more crucial than before, one often hears, "This is too difficult!" or "Is it really necessary?" or "Isn't this dangerous?" In the early days, the superficiality inherent in an incomplete approach to reeducation not only led to limited learning, it was also used by superiors and subordinates to cover themselves. Today superiors and subordinates may seek to protect themselves by raising the specter of "danger" and "Pandora's box." We believe that if concepts such as decentralization, empowerment, and personal responsibility are to persevere and encourage continuous improvement, the connection between the organizational and the interpersonal will have to be made.

Activity Costing

The following is an account of Robert Kaplan's attempts to introduce firms to **activity-based costing** (ABC), an information system aimed at improving organizational performance by enabling more precise attribution of costs and profitability to product lines (Argyris and Kaplan, 1992). Kaplan and his colleagues have developed an explicit structure for sponsoring and implementing an ABC project. Typically they begin with an activity-based cost model of organizational expenses and profitability which often reveals "many unexpectedly higher cost activities, processes, products, and customers"(p. 7) and proceeds to an action phase in which "management acts on the insights revealed by the ABC model to produce improved organizational performance."(p. 8) Kaplan and his colleagues distinguish key roles in this process: advocates for change, sponsors who have the ability to approve the required changes, change agents who take on the task of proving the concept and developing the more accurate information it requires, and targets, "the person or group whose behavior…is expected to change based on the newly revealed information."(p. 8)

Kaplan and his colleagues learned that they would regularly encounter resistance to action on improved information made available by ABC. Successful introduction of the system in one division of a firm was often followed by failure to disseminate it throughout the firm. One of Kaplan's manager-clients told him,

> I'm not convinced yet that the organization is geared to making difficult decisions based on information. It took us five years to drop a product line that we knew was not making money for us. If we're not prepared to take tough decisions, we don't need a fancy new information system.

In reponse to such resistance, Kaplan worked with some of his clients to develop "organizational enablers," such as performance measures keyed to incentives, formation of task forces and introduction of group training exercises. But these enablers often proved insufficient to elicit managers' internal commitment to the changes necessary for successful implementation of ABC. Subtle forces still exist inhibiting the acceptance of new ideas whenever technical theories challenge existing organizational norms and long-established ways of doing business, thereby threatening or embarrassing "people who have much of their professional and self-feelings identified with decisions, actions, and organizational structures implemented in the past." (p. 13) For example, the analysis may reveal that "certain favored product lines or customers are highly unprofitable," and product managers responsible for introducing and maintaining these lines or the account managers responsible for the highly unprofitable customers "become threatened by the quantitative and defensible evidence of their value-destroying activities."(p. 16) Or managers may be embarrassed "by the explicit recognition of excess capacity in areas under their authority," or more generally, by the recognition that their traditional cost and performance measurement systems have "led to bad decisions…and a lack of focus on wasteful activities."(p. 17) The experience of threat or embarrassment typically gives rise to defensive reasoning, as illustrated by the following:

- It is better to fail with existing procedures than to fail trying something new, especially where business is okay and no one is really up against the wall. Believe me, I know.

- People are more used to managing expenses than the behavior that drives the expenses. That's the reality of organizational life.

When champions of ABC seek to overcome such defenses, they often adopt strategies of change that exacerbate the defenses. In one instance, a top manager bypassed divisional managers, going directly to the factory to develop the ABC model, without seeking divisional managers' approval or precommitment to the changes that would be required once the large number of unprofitable products were revealed. He avoided early confrontation with these managers by concentrating on building a defensible model of operations, inoculating himself against the resistance he anticipated by asking the controller and data processing manager to make an independent confirmation of the analysis. Ultimately, the division's executives still rejected the analysis. And by framing the debate as "a conflict between an analytic, rational approach versus the executives' ignorance and resistance to change, he provided himself with an excuse that absolved him from blame for the lack of effective action," which he had anticipated. (p. 17)

Argyris and Kaplan conclude their analysis by observing

> In every change that involves the introduction of a new technical theory of action whose correct implementation could be embarrassing or threatening, the advocates, sponsors, change agents, and targets who use the generic implementation approach will still face the challenge of dealing with the defensive reasoning of organizational participants, including themselves. (p. 18)

Studies of TQM

Total Quality Management (TQM), introduced in Japan by W. Edwards Deming just after World War II, has had a 50-year history. Its transfer to the United States began in earnest in the early 1980s, following American management's awakening to the fact that Japan was outperforming U.S. industry not only in costs but in quality and that Japan's superior performance was due, in no small measure, to its practice of continuous quality improvement based on Deming's theory and methods. Throughout the 1980s, TQM grew steadily in its scope of adoption and prestige. By the early 1990s, however, its popularity had peaked, and what Beer (1994) describes as a "literature of disillusionment" had begun to appear.[3] We discuss two examples of recent essays in which the authors reflect on the mixed record of TQM interventions, the nature of the resistance TQM has provoked, and the limits of the TQM methodology.

Schneiderman (1992) writes as a professional TQM advocate and teacher, drawing on long experience in teaching organizations to implement TQM. His article is addressed to the naysayers, but it also reveals a thoughtful analysis of TQM's limits. He begins with a now familiar description of TQM which includes three main elements:

1. identification and flowcharting of component organizational processes, such as manufacturing, product development, filing, and telephone answering,

2. framing each such process as a partnership of supplier and customer and accompanying it with explicit metrics and standards for its performance, and

3. involving all workers engaged in a process in continuous, unrelenting process improvement through the identification and elimination of defects.

Next, Schneiderman reports on his study of "nearly 100 cases of exemplary use of the PDCA (Plan-Do-Check-Act) cycle." These are some of his main findings:

- The rate of improvement was constant, which Schneiderman interprets in terms of the concept of "half-life." A half-life of 6 months for a process improvement activity means that there is a 50 percent reduction in defect level every 6 months. (p. 6)

- As process complexity increased, the rate of continuous improvement declined. This was especially true where the "complexity" was "organizational." "With multiple managers who are not part of the team and often have conflicting goals, the improvement process slows."(p. 11)

- The complexity of processes most in need of improvement in an organization increases with organizational level.

---

[3] See Michael Beer, "Developing an Organization Capable of Implementing Strategy and Learning," Harvard Business School mimeo, September 1994. On page 2, Beer writes that "70% of all corporations report that TQM has not lived up to their expectations (Spector and Beer, 1994)."

Success of the quality movement in Japan led to "the natural desire to move improvement activity to the ranks of management," but "QC Circles were trained to avoid, if possible, problems that involved human behavior, particularly when the behavior was that of others outside of the team, and to focus instead on machines, materials, and methods."(p. 21)

- TQM tools applied to complex management problems may produce a "false sense of rigor." They seem to "cut through the ambiguity that surrounds complex problems. But the ambiguity is real; it is the forced solution that is unreal."(p. 27) Managers like other workers "repeatedly make good decisions in complex situations based on their experience or gut feel...[Their solutions] are often better than the descriptions that we force-fit into our analytical frameworks."(p. 27) But managers are often caught in dilemmas they find unacceptable when their intuitions put them at odds with the consensual conclusion that has been reached by a TQM team.

- A more fundamental limit of TQM, as practiced today, is that it fails to address the dynamic interactions that exist in complex systems, interactions that make it difficult to answer questions about the relative importance of multiple causes of defects in a process. Top management struggles with critical processes in which causal linkages are at best obscure. Consider the proposition that "increasing compensation will reduce labor turnover." What if job satisfaction, not compensation, is the real issue, and employees, not wanting to burn their bridges, camouflage the real causes of unwanted attrition? Or consider the proposition that "centralization improves efficiency." Why, then, do most reorganizations follow a pendulum that swings between centralization and decentralization?

Schneiderman concludes that TQM, as presently practiced, is limited. He even leans toward Ackoff's argument (1981) that "most current processes are so outdated and incapable of being improved in a timely way that they should be scrapped and replaced with idealized redesigns." Nevertheless, he believes "the improvement process remains the same."(p. 35) He states that cross-functional problems of medium complexity can be remedied, in some cases, through the use of advanced TQM tools (the "7-management tools"), though "it is important to use them thoughtfully," and "we must remember that consensus doesn't always lead to the best answer." Finally, he suggests that highly complex, interactive, dynamic problems which "seem to create the greatest amount of pain both inside and outside our organizations," might yield to the increased use of simulation modeling. (p. 39)

Mallinger (1993) describes his experience as "change agent" in a company that proved relatively ineffective in its attempts to implement TQM. He spent a one-year sabbatical as participant/observer of a manufacturing division in a multibillion dollar Fortune 500 company. The corporate CEO, in response to financial and schedule pressures, announced a reorganization that drastically reduced management levels from 9 to 5 and cut management personnel by about 2000 people. The CEO then ordered the manufacturing division to implement TQM.

After 5 months of training and attempted implementation and an expenditure of $11 million, the TQM program was halted, Mallinger reports, because of "a noticeable lack of transfer of TQM skills presented in training to the rework and delivery schedule problems faced by the company."(p. 11)

A year later, with a much-reduced training staff, the TQM intervention was begun again on the basis of of an iterative approach to data gathering and intervention design. This time, a "lack of tribal knowledge" held by experienced managers, due in part to the lay-offs, led to a rise in skepticism about the process. Mallinger reports, based on numerous discussions with the division vice presidents, that TQM was not a priority and was seen, indeed, as an obstacle. "Although they each acknowledged the need for change, their actual behavior was quite different from their stated objectives."(p. 15) In one case a division vice president who indicated a desire to incorporate TQM as one of his five department goals for the year left a meeting after telling his human resource liaison staff to work out the plan to "fix my people." Apparently, the vice president saw TQM as a set of training techniques to improve the productivity of first-line managers rather than as a "commitment to mutual, proactive team planning." This individual seemed to think he would meet his obligation to be a TQM department, as ordered by the corporate CEO, by head count.

Middle managers also expressed skepticism and distrust, as indicated by comments such as, "Programs come and go around here, as do the people who support them." Shop floor people became increasingly discontented when the lay-offs began and advertised changes failed to occur. They felt their union leaders were joining their managers in taking them "down the road to hell." In one department, upper-level managers who had agreed to become active participants in the transformation process, dropped out of training meetings after the first hour of a twenty-four hour training program, claiming they had emergency meetings to attend. The first-level supervisors inferred that TQM had low priority for senior management and that they themselves had little value for the organization. They increased their skepticism of TQM and their distrust of their senior bosses. "No significant changes in performance within the business unit were reported two weeks, one month, or five months after training, and the intervention was curtailed."(p. 19)

As job insecurity increased with continuing lay-offs, the TQM team were increasingly seen as "hitmen on the prowl for fodder for the next round of reductions-in-force."

Mallinger reports further that he found no evidence that a "risk taking, empowered environment" was in place. On the contrary, he found a pervasive climate of fear. This was illustrated by a meeting that the TQM team head, the human resources general manager, and the human resources vice president held with the president to brief him on the progress of the Phase II TQM model. The primary agenda was to sell the TQM design to the president rather than address issues of resistance such as those just described. Mallinger states,

> The meeting took on a "we've got the answer now" message. I observed both the VP and GM agreeing with the president's philosophy and responding to each of his questions regarding TQM in a way that suggested that we've got the "bases covered." It was evident to me that the project leader, who made the presentation, was uncomfortable raising substantive issues for fear of embarrassing his bosses. (p. 23)

Mallinger's report of his own behavior at the meeting is also of interest. He states that he "felt a responsibility not to collaborate in the ruse" but was also careful not to discomfort the HR managers. In hindsight, though, he felt he should have been more direct. What he did was to

> ...indicate to the president that the culture may be resistant to the changes that TQM advocates. His response was immediate: "First you change the system, then the culture will follow."...The GM strongly agreed with the president, and the discussion of organizational culture ended."(p. 24)

The underlying meaning of what took place in the meeting, as Mallinger saw it, was to "not bring bad news to the President," a pattern he later observed at all levels of management.

The lessons Mallinger draws from this example are several. They include the need to form partnerships between the business unit under study and the elements outside it, to increase organization members' ownership of the TQM process by giving them greater input into its planning, and to encourage subordinates to engage in open discussion of troublesome issues in TQM implementation and in open expression of their fears and hopes for the process. However, Mallinger stops short of suggesting how, in corporate cultures like the one he observed, such lessons might actually be put into practice.

Roth's Study of Business Process Reengineering in Business Service Companies

George Roth's doctoral dissertation, written at MIT's Sloan School of Management (Roth, 1993), is a detailed analysis of attempts in two business service companies to improve productivity and quality of service through interventions that combined the introduction of new information technology with **Business Process Reengineering**. Roth defines this term, following CSC Index Inc., as "the concept of fundamentally changing the way work is performed in order to achieve radical performance improvements in speed, cost, and quality."

Roth undertook a year-long study of the introduction of imaging systems coupled with process reengineering in two insurance company subsidiaries. One of these, which he calls Dover Service Company, managed mutual fund investments for a financial services operation; the other, Harwick, provided service for life insurance policies. Both of these companies had similar work activities: processing paper-based information, answering customers' telephone inquiries, and performing business transactions on computer systems. Both were engaged in reengineering customer service and paper-processing operations through the development of imaging system applications which were intended to take the place of paper processing and were based on the same image system technology.

Roth organizes both of his studies around a stage model of the reengineering process that begins with strategy formulation and proceeds through phases of systems selection, preparation, implementation, and observation of use and outcomes. As he traces the development of the two projects through these stages, he describes the roles, activities, and views of four stakeholder groups:

1. *executives* (CEOs, presidents, COOs, and senior vice presidents), who had a role in formulating strategy and making decisions about imaging systems;
2. *managers*, who had line responsibility for daily business operations,
3. *technologists*, who were responsible for systems specification, development, installation, and operation, and
4. *workers*, the users of the imaging technology, who processed documents, responded to phone calls, and serviced customer requests.

Although the contexts of the two companies and their patterns of systems development and implementation are somewhat different, Roth's findings in the two cases are basically similar.

He finds in both studies that the anticipated benefits in service quality, speed, and productivity did not materialize. At Dover he writes,

> A year later in May 1993, there were many changes but little effect on technological change outcomes. Use of the new account imaging application never resumed. Managers were still uncertain of where imaging system benefits would occur and how they would have a greater role in specifying changes. The Processing Department was allowed to hire only one person and assigned one manager part-time to work on imaging system developments. A new project to front-end scan all incoming documents in the mail room was undertaken and completed. This imaging application provided good statistics and management reports, but it did not produce productivity benefits, and documents continued to be processed in paper form. (p. 167)

At Harwick, Roth reports on outcomes across some eight subprojects. Across the board, he writes, staffing levels in the two departments he focused on (Customer Service and Universal Life) were reduced by 23 percent, and "imaging system implementation effects on work, workers, and managers were not auspicious."(p. 244)

In Customer Service, Roth reports that one project, "UltraFind," designed to assist consultants in servicing customers over the phone, was found five months after implementation to provide capabilities required by "only one out of fifteen customer calls."(p. 249) and that "UltraFind was simply too slow to provide benefits for consultants' work."(p. 251) In the case of TIP, a paper processing system for company reps, Roth found that "reps required

3.3 times longer to process documents on TIP than to use paper documents and TAA (the preexisting system). (p. 256)

At Universal Life, an image processing application, ULIP (Universal Life Image Processing), replaced paper documents in workers' processing of cash items, franchise updates, loans, and the like. Roth reports that "workers' initial enthusiasm for ULIP waned when they were unable to process documents faster than their previous paper-based methods."(p. 261) Document processing time increased by a factor of 1.8, and questionnaire data showed "deterioration in workers' attitudes and work perceptions."(p. 265) Roth characterizes one application, CC (Correspondence Creation), designed to help word-processing workers by allowing them to select form letters from a menu, as successful. Correspondence consultants showed a 26 percent increase in productivity, and their responses to open-ended questions were more positive than those of any other workers. (p. 275) Roth points out, however, that these responses were the exception rather than the norm for workers and managers.

What is especially interesting is not so much that Roth found an absence of anticipated increases in measurable productivity, quality of service, and worker attitude and performance, outcomes that may or may not be typical of the consequences of most business process reengineering, but that he described the interactions among stakeholder groups in the reengineering processes to which he partly attributes the disappointing project outcomes. Roth states that,

> The two organizations' inabilities to create conditions in which stakeholders could communicate with one another led to fundamental difficulties in managing technological change and unexpected negative consequences. Stakeholders in technological change processes were unable to reconcile underlying assumptions, avoid miscommunications, or create shared meaning for imaging systems and their organizational implications. As a result, the more powerful stakeholder groups' ideas and agendas were promoted through imaging system activities. Technologists dominated the technological change process. (p. 299)

Roth gives many examples of what he means by "fundamental difficulties" of interaction. At Dover, for example, a line manager said that "he did not trust technologists because they withheld information and were unwilling to listen to his suggestions."(p. 157) He found that the technologists could not be influenced. He wanted his own specialists to help refine and adapt the application, but he was unable to secure resources for them to do so. Another manager complained that he relied on the technologists because they had chosen the imaging system and knew how to implement it, but "they applied [the system] broadly across the business process, without regard for whether it was appropriate, or for what business changes were required."(p. 158) Still another manager said that when change issues surfaced, "there was no process in place for deciding them," meetings were unsatisfactory (because they were dominated by technologists), and "there was no dialogue outside of the meetings."

What is striking about both of Roth's case examples is that, in spite of the disappointing data reported by managers and workers and independently ascertained by him, the top executives declared their projects to be resounding successes. Dwyer, the COO at Harwick, who had been hired to make organizational improvements, told Roth that "although she was aware of some difficulties," she believed that business objectives had been met, and she touted the project's success to the industry at large. At Dover, Bryant, the president, had a similarly positive evaluation of his reengineering project. Managers believed that Bryant held this view because he was fed only positive information; the problems were kept from him. They also believed that Bryant colluded with the masking of negative information because "he did not create conditions of intense scrutiny and involvement among his staff."(p. 138) And when lower-level managers tried to blow the whistle on this reporting process, they were punished. One manager said that she was floored when she saw a report indicating that the system had "98 percent up time," since she had her own experience of system failure. The technologist she first approached told her that, if she had problems with the reporting, she should call the project manager. When she did so, she was told that "it was reported that way because Craig (the CEO) wanted it that way." This manager concluded that Bryant had only received information that the project was going well and that the imaging system's problems and its real impact were never discussed at Bryant's staff meetings. The manager eventually "withdrew her attention from the imaging project because .. 'we aren't getting anywhere with [it] and I have other things to do.'"(p. 138)

Roth concludes his analysis as follows:

> Technologists had enough power in both organizations to coerce workers and managers to accept and use applications, but not enough power to assure applications' success. Technologists did, however, wield enough power to report mostly successful results despite contrary evidence in outcomes. (p. 302)

Beer's Study of His SHRM Intervention At Alpha Medical

Michael Beer's account of his intervention in the Alpha Medical Corporation (Beer, 1994) is an unusually full and frank exposition of an attempt to develop, not a one-time change, but an organization capable of the kind of "continuous learning" suited to "the kind of strategic change required by competitive forces."(p. 6) Beer deliberately sought to bring about the internalization of a continuing organizational learning process that would link "hard" and "soft" elements of the organization. In his view, such a process must be systemic and iterative; it must establish a partnership between upper and lower levels of the organization; and it must "find some means for making normally hidden organizational and managerial behavior transparent."(pp. 7–8) In short, Beer's intervention was directly addressed to the kinds of behavioral resistances the authors, cited earlier, said they encountered when they undertook or observed attempts to undertake interventions based on decentralization and management empowerment, TQM, or reengineering. It can also be seen as an attempt to create what Schein (1992) calls a "learning culture."

In Beer's Strategic Human Resource Management (SHRM) intervention, he hoped to link strategic change to a continuing process of organizational learning in the sense that "experience in implementing the new [strategic] design [would be] used to redesign the organization to align with limitations in human capabilities, or further changes in the environment discovered along the way."(p. 8) Beer began with "strategic profiling," and went on to assess "organizational ability to reframe and implement new strategy matched to changing business realities."(p. 9) These and later steps were conducted by an employee task force made up of "the unit's best employees one or two levels below the top team." This team operated within structures that were designed to promote the discussion of findings and issues that might otherwise remain undiscussable. In the early profiling meeting,

> While management listens, the [task force] sits in the middle of the room and discusses their findings [from investigations of the organization's ability to implement its new strategy], organized into themes. This "fishbowl" discussion, interrupted at the end of each theme for questions of clarification from the top management team, typically goes on for several hours. (p. 10)

The organizational diagnosis, jointly conducted by the task force and top management, went on to identify "key design levers and human resource policies within the unit, including the top team itself, which are at the root of the problems identified by the task force." Subsequently, the participants worked out a vision, philosophy of management, organizational design, and action plan for implementing and managing strategic change. (p. 11) Among the "barriers to implementation" identified in this process were several that Beer believes to have been "undoubtedly responsible" for the failure of such enabling interventions as total quality management, reengineering, and employee involvement, including unclear or conflicting strategic priorities; difficulties in how the top team works together, top-down management style, poor interfunctional/divisional coordination, poor up/down communication, and deficiencies in career development and management competencies.

Participants in the SHRM intervention reported that it "allowed us to discuss the undiscussable...[putting] things on the table that would have taken [us] years," giving rise along the way to a sense that "we didn't know what we were getting into" and anxious jokes about the messenger being shot. Beer believes that because the project's data had been generated by employees whom the managers had chosen as the best, the managers accepted the data "as valid and relevant, despite the fact that many issues point to their own effectiveness as managers."(p. 15)

Over the longer term, however, the outcomes of this intervention were viewed as mixed. Some intended objectives were achieved; others were not. Beer's surveys and interviews showed the following pattern: There was high commitment to the process of change at the top of the organization but less at the bottom (p. 16), and there was only modest change in overcoming barriers and accomplishing strategic tasks. The most change was in top-team effectiveness and cross-functional coordination; the least, in employee perception that top management rewards and promotes employees on the basis of their skill in managing and leading others and on their willingness to raise difficult issues with higher management.

Clearly Beer concludes, top management "had not created a partnership with employees and a sense of group responsibility for producing strategic results."(p. 18) SHRM remained invisible at lower levels of the organization and remained limited by "hierarchical assumptions about how decisions should be made."(p. 17) In all but a few instances, higher management did not review SHRM results and follow them up, mainly, Beer believes, because of "...their own discomfort and lack of skill in discussing difficult issues with subordinates."(p. 19) Beer observes that such discussion

....requires interpersonal competence and management values that the process itself is designed to develop...Though SHRM successfully opens a window for open dialogue, it apparently does not develop interpersonal and organizational capability to sustain that dialogue.(p. 20)

Beer's final word on his intervention is that a competitive world requires organizational capacity for self-design, which calls for management processes and skills to "engage in an open, fact-based conversation" about "difficult and often painful" issues. Such skills "have not yet been invented," he believes. They require "interpersonal behavior regarded by many managers as an 'unnatural act.'"(p. 22) It remains to be seen, he concludes, "whether these skills can be developed and/or whether organizations must obtain them through selection."(p. 23) In either case, Beer asserts that these are "core skills for an effective organization," whether managers and their consultants recognize them to be so, and "they will be in greater demand as organizational adaptability becomes important in a more competitive world."(p. 23)

Lessons from the Two Sets of Studies

The Two Gaps.

We have examined two sets of studies: the first deals with episodes in the lives of business firms in which organizational learning or adaptation occurred "naturally"; the second deals with interventions designed around various types of enablers that were intended to enhance organizational capability for productive learning.

The first set of studies (Van de Ven and Polley, Burgelman) reveal a *gap of explanation.* In both of the organizations studied, there were mixed results; there was some evidence of productive organizational learning, coupled with evidence that the organization had made only a partial or delayed response to data that could and should have been interpreted as calling for a significant change of course. Dynamically conservative, these organizations tended to persist in their previously established patterns of thought and action, and in so persisting, failed to act on what some of their members knew. During critical periods of decision, managers exhibited some patterns of inquiry that were distorted, overly constrained, and ineffective. The researchers take notice of these patterns, but they stop short of emphasizing or exploring them.

The two studies provide incomplete explanations of their mixed results. They do not fully explain first-order errors, such as the firm's failure to bring managerial attention to bear on signs of trouble that were known to insiders in the early stages of the TAP case, or in Burgelman's study, Intel's lagging response to the shift in the DRAM market and its competitive position in that market. They do not at all explain the second-order errors that underlie first-order errors, namely, how key managers remained individually and collectively unaware of the firm's lagging response to important mismatches between the assumptions that guided organizational action and the changing patterns of internal or external reality, and how the organization kept undiscussable the issues raised by knowledge already privately held by some of its members.

The second set of studies (of decentralization during the Cordiner regime at GE, Activity-Based Costing, TQM, Reengineering, and SHRM) reveals a *gap of implementation.* The studies show that mixed results also followed from attempts to introduce enablers of productive organizational learning, that is, techniques and information systems (ABC), new formal structures (decentralization and flattening, creation of inquiry units, as in SHRM), principles and procedures for the development of a learning culture (TQM, Reengineering, and SHRM). These interventions resulted in only partial or temporary improvement in organizational performance. For example, Cordiner's introduction of decentralization at GE was subverted, over time, by organizational games of authority, deception, and control. The diffusion of Activity-Based Costing was stymied by the defenses it stimulated on the part of managers who were threatened or embarrassed by the information it would bring to light. The study of TQM interventions showed a declining rate of improvement in performance where the issues involved problems of behavior, such as conflicting goals and interests held by multiple managers, especially at higher levels of the hierarchy.

The studies of TQM, Reengineering, and SHRM document the gap of implementation. Some of them (Beer, Schneiderman) point directly to the importance of constrained and/or distorted organizational inquiry but offer no general theory to account for it. In some instances, the researchers suggest hypotheses to account for the observed results of the interventions they studied, but their attempts to explain mixed outcomes by reference to cognitive limitations, interest theory, management values, and political games are only partly satisfactory. These hypotheses do not fully explain the first-order errors the researchers have identified in their cases. And they do not at all explain the second-order errors *we* find in their cases: the organization's being unaware of its inability to act on what it knew or to detect and correct error.

We have argued that the mixed outcomes and the limits of productive learning revealed by both groups of studies are attributable to the persistence of Model O-I learning systems, reinforced by the Model I theories-in-use of individuals whose thought and action are partly constrained by these systems. Under conditions of embarrassment or threat, these O-I systems distort processes of organizational inquiry. They give rise to defensive routines that block inquiry, they make critically important issues and dilemmas undiscussable, they prevent organizations from acting on what some of their members know, and they reinforce organizational awareness of the ability to detect and correct error.

We turn now to a discussion of the implications of our analysis for the principal challenges to a theory of productive organizational learning. We explore how our theory-of-action account of the gaps of explanation and implementation bears on the several doubts raised by learning skeptics about organizational learning:

1. its meaningfulness,
2. its desirability,
3. the capability of real-world organizations to engage in productive versions of it, and
4. the efficacy of interventions aimed at enhancing it.

The Paradox of "Organizational Learning"

The meaning of "organizational learning" hinges, as we have seen, on the crucial issue of the levels of aggregation at which organizational phenomena are described and explained and at which prescriptions for organizational action are directed. Our analyses of the two groups of studies show that one cannot account for the observed higher-level phenomena of organizational learning, that is, those that seem important to researchers concerned with strategy making or technological innovation, without referring to individual and interpersonal processes of inquiry. The feedback loops contained in our cause-maps and models of O-I learning systems show crucially important causal linkages among three levels of aggregation: interpersonal inquiry, interactions among organizational subunits, and the patterns of action and learning characteristic of whole organizations. We have argued that we should also treat as organizational the kinds of processes that shape the phenomena we take to be organizational in the first instance.

Unless we refer to the level of interpersonal inquiry, we cannot:

    a. explain the empirically discovered phenomena of limited organizational learning,

    b. resolve plausible but conflicting explanatory hypotheses about limited organizational learning,

    c. produce an explanation useful for redesigning practices so as to overcome barriers to productive organizational learning.

The Meaning of "Productive" Organizational Learning

What do these examples of mixed results tell us about the nature of productive, especially double-loop, organizational learning?

They indicate the occurrence of some double-loop changes in organizational outcomes at the level of theory of action. But these changes are only temporary (one-shot) or affect only a part of the organization or affect only some key values and assumptions of organizational theory of action and not others. In both groups of examples, the organization's theory-in-use for organizational inquiry did not undergo double-loop change. Although in Beer's case the intervenor did seek to inject Model II values into organizational inquiry, the injection did not last beyond the period of intervention.

It is clear, then, that it is possible for limited double-loop learning to occur at the level of outcomes in organizational theory of action without double-loop learning in processes of organizational inquiry. We have argued that whatever values may be espoused for organizational learning—single-loop, instrumental improvement in organizational performance, or double-loop change in the criteria by which organizational improvement is measured—their sustained achievement depends on the organization's continuing ability to engage in double-loop organizational inquiry. The Model II values that govern double-loop organizational inquiry are essential to the sustained achievement of other criteria for productive learning, for example, sustained and timely adaptive learning in technological innovation (Van de Ven and Polley), the timely reconciliation of formal strategy with a changing strategic situation (Burgelman), or the maintenance of the productive effects of enablers, such as decentralization and management empowerment (as in Cordiner at GE), or of structures for enhanced organizational inquiry (as in Beer's SHRM intervention).

The Model II values that govern double-loop organizational inquiry are foundational to sustained productive organizational learning. By the same token, as we have shown in each of the studies we have discussed, double-loop organizational inquiry with its Model II values is required in order to disrupt the defensive routines that preserve the organizational status quo in situations of ambiguity or uncertainty by keeping threatening issues undiscussable and by keeping participants unaware of how they help to perpetuate those routines.

Our emphasis on Model II values for double-loop inquiry does not obviate the issue of learning for evil ends. In any given instance, the objectives of organizational learning and the values that inform those objectives must be examined. We would argue, however, that double-loop inquiry, which seeks to illuminate issues and dilemmas we might otherwise suppress or of which we might otherwise remain unaware, offers the most likely route to such examination.

Threats to Productive Organizational Learning

In Chapter 8 we discussed three kinds of threats: to coherent organizational action, to cognitive capability for learning, and to effective implementation of lessons drawn from experience.

The issue of *coherence* arises in several of the cases we analysed in this chapter, most obviously in Van de Ven and Polley's and Burgelman's cases. In all of these cases, there was evidence of incoherence in relationships between middle and top management, as well as among divisions at the level of middle management. Top and middle managers or divisions such as R&D and Fabrication, diverged from one another, enacted contrary policies, or engaged in a kind of parallel play, pursuing independent policies without coordination. Burgelman now argues that in the early stages of his example this lack of coherence proved actually to be useful since it allowed DRAM development to go on beyond the point when at least some people in the company clearly saw that Intel no longer had a competitive edge in the DRAM business. The result was that the company could eventually take advantage of the unanticipated benefits of that development for the microprocessor business that it was (by then) coming to see as the wave of the future. In this case, if we accept Burgelman's analysis, a vein of technological development undertaken for the sake of one business proved unexpectedly to be useful for another business. Such things happen. But the outcome might have been less rosy. At crucial moments in Van de Ven and Polley's story of the TAP development and in Roth's story of Business Process Reengineering at Dover and Harwick, analogous situations arose when TAP's development and the reengineering processes continued beyond the points at which they should have been subjected to critical scrutiny. In these instances, according to the authors, the results were negative.

What lessons should we draw from such occurrences? We certainly should not conclude that all programs of technological development undertaken for the sake of a business now seen as obsolescent should be continued because they might turn out to be useful for another business. On what basis, then, should one distinguish projects worth supporting from those that ought not to be supported? Even to raise this question is to pose the issue of awareness. If organizational inquirers are not aware of an existing incoherence in policies enacted by different levels or groups of managers and if they are not capable of subjecting that incoherence to public scrutiny, then how could such discriminaton be made? In both the Van de Ven and Polley and Burgelman cases, managerial awareness and public discussion of disjointed policies would have required double-loop inquiry into the issues that provoked threat or embarrassment and triggered organizational defensive routines—inquiry comparable to the inquiry undertaken by the CEO and directors of the management consulting firm described in Chapter 7. The incoherence that might be taken as evidence of lack of capability for productive learning in real-world organizations, giving rise to generalizations of the kind that March and like-minded scholars have proposed, could also be seen—and is in fact seen, from the theory-of-action perspective—as an occasion for double-loop inquiry.

All of the cases we have considered in this chapter provide evidence that could be attributed to *limited cognitive capability for productive organizational learning.* The question is how we ought to interpret this evidence.

In several of these cases, threats to valid inference arose. ιn most of them, uncertainty and ambiguity surrounded the causes of some critically important effects of organizational action. In some instances (Intel), managers faced with uncertainty fell into competence traps or engaged in superstitious learning. In other instances (TAP), managers failed to focus concerted attention on signs of trouble that ought to have cast doubt on the assumptions that underlay established organizational policies. In most of the cases of attempts to introduce enablers to improve organizational capability for productive learning, managers persisted in a course of action about which some members of the organization had significant grounds for doubt, yet the information and interpretations held by these managers did not give rise to a concerted, public critique of the assumptions that underlay organizational action.

Should we argue, as March and others have done, that such instances of first-order error provide further evidence for the general proposition that organizations lack cognitive capability for productive learning from experience? Our position is that such instances do not, of themselves, reveal limited cogitive capability. Rather, a close inspection of the evidence compiled by the authors of the case studies reveals a pattern of organizational defenses that reinforce a prevailing blindness to first-order error, a blindness that makes such errors uncorrectable and their underlying, mistaken assumptions self-sealing. The question of cognitive capability must remain moot since during the time periods in question, the fact that organization members were unaware of or unwilling to discuss the relevant issues, prevented the organization from applying to them whatever cognitive capabilty it had. There is, indeed, some evidence, from the authors' account of patterns of inquiry carried out in the later stages of the Intel and the TAP cases, that both organizations possessed the ability to engage in complex and refined exercises of error detection, causal analysis, and error correction.

There is, of course, no guarantee that if the managers in these cases had been aware of their first-order errors and had subjected them to public discussion and critical analysis, they would have succeeded in correcting them. In the world of management, as of science, there is no guarantee against persistent error. But there is also no a priori reason to attribute persistent first-order error to the limits of cognitive capability *when there is manifest evidence that a prevailing pattern of defensive behavior blocks the exercise of that capability, whatever its strengths or limitations may be.* The much more important issue raised by our analysis of the case material is the need and potential for double-loop inquiry into the patterns of second-order error, the limited learning systems whose persistence makes first-order error unassailable. This issue is central to the gap of implementation and critical to the design of interventions aimed at enabling productive organizational learning.

Moreover, from the perspective of scholarly research on organizational learning, a robust test of propositions about the cognitive capability of organizations depends on making organizational actors aware of, and helping them to overcome, the defenses that blind them to first-order errors. For in the absence of such an intervention, how could one tell whether an organization's vulnerability to such threats to valid inference as competence traps and superstitious learning is due to the organization's limited cognitive capability or to the effects of its organizational defensive routines?

Conceivably, researchers might argue along the lines of the behavioral theory of the firm that defensive routines are unalterable facts of organizational life that should be "folded into" the attribution of limited cognitive capability. We would agree that patterns of organizational defensiveness are widespread and deeply embedded in the behavioral worlds of organizations. But an intervention of the kind reported in Chapter 7 and others like it (see Argyris, 1990, 1993), stand as existence proofs of the possibility of double-loop inquiry that breaks through the constraints of O-I behavioral worlds. In the wide-ranging universe of organizational life, such episodes must be counted as rare events. Nevertheless, they cast doubt on the validity of any general attribution of limited cognitive capability and point the way to future programs of intervention and research.

Overcoming Impediments to Productive Organizational Learning

Our analysis of case material related to decentralization, TQM, Activity-Based Costing, Reengineering, and SHRM, indicates that organizational enablers can induce productive organizational learning, leading even to temporary double-loop outcomes at the level of organizational theory-in-use, when the issues are neither embarrassing nor threatening. But under conditions of embarrassment or threat, we find that the O-I learning systems of the organizations tend over time to subvert the enabling interventions.

We believe that our analysis helps to explain the characteristic life cycles of such organizational fixes as TQM, Flat Organization, Reengineering, and Management Empowerment. In each such instance, a prescription for organizational reform appears on the horizon, supported by plausible-sounding theory and stories of successful implementation by early adopters. Often at the core of the reform there lies a significant insight, for example, managers *should* be freed up to take on greater responsibility and make greater use of local knowledge, or organizational processes *should* be rethought in the light of the possibilities opened up by advanced information technology. Usually, however, the prescription is converted by its advocates and the consultants who undertake its dissemination into a readily understandable package of procedures. Not infrequently, the package is accompanied by an ideology that takes on quasi-religious overtones. Organization managers, thirsty for solutions to the persistent predicaments in which they find themselves and impatient with calls to wrestle with the complexity of the predicaments or with their own possible collusion in reinforcing them, latch onto the package. A bandwagon effect ensues as managers adopt the package because managers around them are adopting it. Then over time, as experience with the reform builds up and as good intentions are subverted by organizational defensive routines and their associated Model I theories-in-use, a literature of disillusionment begins to appear. Then normal cynicism begins to reassert itself. Lower-level managers begin to mutter that those at the top never really meant it, and top-level managers express frustration at the intractable resistance to change exhibited by those below them. People begin to say, "We tried that!" and a readiness for the next reform package begins to take shape.

Nevertheless, as we have argued, there are examples of rare events in which individual members of organizations show themselves willing and able to engage the complexity of the limited learning systems in which they operate, to examine their own skilled contributions to the maintenance of those systems, and to learn to move toward the Model II values, strategies, and assumptions that enable them to disrupt prevailing organizational defensive routines. Perhaps as Beer and others have suggested, some managers who have not experienced such rare events but have experienced the reforms described in literatures of disillusionment are growing in readiness to wrestle with complexity and to explore the patterns of thought and action through which they contribute to their own disillusionment.

These conclusions hold important implications for practice and research.

Practitioners who want to increase their organization's capability for continuing productive learning, especially of the double-loop variety, should learn to improve the performance of organizational inquiry, which requires double-loop learning in their own theories-in-use.

Researchers who want only to explain the phenomena of limited organizational learning should attend to the directly observable data of organizational inquiry which must, in turn, be linked to higher levels of aggregation. This strategy of attention is all the more appropriate for researchers who want to produce usable knowledge that can help practitioners build organizational capability for productive learning. In both cases, researchers would do well to reframe their research as action research undertaken in collaboration with practitioners who seek to build capability for enhancing and expanding the rare events of productive organizational learning.

10

Strategy and Learning: Making Prescriptions Actionable by Wim Overmeer

The Split in the Field of Strategic Management

The field of strategic management addresses the problems of managing dynamic changes in the relationship between a firm's actions and its environment. Over the last two decades, even the largest and most venerable firms have experienced difficulties in responding to shifts in their environments. Those authors in the field of strategic management who are interested in advising managers about the strategic problems of their firms have become increasingly polarized around two very different sets of ideas for strategy making.

The older view, exemplified by the work of Kenneth Andrews and Michael Porter, prescribes a *rational* process of strategy making. It holds that a firm can dominate and harvest a selected environmental niche by attending to the dominant factors that govern the behavior of the niche and by seeking a close fit between corporate action and the niche environment. The strategic task of the corporate office is twofold. The first task is to make a cross-sectional analysis of the environment and formulate a corporate strategy. The next is to position the firm as a whole, coordinating its actions and administering its strategy through an orderly process of implementation that consists in rearranging organizational structures and processes.

The opposite view, exemplified by the work of Henry Mintzberg, describes a *natural* process of strategy making that takes the form of an interplay between deliberate and emergent processes. It shows, using longitudinal studies of the changing patterns of behavior through which the firm responds to environmental change, that managers anywhere in a firm may craft a new business strategy, an emerging strategy. When the misfit between the environment and the firm's formally established pattern of action (the deliberate strategy) becomes too large, the firm will draw on its stock of emerging strategies to construct a new configuration, thereby establishing a new fit with the environment, leading to a new deliberate strategy.

These two perspectives take polar positions on the relation between thinking and doing. The first view focuses on formulating a strategic intent and planning how to accomplish it. It is based on the assumption that a firm's strategy should be made explicit and should be deliberated prior to taking action to assure its effectiveness in the face of otherwise overwhelming complexity and chaos. The second view holds that "intent is cheap"; that planners "too often cry wolf," numbing the sensitivity of managers to signs of discontinuous change; and that "the paraphernalia of the strategy industry" (i.e., the recommendations made by strategists) get in the way of the process by which individual managers anywhere in the organization may creatively respond to changes in the environment.

Yet, at the end of the day, despite their radically different positions on strategy making, proponents of both perspectives hold two assumptions in common. The first is that strategy making is grounded in an *artistic* sense, that of either the CEO who functions as "the architect of corporate purpose" (Andrews, 1980, pp. 11 and 129), or the creative manager who operates as a "craftsman" of strategy (Mintzberg, 1987). Both metaphors, of "architect" and "craftsman," are associated with the notion that managers "can do more than they can tell" (Polany, 1957; Schön, 1983). The second shared assumption is the requirement for an explicit corporate strategy. Even Mintzberg acknowledges that the development of emergent strategies depends on the guidance provided by an umbrella strategy or a formulation of overall mission. Beyond these common assumptions, proponents of both views, faced with major shifts in corporate environments, have converged more recently on a shared prescription: the imperative of strategic learning. In their recent attention to this imperative, they suggest different mechanisms of strategic learning—the selection of internally generated variations (Burgelman, 1983), the interaction between strategy formulation and its implementation (Andrews, 1980), or the interaction between deliberate and emergent strategy (Mintzberg, 1987).

However, neither the "rational" nor the "natural" theorists of strategy making have been articulate about how to bring about the interactions they take, respectively, to be essential to strategic learning or how to overcome barriers to their achievement. Neither side has much to say about what managers would actually do when they follow its prescriptions or what ensuing problems they might expect to encounter. The action proposals of the authors on both sides seem to have been afterthoughts of theorizing; they are described as though they were self-evident, if only the right prescriptions were followed or if only managers were able to manage without interference. While strategic learning stands (within the first view) for a change in plans and for a change in patterns of corporate behavior (within the second)[1], neither view gives much emphasis to the problem of realizing strategy: framing strategic intent and taking action to bring intention to reality. Both views display a particular inattentiveness to mismatches between intent and realization and offer little to guide our thinking about them.

Inattentiveness to the Gap Between Intent and Realization
The rational view presents the realization of strategy as a process of imposing strategic intent through the implementation of a comprehensive strategy; it assumes that strategic intentions, and designs for their achievement, will not be challenged in the course of implementation. A theory of action perspective would lead us to ask, "To what extent does a given design actually realize a particular strategic intention? How do designers get to know about mismatches between intent and realization? And how do they respond to these mismatches as they implement their design?" More generally, we would ask, "How do designers test their design in action, and how good is the test?"

Consider, for instance Doz & Prahalad (1987), in which the authors report on the research that subsequently led to the idea of "strategic intent" (Hamel & Prahalad, 1989). The authors found that some managers, in newly created product divisions of large, geographically dispersed, multinational firms, had developed a vision about the nature of Japanese competition. These managers started working toward legitimizing their vision by "undermining the legitimacy of prevalent conventional wisdom" (based on regional organizations). They "would not always discuss their vision openly" because they felt that, within the existing behavioral world of their organizations, their ideas were "too tentative and too fragile." Rather than "sell their vision," they created a sense of impending crisis by

---

[1] Both are a version of "win, stay; lose, change is enough" (Weick, 1979).

"emphasizing and reinterpreting performance decline". A theory of action perspective would predict that such "subversive"[2] organizational tactics would reinforce the existing behavioral world of the firms (low trust, low risk taking, high levels of competitiveness) and would lead to unrealistic designs for organizational action whose implementation would be marred by the very organizational dynamics the users of the tactics were trying to circumvent.[3]

The natural view of strategy making focuses on emerging strategies[4] that respond to environmental change; it assumes that the managers who develop these strategies, like potters crafting a vase, have tacit knowledge about them or private ways of enacting them that cannot be made explicit. During a revolutionary episode, various ideas naturally merge into a new gestalt that becomes, retroactively, the new deliberate strategy of the firm. From a theory of action perspective, we would ask questions such as, How are emergent strategies actually kept "dormant," or "in check," until a revolutionary change occurs? Which emergent strategies are drawn on, which are not, and how is this selection managed? How are several emergent strategies integrated during an episode of change? How do one or more pent up, emergent strategies disseminate quickly, at what cost, and through what kinds of "mutual adaptation" among managers? More generally, we would ask, What organizational practices are used during episodes of revolutionary strategic change, and what are the unintended consequences of their use?

Consider Quinn (1980), who explicitly rejects formal planning based on the rational view on the grounds that important strategic decisions take place outside of rigid planning systems. He advocates

---

[2] From a personal conversation with Yves Doz during the Strategic Management Conference in Cambridge, UK, December 1990; further worked out in Doz & Thanheizer (1992).

[3] This is confirmed by the organizational problems later experienced by Philips, one of the firms studied by Doz and Prahalad. The author of this chapter discussed this point with Philips' internal organizational consultants at the time. The internal consultants reported that, after "the matrix was tilted" by the CEO, reallocating formal authority from the general managers of "national organizations" to general managers of "product division," the new Product Division heads began to act like the heads of the "national organizations," that is, like "barons."

[4] The "variations" or "mutations" created in the "reproductive system."

(p.129) that top managers should follow a few proposals through their informal networks. He goes on to say that they should

> encourage concepts they favor, let undesired or weakly supported options die through inaction, and establish hurdles or tests for strongly favored ideas they might not agree with but did not want to oppose directly, [and] kill options through subordinates rather than directly.

The theory of action perspective would predict that this kind of top management behavior is likely to be replicated by emergent strategy managers and to generate a highly politicized game not unlike what happens in the formal planning system it tries to remedy.

In order to bridge the gap between design and implementation inherent in the rational view, and the gap between emergent and deliberate strategy inherent in the evolutionary framework, one would have to deal with the kinds of questions raised earlier. Yet the proponents of neither the rational nor the natural view have done so. They have been selectively inattentive to the ways in which their advice may create organizational dynamics that undermine that very advice. The rational view studies best practices in various firms in order to distill lessons, which it then introduces as broad guidelines for action or as generic principles on which specific strategies ought to be modeled. The natural view focuses on patterns of corporate behavior over time, often drawing on information from archives studied in retrospect. Within each perspective, the authors, such as Doz and Prahalad or Quinn, spot organizational defensive routines. However, they ignore the impact their advice is likely to have on existing organizational dynamics informed by those routines.

By leaving out what actually happens during the implementation of strategy (within the rational view) or during the integration of emergent and deliberate strategy (within the evolutionary view) and without helping managers to address these issues, both perspectives tend to ignore a crucial element of strategic management: the *realtime* microactions through which managers respond to the challenges to implementation or integration that are likely to arise when the environment and strategy of a corporation undergo major change. As a result, both views tend to be inattentive to the defensive routines, individual or organizational, that are prevalent during the implementation of a strategy or the integration of an emerging with a deliberate strategy. As we will illustrate in this chapter, such defensive routines have a profound impact on an organization's ability to realize its strategic intent and engage in strategic learning.

Realizing Strategy As Probing the Environment

How, then, from the prospective point of view of practicing managers, shall we think about a process of strategy making that encompasses realization as well as intent?

First, a firm's strategy making is grounded in its managers' artistic sense of a changing environment. Because managers may see and do more than they can tell, their strategic designs may not be fully articulated. This is not to say that managers should not try to make their ideas about strategy explicit or that they cannot succeed in articulating them to the point where others can understand and comment on them. In response to the helpful inquiry of others, managers may learn to articulate their ideas more fully, frame them as hypotheses, and test them publicly. Moreover, as a strategic design is enacted, it becomes more susceptible to articulation and testing.

Second, major trends in the contemporary, globalizing environment of corporations have the effect of increasing the rate and complexity of nontrivial change. For instance, the integration of generative technologies, such as computers, semiconductors, and telecommunications, leads to new and unexpected products, indeed, to whole new industries, and, in turn, either calls for the drastic restructuring of existing industries or makes them obsolescent. The trends of market deregulation, privatization of government-owned firms, and retreat of governments from many sectors of the economy remove many of the layers of protection on which firms could traditionally rely, even as they may create new layers of protection. The competitive landscape is being transformed by the appearance of strong competition from newly industrialized countries; the imposition of General Agreement on Trade and Tariffs (GATT) rules; the creation of regional trade blocks such as the North American Free Trade Agreement (NAFTA), the European Union (EU); the Association of South East Asian Nations (ASEAN); and the opening of emerging markets like China, India, and Indonesia. These trends, by themselves and in combination, create increasingly complex corporate environments in which managers find themselves unable to make full and accurate predictions about the nature and the rate of change or about likely organizational responses to such change. These phenomena give a new meaning to the familiar observation that human beings, limited in their capacity to process information, are subject to bounded rationality (Cyert and March, 1963).

Third, the interaction of artistic responses of managers at various levels of the firm within an increasingly complex and fast-changing environment, gives rise to a strategic "conversation" between the firm and its environment. It makes sense to think of a firm as engaging in a reciprocal transaction with its environment through which it takes stock of a new environmental situation, "speaks" to that situation through the design and implementation of new strategic moves, and receives (at times) surprising "back talk" from the environment, in response to which it is led to rethink its appreciation of the environment and to restructure its strategy.

Fourth, managers who are part of such a strategic conversation are sometimes compelled to make moves in real time in response to changing situations that turn out to be inconsistent with strategic intent in a way that the rational approach does not explain. Sometimes managers make moves that do not result in completed behavior and, therefore, do not constitute emergent behavior. Nevertheless they learn lessons that may have an important influence on how they think about the firm's strategies and its possible future moves, in a way that the natural approach does not explain.

Fifth, inconsistent moves (e.g., discovery of an error or a surprising response from customers) and incomplete moves (e.g., an unexpected nontariff barrier to entry into a foreign market) may have for a firm's strategy consequences that have to be constructed and assessed through an organizational process geared to strategic learning.

Sixth, where managers may see or do more than they can tell, where they have limited capacity to process information, where their moves may be inconsistent with their articulated intentions, and where they may learn from incomplete moves, the realization of strategy should be framed as *a probe* into the corporate environment. The idea of a probe, an exploratory move into the environment, alerts managers to the possibility that the realization of strategy may yield new, nontrivial information, first, about what the designers saw but could not fully tell, and, second, about previously unappreciated features of the environment that must now be taken into account.

Seventh, the realization of strategy therefore involves a second-order design process: not only should the design of a strategy be considered and tested as a hypothesis about the firm's environment, but the resulting strategic action should itself be treated as a probe into that environment, potentially revealing new information about that environment and about the designer's ideas. This reframing of the strategy-making process, as one in which actions taken to realize strategy are also seen as design moves and exploratory probes, begins to undo the long-standing dichotomy between strategy formulation and strategy implementation, or between intended and emergent strategy.

Framing the realization of a new strategy as a probe into the environment means that designers and implementors of strategy should not only impose their intended strategy on a given corporate situation but should also remain open to new information about the environment that may require nontrivial changes in strategy. This framing calls for an active stance on the part of:

1. designers, who should seek information to test, and especially to disconfirm, their reasoning about the environment,

2. implementors, who should seek information to test whether the firm's actions actually realize strategic intent, and

3. designers and implementors together, who should seek information that could lead to nontrivial changes in strategy, so as to pursue the new opportunities that emerge or the new challenges that present themselves.

Hence, "realization of strategy" conveys not only the idea of "implementation" (literally, "arranging the tools"), but also the idea of "becoming aware," or "discovery."

Requirements for Organizational Learning

Framing the realization of a new strategy as a probe into the environment is distinctly different from seeing it as merely imposing strategic intent through rigorous implementation or as behavioral adaptation to a change in the environment through trial-and-error learning. In the former, intent is seen as a given, once it has been established; in the latter, intent is seemingly ignored. Both of these approaches rest on the key assumption that new information will not challenge explicit or implicit intentions or how the actors think about pursuing their enactment. As a result, both approaches run two significant risks. First, managers may ignore information that points to mismatches between intention and action, especially those that cannot be corrected by a mere change in strategies of instrumental action (that is, single-loop learning, within the theory of action perspective). Second, very sensitive managers who may be aware of such information and equally aware that a change in behavior will not be sufficient to deal with it may become exasperated to find that they do not know how to think beyond merely changing behavior. The idea of strategy as a probe into the environment tries to remedy this state of affairs by specifically leaving open the possibility that strategic intent, and how the actors think about its realization can and should be challenged.

Framing realization of strategy as a probe calls for a proactive process of organizing joint monitoring, evaluation, and inquiry on the part of both designers and implementors. This process of organizational inquiry or corporate inquiry (if it takes place in a corporation and cuts across strategic business units) needs to be actively pursued, and it is different from merely receiving feedback. Organizational inquiry, consisting in actively constructing and sorting out puzzles generated in the process of probing, is essential to the firm's strategic conversation with its environment and central to the fostering of strategic learning. From the rational perspective, such organizational inquiry requires interpenetrating processes of strategy design and implementation through the joint reflection of designers and implementors on the strategy they have realized and the puzzles it contains. From the natural perspective, it requires those who work from or within the deliberate strategy of the firm to engage in joint reflection with those who are involved in developing emergent strategies.

In order to create an organizational environment conducive to such inquiry and to strategic learning, the members of the organization must be able to *learn strategically*. This means that managers should learn to create an organizational environment in which

1. designers who see more than they can tell are encouraged and helped to make their ideas explicit, so as to test them rather than withhold them,

2. implementors are encouraged and helped to surface their questions about the design and their worries about implementation, rather than withhold their contributions and concerns, and

3. both designers and implementors are helped to see that they are subject to bounded rationality and must, therefore, actively seek out evidence during the realization of strategy that may disconfirm their reasoning and lead to new information about the environment.

Under these conditions, it is possible for an organization to rely on and develop the artistic sense of its managers.

While organizational inquiry of this kind does sometimes happen in practice or, at least, designers and implementors do attempt to engage in it, it is not nearly as self-evident or automatic as the literature tends to assume.[5] Its exploration is crucially important for

---

[5] It is only self-evident and automatic to the extent that single-loop and deuterosingle-loop learning have become an institutionalized ability of the best firms.

researchers who are interested in helping practicing managers set and solve the problems they experience in realizing strategy.

It is here that the theory-of-action perspective on organizational learning can be helpful. In contemporary corporate environments, both designers and implementors are increasingly confronted with challenging, nontrivial information that questions important design assumptions and policies for implementation and thereby challenges the competence of designers and implementors. The theory-of-action perspective predicts that both designers and implementors are likely to experience such challenges as potentially threatening and embarrassing. In a Model I world, threatening or embarrassing information tends to trigger individual defenses and lead to the emergence of organizational defensive routines. These, in turn, add new levels of complexity to an already complex strategic situation. They may prevent managers from jointly reflecting on the efficacy of the strategy and keep them from discovering new information about the corporate environment. Hence, the managers may not perceive emerging opportunities and challenges that call for a rethinking of the strategy or its implementation. Defensive routines may lead to a disjunction between processes of design and implementation which may, in turn, lead to further distancing between designers and implementors and to unilateral attempts by the designers to get at important information, bypassing the implementors and setting the stage for a new layer of defenses. Such a process may make the productive interplay between design and implementation increasingly difficult.

In the following sections the idea of realizing strategy as a probe into the corporate environment will be illustrated, and the consequent requirements for organizational learning will be outlined. Strategic and organizational change will be discussed in the case of a firm I called "Citadel," a firm with a long history of strategic probing and learning.

The Outside-in View: Citadel's Theory-in-use for Probing the Environment

In the early 1980s, Citadel, a renowned, medium-sized real estate development firm, experienced a major shift in its environment which led it to abandon its long-standing program of low-income housing and enter into a new field, the development and management of hotels. At the same time, Citadel chose to continue developing luxury office buildings. It's new hotel group, which planned and operated the hotels, and its project management group, which supervised hotel construction, were soon involved in a series of minor disagree-

*ments. By the mid-1980s, these had escalated into major organizational con-
flicts that embroiled most senior managers, sapped their energy, and led them
to feel a loss of creative energy and strategic control over the firm.*

*Citadel's top management framed this problem as a conflict between
the two divisions and began to look for changes in organizational structure
that would alleviate it. Preliminary talks revealed that middle managers in the
two divisions saw themselves as locked in contention over incompatible differences in real estate development practice. The hotel group wanted to build
"cookie-cutter" hotels; the project management group favored "unique" office buildings. According to the hotel group managers, Citadel had a revolutionary concept for hotel development, and they thought the company should
take immediate advantage of its window of opportunity in the hotel market.
The project management group argued, on the contrary, that Citadel "was
about" and, therefore, ought to focus on large-scale, luxury office projects
that might also hold a hotel project.*

*An investigation carried out by the researcher (Overmeer) in cooper-
ation with Citadel's strategic planner, revealed that members of the two
groups could not resolve their differences and that each group, in its daily
work, felt threatened or embarrassed by the demands imposed by the other.
The same inquiry revealed that conflict between two development practices,
analogous to hotels and project management, had been a recurrent theme in
Citadel's history, going back at least to the early 1960s. As these conflicts
flared up episodically, they would trigger defensive actions and reactions that
reinforced one another, giving rise to further eruptions of conflict.
Increasingly, this pattern of defensive behavior had come to inhibit the productive interplay between strategy designers and implementors, undermining
the quality of the firm's probes into the environment, the strategic choices
available to it, and the capability for strategic learning that had made it a formidable competitor in the past.*

*In order to get beneath the differences between groups of senior man-
agers, the researcher created a map in which he plotted similar, completed development projects over time (see figure on page 262). This was a first step in
his attempt to construct the firm's theory-in-use for strategy making. The map
showed a remarkably rich, complex, and consistent pattern characteristic of
Citadel's strategic conversation with its shifting environment. Within this conversation, Citadel's multiple probes into the environment seemed to be governed by a limited number of rules, of which the most important were the
following:*

1. *Each group of similar projects represented a quick and early strategic move in response to a Federal or local government initiative.*

2. *Within a given group of projects, individual projects existed at different stages of development, which allowed lessons from earlier*

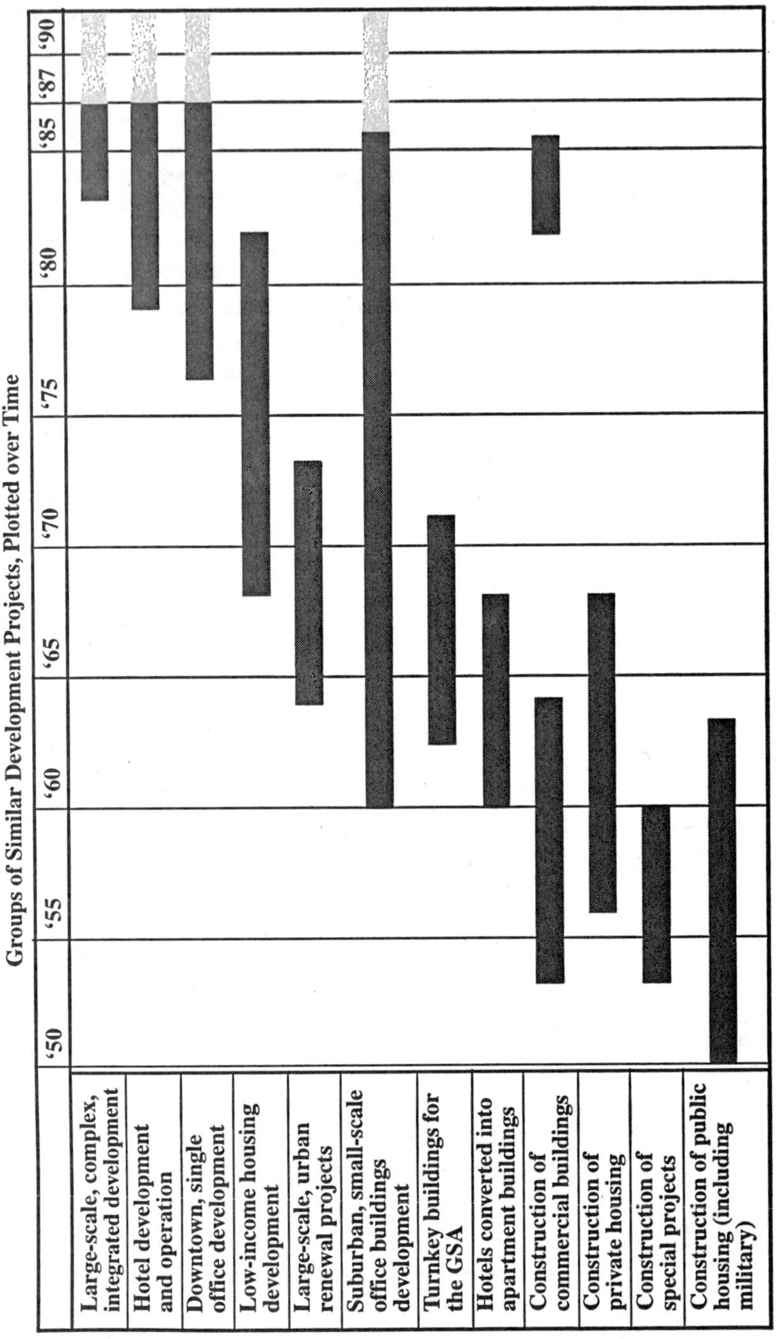
Groups of Similar Development Projects, Plotted over Time
'50
'55
'60
'65
'70
'75
'80
'85
'87
'90
Large-scale, complex, integrated development
Hotel development and operation
Downtown, single office development
Low-income housing development
Large-scale, urban renewal projects
Suburban, small-scale office buildings development
Turnkey buildings for the GSA
Hotels converted into apartment buildings
Construction of commercial buildings
Construction of private housing
Construction of special projects
Construction of public housing (including military)

projects to be used in later ones. Groups of projects were also staged in a learning sequence.

3. *Each group of similar projects was deliberately undertaken as a probe into the environment.*

4. *Each group of projects would shape a larger program initiative, as well as emerge over time as a "typical" Citadel project, clearly identifiable by insiders in the industry.*

5. *In any given time period, the firm was always involved in several series of projects, thereby spreading risks.*

6. *The firm always carried out groups of projects in two counter-cyclical domains of real estate development practice, such as privately financed luxury office buildings and publicly financed low-income housing.*

7. *The firm switched attention between domains, depending on the level of initiative in its surroundings. As a result, it created, in a volatile corporate environment, a continuous and relative stable flow of projects.*

8. *The firm's two real estate practices were complementary. For example, "unique" office projects were pursued as a kind of real-time R&D, challenging the firm to develop new capabilities which were subsequently brought to bear on "cookie-cutter" housing projects, which generated the cash to start developing office buildings.*[6]

Over roughly four decades, these rules for probing the environment had remained remarkably constant. They constituted the firm's global theory-in-use for probing the environment through which it had grown from renovating storefronts in 1946 to a program in which it was simultaneously building several large-scale, integrated, mixed-use landmark projects as well as a string of first-class hotel projects by 1986. At the same time, the firm's pattern of strategic behavior also displayed several kinds of discontinuities. These included

1. *a pulsing oscillation between geographical expansion and abrupt retreat, paralleled by swings in turnover,*

---

6 For a detailed discussion, see W.J.A.M. Overmeer, "Strategy Design, Learning and Realization: Exploring Designing Under Conditions of Major Change" in Howard Thomas (ed.), *Proceedings of the Strategic Management Society Conference* on Renaissance: the transformation of economic enterprise, London: John Wiley & Sons, 1996.

2. *the financial failure of several large projects in the early 1970s, which put the firm's continued existence in jeopardy,*

3. *a quantum leap in turnover shortly after 1980 and a rapidly increasing portfolio of completed projects.*

Over the roughly forty-year interval, Citadel's consistent pattern of strategic behavior, together with its discontinuities, revealed roughly eight-year periods in which there was a steady pattern of ongoing probing, punctuated by episodes of experimental probing during the early 1950s, 1960s, 1970s, and 1980s, each time in response to a discontinuity in the firm's environment.

Nobody in Citadel had ever attempted to construct such a map with its accompanying inferences about the logic of the firm's strategic moves. The map revealed that the firm had pursued both cookie-cutter and unique projects in a symbiotic way through an intricate set of largely tacit rules. Each such rule, and sometimes a subset of a few rules, was known to one or more managers or would be recognizable by them if it were stated. But no one in the firm had a complete picture of the map as a whole, nor had they ever tried to concert their respective images. The firm could do more than its managers could tell, and the managers had limited access to the firm's global theory-in-use for probing its environment.

This global theory-in-use differs from strategic intent, in that it was partly tacit; it accounted for the firm's patterns of behavior; it was remarkably constant over time; and, as we shall see, it was remarkably resistant to change. It also differs from the idea of "emergent strategy," in that each series of similar projects constituted a deliberate strategic move with features typical of Citadel. These moves were not disjointed responses to shifts in the environment; over time they displayed a pattern consistent with Citadel's global theory-in-use for probing its environment.

The Inside-out View: Probing the Environment and the Firm's Behavioral World

Seen from the outside-in, Citadel had completed probe after probe during its first three and a half decades. And, in response to a volatile context, it had very successfully switched strategic attention between two counter-cyclical development programs, drawing on two complementary real estate practices. Seen from the inside-out, however, through the lens of interviews with Citadel's managers, the synergy between the two complementary practices had become increasingly problematic with each new switch of attention.

In the second half of the 1970s, prior to Citadel's major strategic change, disagreements between Joe, the CEO and cofounder, and John, the head of the construction division, had come to a head. Joe was widely re-

spected for the high-quality, unique, landmark projects that Citadel had developed in the 1960s and early 1970s. During the last two of these projects, however, he had added an extra wing at the urging of the project architect, only to be stuck after project completion with excess space. These two projects had jeopardized the firm's continuity, and managers working for Joe had concluded that he needed to be protected from himself. During the same period, John had build out-of-town cookie-cutter housing projects, the strategic focus in the 1970s. While John had never produced a loss, some of Joe's assistants believed that he deliberately overestimated construction budgets in order to avoid the embarrassment of going over budget. These assistants had responded, unilaterally, by taking 10 percent off of the budgets submitted by John; John responded, they believed, by adding an additional 10 percent to his next budget, and so on. This escalating pattern led to unreliable information about project costs, despite the introduction of a computerized information system that was intended to remedy the problem. As the designer of the information system complained,

> You can tell it whatever you want and use it as a protective shield and prevent control through computer systems.

By the late 1970s, Joe sensed a gradual but major shift in Citadel's stagnant local environment and began to switch the firm's attention back to unique projects by developing a mid-sized, downtown office building. Due to the architectural complexity of this project, its proximity to a subway tunnel, new and changing city regulations, and a troubled joint venture relationship, Joe became deeply involved. According to John,

> It was different working in the hometown. It was a high-visibility project, so the CEO was much more involved. Oversight was much closer. Anything the architect wanted was approved by the CEO.

At the same time, Joe complained that John "played it close to the vest," "bulldozed his way over the architect," and "acted as if he understood it all."

Feeling constrained by this conflictual relationship, Joe called in a management consultant, psychoanalytically trained, who proceeded to study the situation. The consultant reported "endless hard bargaining" and "anger over minutiae." He saw "an intolerable situation," and framed the problem as a "tyranny" and a "power struggle" which "undermined the creative position of the development people." In order to "free up creative energy" and "break the dependency" between Joe and John, the consultant proposed creating a third force in the form of a project manager who would act as a memory device for construction data and a containment vessel for conflict and who could interrupt the flow of action until the CEO could *"come in and make decisions." Joe accepted this advice. Moreover, without informing the construction division, Joe decided that the division would have to become a profit center so that it might be sold in the future.*

Thus an underlying conflict arose between the CEO, steeped in the practice of unique office buildings with an open-ended design process, and the head of construction, steeped in the practice of cookie-cutter housing projects. One's demands led to threatening or embarrassing situations for the other, who was usually, in turn, unable to reconcile the first party's demands with his own image of practice. Each party responded by making unilateral attempts to control the situation and protect his own practice. Neither, as it turned out, could talk across practices or step back to see how it might be possible to reconcile conflicting norms for performance.

Unable to address the intraorganizational conflict that diverted their attention from the need to respond to shifts in the corporate environment, the business planners and developers who functioned as Citadel's strategy designers, distanced themselves from conflicts with the implementors (the construction division) by executing a highly defensive change in organizational structure. In so doing, they also disconnected themselves from a valuable source of information about cookie-cutter construction.

Disconnected Probing During A Major Shift in the Environment

By 1980, faced with a declining housing market, Citadel's senior managers engaged in a planning process not unlike the one described by Andrews (1980). They identified unique, luxury office skyscrapers in their hometown as the new strategic domain, and they enacted the firm's switching rule for strategic attention. However, the new strategic intent was challenged as soon as the managers tried to realize it, and the planning process turned out to be merely the beginning of a longer-term process of strategic change. Over a period of two years, management initiated a series of strategic moves, each of which failed, leading to new and increasingly more urgent strategic predicaments to which they responded by making additional moves that were either incomplete or inconsistent with strategic intent.

In retrospect, these multiple moves made up a complex process of probing the environment during which the firm tried to enact the theory-in-use for probing that it had developed under less challenging circumstances. Over a period of two years, this theory-in-use failed to achieve its objectives; but in the process of imposing it, a strategy for hotel development emerged. In the course of developing a large office skyscraper, Citadel found that it could not pass an approval process. In response, it added on a hotel, which came to be seen as a strategic invention: unique projects in which of-

fices were integrated with a hotel. Citadel's managers soon learned that it would be very difficult to locate opportunities for additional office-hotel projects. Nevertheless, their search for such opportunities revealed a regional and later national niche for luxury suites hotels. Management now believed it had stumbled upon a revolutionary hotel concept that it could ride on the wave of the future. After two years of instability and with its back against the wall (laying off employees that held some of the firm's core competence), Citadel's managers finally embarked on a new program that consisted initially of five hotels. Contrary to the natural theory of strategic change, this emerging strategy was not kept dormant and in check, only to spread rapidly during a later quantum leap; rather, it took the form of an anomalous move (the introduction of a hotel attached to an office skyscraper) which was repeatedly reframed in the course of a series of moves that management made as it faced new strategic predicaments.

By the time Citadel's top managers decided on a hotel program, they saw it as a replacement for their housing program and erroneously as counter-cyclical to their office program. They were confident that hotel development and management, which they erroneously saw as a combination of office development and housing management, was something the firm knew how to do. They believed this despite the fact that they had never developed large and complex hotel projects in a cookie-cutter fashion, had never managed a hotel, (let alone a chain of hotels), and were disconnected from a source of knowledge about this type of cookie-cutter project.

The process of probing just described, characterized by the operation of a partly tacit theory-in-use, by repeated failures of strategic moves and resulting strategic predicaments, by changes in the significance of one move under the influence of subsequent moves, and by the erroneous framing of new strategy in terms of familiar programs, differs significantly from both the rational and the natural descriptions of strategic change.

Realizing Strategy and the Emergence of Defensive Routines

Between 1983 and 1986, as Citadel tried to realize its new strategy, its managers were confronted with a new family of predicaments.

The Corporate Strategy Was Challenged. *Soon after the hotel program started, a new mayor was elected in Citadel's hometown, and Citadel was able to secure two more unique, large-scale, integrated projects. The resulting concurrent demand for new resources for the two programs, which Citadel had taken to be counter-cyclical, led to a strategic dilemma: either top management would have to switch its attention back to office projects, or* *it would have to achieve a critical mass in hotel development, taking advantage of the window of opportunity, so as to be able to spread its overhead costs over many projects. During the next two years, the managers tried to address this dilemma in several ways:*

1. *holding a traditional strategic planning session which only succeeded in papering over differences through the formulation of an abstract mission statement,*

2. *studying the financial risks and exposure and calling for a balanced portfolio, and*

3. *changing the compensation package for the hotel group.*

The use of these traditional strategic management techniques showed that Citadel recognized it was at a crossroad, but it did not resolve the issue. Senior managers continued to focus on deal making, postponing action for almost two years.

The Design of the Hotel Program Was Challenged. *Citadel's top management had designed a construction process for cookie-cutter hotels, premised on:*

1. *the replication of a computer-based footprint at five locations,*

2. *a minimum-scope standard design to which options could be added later,*

3. *a fast-track construction process,*

4. *a stringent change order system, and*

5. *a healthy conflict between the hotel planners and the project managers (PMs) who were building the hotels.*

However, as Citadel's managers probed the new hotel environment, their key assumptions were disconfirmed. First, instead of the one type of hotel it had planned, Citadel was forced to develop four types. Second, the first five suites hotels were developed simultaneously rather than sequentially because of delays due to negotiations and site problems. Third, hotels turned out to be more expensive than expected, which meant that Citadel would need more hotels and would have to devote more top management attention to deal making. Fourth, the window of opportunity turned out to be very brief, and Citadel had to speed up development in order to stay ahead of competition. Fifth, in order to make its hotels more competitive, Citadel made several important design changes which led to higher costs and again required more hotels. Finally, because it proved necessary to use different hotel footprints under different local circumstances, hotels were not nearly the cookie-cutter exercises they were expected to be, with the result that costs, especially architectural costs, again increased. Thus the process of re-

alizing the new strategy challenged several of the rules built into the firm's theory-in-use for probing its environment—in particular, the rule that projects should be staged so as to permit lessons drawn from one project to inform the next.

A Conflict in the Field Came Gradually to the Fore. *Conflicts between the hotel group and the project management group significantly undermined the quality of Citadel's strategic probing of the hotel environment.*

During initial explorations, young project managers, initially hired to do unique luxury buildings, thought the cookie-cutter hotel design was tacky and not what Citadel was all about. The first PM (and later vice president), Karl, reported that he felt caught in an internal conflict; he provided absolutely no feedback to the more experienced hotel planners, and he dismissed their approach as "mere marketing."

During the planning stage, Karl quickly attributed to the planners that their construction budgets were a joke from the beginning, deliberately underestimated, so that he would be forced to work harder. After coming close to burn-out and being dismissed by the planners as their "cranker," he eventually put up with their numbers because, as he said, he "had no idea how to challenge them."

During the design stage, when the PMs could not get the technical information they wanted from the planners, they began to doubt the competence of the planners and to mistrust the hotel managers.

During construction, the minimum scope for hotel design was expanded, first by senior management who wanted to make the hotels more competitive in view of moves made by other hotel chains, and later by "demands" of the hotel managers, hired after the hotel design had been completed, who insisted on design changes and on ironing out errors if they (the hotel managers) were to be held responsible for the bottom line. As a result, the PMs who had harnessed the architect on a daily basis and held the line on the budget with the construction group, felt that their authority was severely undermined. They complained,

> *You lose all credibility with the designer and the contractor, and [you're] left with a feeling of being out of it.*

To gain control of the budgeting process, the project management group created a rigorous system for tracking and approving change orders. When the CEO and the head of the architectural firm tried to thrash out problems quietly, as they had done in the old days, they irked the PMs and the construction managers even more. The PMs wanted to prevent the CEO from adding extra costs and to protect their own authority. During construction of the fifth hotel, when Joe began to take an active role in correcting errors, the vice president of the project management group privately wondered, exasperatedly, "Is this any way to run an airline?" Some PMs reported that they preferred working on "cookie-cutter" hotels far away from the home office, free from what they saw as interference on the part of senior management.

Hence, some two years into the hotel program, through a gradual process of escalation, the project management group and the hotel group replicated the same dynamics the firm had experienced during the late 1970s between the CEO, Joe, and the construction manager, John, a problem for which the creation of the role of project manager had been seen as the structural solution. Moreover, the unresolved tension between business development and construction, dating from the late 1970s, was still present in the mid-1980s, and it compounded the problems of the hotel development process. In turn, this complicated the relationship between the hotel group and the project management group, which had become increasingly tense as the hotel program's intent and design were challenged. Finally, the top managers, each of whom held responsibility for one of the firm's main programs, focused on deal making for their own program, while they stayed away from conflicts in the field and put off addressing the firm's strategic dilemma.

Probing the Environment, Strategic Learning, and Organizational Defensive Routines

The inability of the principal actors to engage their conflicts productively triggered new layers of defenses, which undermined the quality of the firm's strategic probes and of its strategic learning.

After the construction of five hotels, the PMs reported to the researcher that they felt reasonably seasoned and that they had constructed an anatomy of the process. Senior managers, they felt, were being snookered by hotel executives who pushed for fads. The resulting design changes were "hiccups at the tail end," which prevented the steamroller of fast-track construction from doing its work. Consequently, the PMs began to dig in. They refused to make the design changes requested by the hotel managers, claiming either that there was no money for them or that the changes were technically unfeasible, mimicking the arguments the hotel group had made in the planning stage. Because design issues often came up as minor problems, the hotel group managers began, contrary to agreed-on company policy, to push issues out into the field, asking individual hotel managers to take up these problems with the PMs. The hotel vice president stated:

> *I pushed the issues to the field. Let them do it. It reduces the issues; they make the trade-offs in the field; they cross-fertilize; nobody knows how and nobody cares.*

At the same time, the top manager overseeing the hotel program had begun purposely to stay away from certain issues, especially when he lacked the necessary technical knowledge.

The intensity of this organizational conflict became such that managers feared that inquiry into it would make it worse. For instance, when a fire alarm system was installed in the wrong place, the liaison between the hotel and development groups stated,

> *There seems to be no way out...it seems everybody's fault...personally, I find it most frustrating because it is still an unresolved question out there...not that I am going to lose any sleep over it...it could be made into an issue, [but] it is probably not worth doing something about it...*

Most of the back-of-the-house systems (where hotels differ from office buildings) gave rise to similar evaluations. The liaison concluded that "hopefully the construction group will gain more experience." The hotel group VP wanted to capture his own construction budget, so that when construction was completed, his group could go in and correct design errors already cast in concrete.

When senior management tried to respond to this situation by creating an owners' meeting for each project, where key actors could review the problems, the PMs decided for themselves that they were not going to use that forum to put somebody [from the hotel group] up against the wall. The PMs' lack of confrontation was privately evaluated by top management as "the PMs blowing it." At the same time, top managers had concluded that the PMs used the owners' meetings as a medium of exposure for themselves, that they had become popularity contests, and that there was a need for fewer but more meaningful meetings. The seriousness of the problems was becoming clear, as indicated by one of the top managers, who during the fifth hotel project said,

> *We lost control over the budget. We found out afterwards that we saved a million dollars, but it could have been the other way around.*

This project had been in the firm's own backyard and frequently visited by the CEO. The top manager wondered what might happen if Citadel were to develop hotels several thousands of miles away.

In order to address what the CEO framed as unhealthy conflicts due to cultural and power difference between the young and very bright PMs and the seasoned and mature hotel managers, he again called in the consultant Citadel had used at times during the 1980s. This time, the consultant said,

> *An individual carves out a vision and builds an organization that will help him to do it. If somebody is insecure, they will simply make the struc-*

ture protect them. If we can understand where the sensitivities are, the nature of their defenses, we could begin to see some degrees of freedom.

After the consultant had interviewed the two hotel group senior managers, top management called a series of high-level meetings in order to get to know "the current perceptions" and have "a very candid discussion, so that we can discuss personalities in an open fashion." But top management did not invite the major actors such as the president and vice presidents of the hotel group, the development group, and the construction group. Privately hotel group managers immediately sensed a unilateral change in the ground rules employed by top management, and apparently, the consultant did not alert top management to the defensive reactions they were creating. During the meetings, the consultant reported:

1. the PMs were "nit-picking to avoid responsibility," and
2. the senior hotel group managers did not have the "seasoned background" they pretended to have, and he attributed to them that they knew it.

Hence, he stated during the meeting with the top management group,

They worry about their authority when it is questioned by the PMs. They come across as strong and assertive to cover up their insecurities, they have bravado now, they are a fortress, they are a Siamese twin requiring surgery before it is too late.

Top managers responded that the organization "got battered," and that "the daughter is taking over the mother." They concluded that,

[We] should be unified and uniform in [our] point of view regarding the basic issues. If they smell [otherwise], then we get a struggle for the palace power.

At the consultant's advice, top management decided again to change the formal structure of the organization. They did this to protect themselves and to create—much as they had done in the 1970s with the construction group—a role that would challenge the group they saw threatening them. They decided to split up hotel group management, without discussing it with the hotel group managers, and to change their reporting relations to top management.

Not long afterward, Citadel bought another family-owned hotel development company from the Southwest. Then it announced publicly that it would sell the entire hotel group. And finally, it revoked its offer.

In conclusion, the firm not only replayed in the mid-1980s organizational dynamics similar to those of the late 1970s—aggravated now by the reoccurrence of late-1970s dynamics—but top management and its organizational consultant found in the mid-1980s the same solution they had tried *in the late 1970s, even though there was ample evidence to suggest that it had not worked. The organization was caught in a pattern of self-reinforcing actions and reactions and formal organizational change, all based on defensive reasoning.*

Learning Strategically: The Contributions of the Theory of Action Perspective to Strategic Management

The organizational dynamics Citadel's managers created as they engaged in strategy making is an example of dynamics found in a number of firms. A firm with well-intentioned executives, educated at the best professional schools, probes its business environment and changes its business strategy with competence, only to find that it gradually undermines that competence. Neither the rational nor the natural framework accounts for these dynamics or helps to address them. The rational approach does not explain or address how a mismatch between strategy design and its implementation can result from defensiveness, which leads to seemingly irrational behavior—as in Citadel's knowingly casting errors in concrete before opening a hotel, only to correct them afterwards at far higher cost. The natural approach cannot account for the ways in which defensiveness produces an observed lack of integration between emergent and deliberate strategy—in Citadel's case, how defensive interactions among the hotel group, the project management group, and top management led to higher costs of construction that made the firm less competitive. Neither approach accounts for the persistence of a strategy based on erroneous assumptions in the face of seemingly robust management techniques and convincing information.

The Citadel case shows how a defensive O-I pattern of intraorganizational conflict gradually emerges and escalates in the face of a major shift in the environment. In the course of strategy design, erroneous assumptions go unchallenged by implementors, which leads the designers to be inattentive to the predicaments that implementors experience during realization. Newly emerging defensive behavior begins to interact with already existing defensive routines, further cluttering the interactions between designers and implementors. Communication bottlenecks arise as designers and implementors are faced with each other's demands. Minor problems lead to individual button pushing, which leads, in turn, to intergroup button pushing, which leads to escalating organizational conflict. Recurrences of conflicts within periods as brief as a few weeks, and top management's inability to deal with them productively, sap creative energy, create a feeling of a loss of strategic control over the business, and undermine entrepreneurship. These effects trigger new unilateral actions on the part of top management, such as the introduction of structural solutions or the decision to sell a troublesome division, which provide short-term relief but further aggravate defensive dynamics over the long term. Citadel's strategic learning problem moves beyond the scope of competence of its managers, a key characteristic of an O-I limited learning system.

At the core of these dynamics is a conflict between two very different styles of practice, two very different theories of practice (Argyris and Schön, 1974), and the limited ability of executives to deal productively with the conflicting norms of performance that follow from these styles and theories. A struggle for dominance ensues. Each group of managers, faced with the demands of a different practice, feels threatened and/or embarrassed. As the theory of action perspective predicts, groups tend to respond by taking unilateral actions. They try to control the situation and protect themselves so that they can impose their theory of practice onto the situation. Their opposite numbers do likewise. The resulting interpersonal and intergroup dynamics, conflictual and defensive, tend to remain publicly undiscussable. Efforts to address the consequences of these dynamics only succeed in triggering more of the same, which presents members of the firm with a double-bind of organizational inquiry, that is, inquiry into the problem tends to aggravate the problem.

For about two decades, with only occasional flare-ups, the organization had been able to manage the conflict between its two main practices—"unique" office projects with open-ended design and flexible construction processes and "cookie-cutter" housing projects based on a rather fixed design. How had this been accomplished? The managers who practiced the two different styles of real estate development had compartmentalized their work into two different groups, each extending its competence in that style of practice by a series of probes which built on previous similar probes. Osmosis between practices, if it occurred at all, was largely due to the CEO's involvement. At the same time, managers had relied on a set of partly tacit rules, the global theory-in-use for probing, in order to deal with changes in the corporate environment. However, a major shift in the environment, which occurred in the mid-1980s, not only challenged the tacit rules (most prominently, the switching rule), but also disrupted the process of management through compartmentalization.

This gradual but major change in the environment required the different groups to reflect jointly on their practices in order to build new hybrid practices ("cookie-cutter" first-class hotels and soon after, "unique" integrated projects) in the face of the multiple uncertainties that characterized a new and unfamiliar corporate context. This challenge required managers of each of the two practices to articulate and discuss their activities with managers stéeped in another style of practice. It required them not only to invent, produce, and test a new practice through a series of projects, but also to inquire and reflect jointly on the outcomes they were producing. In so doing, they might develop a new kind of competence, uniquely matched to the new environment and typical of that particular firm. This new practice might then develop a new sensitivity and intelligence with respect to later changes in the environment.

How, then, could Citadel's members be helped to develop such a capacity for deutero- and double-loop organizational learning, central to realizing a new strategy and to probing the environment? In order to deal competently with the organization's defensive dynamics, executives would need to learn strategically. This means, for one thing, that they would need to learn to address these dynamics before a shift in the environment led to escalating conflict that would cause them to distance themselves and disconnect themselves from implementors and hence from important design knowledge. Ideally, such learning would start early in the life of an organization (see Argyris, 1993, and Chapter 7 this volume) so as to build in the capacity for deutero- and double-loop learning from the very beginning.[7] It is also possible for managers to take a time-out prior to a major shift in the environment in order to reflect jointly on their practices and to learn a repertoire of skills for talking across practices. For instance, Citadel's managers could have engaged in such a process with the help of a consultant even as this research was taking place, especially when they decided to set up owners' meetings in which all

---

[7] Note: while the organization Argyris studied was new, the senior managers of the organization had experiences in similar previous organizations. It was precisely their explicit joint intent to learn strategically, to avoid what they experienced in their previous work contexts. Their failure to do so provided the powerful impetus for joint reflection on the organizational dynamics they created.

those who were centrally involved in the new strategy would take part. They could have started with the President's puzzle of how a project in the firm's backyard could have come in one million dollars under budget, and how top management only became aware of this after the project was completed.

Inquiry into such a concrete problem, highly relevant to a new project, could bring out the differences in theories of practice held by the major actors, the defensive dynamics that arose around them during each stage of the project, the organizational defensive routines that accumulated, and the consequences of these phenomena for each project and for the firm's probes into its new environment, all of which have been discussed earlier. Members of the firm could learn how to address these dynamics more competently—first by looking at how they might have handled issues that arose in the fifth hotel project, and then how they might handle similar issues in a new project. Once they had developed a repertoire of competent responses to get underneath budget problems, they would be very likely to extend them to deal with other kinds of problems.

Additional inquiry, with the help of a consultant-researcher, might lead the managers to understand that the conflict of demands inherent in their different practices represented "a Citadel kind of a problem" that had been around, in one version or another, for a long time. By mapping these versions over time, as in this case study, and by relating them to the theory-in-use of the firm, the managers could learn that:

1. this kind of problem is going to stay with them,
2. it will be expressed through organizational conflict, and
3. rather than deal with it through political games, they could recognize it and subject it to competent inquiry in a way that would actually extend the kind of strategic learning and probing that have been central at times to the firm's extraordinary strategic competence.

Even a firm as competent as Citadel would face formidable odds if it tried to develop a capability for deutero- and double-loop organizational learning. During research, for instance, it was found that, although the struggle between the two styles of practice was publicly undiscussable, private conversations with Citadel managers provided evidence that:

1. this struggle went back to the early 1960s,

2. members of the firm who had left the firm some fifteen years earlier continued to talk as though they were still responding to one another in the familiar patterns of conflict,

3. present members of the firm had little or no knowledge that the differences between practices had been with the firm for at least 25 years and that they were, in ways, reinventing an old debate,

4. present members had only scattered knowledge about the symbiotic relationship in which the two practices had been joined over the past 25 years, and

5. the conflict between the two practices was framed as "what Citadel was all about."

Moreover, present members of the firm had not stepped back to take account of inconsistencies in their own theories of practice. For instance

1. new series of "cookie-cutter" projects started with a "unique" project,

2. unique projects had cookie-cutter features, in that unique architectural designs were draped around modularized steel support structures,

3. cookie-cutter projects usually had to accommodate to unique local circumstances

4. rather than seeing large-scale integrated projects as opportunities to think through how unique and cookie cutter aspects could be combined, much as hotel projects could have been, managers tended to see them as new battlegrounds for unilateral control and protection for winning and losing.

These formidable odds against strategic learning have led population ecologists in the field of strategy to conclude that firms cannot adjust their imprint and that the firm's survival is largely determined by dynamics at the population level, well beyond the influence of the managers of individual firms—dependent, for example, on the difference between entries and exits of the industry and the resulting population density. While such a perspective is understandable, it offers little help for individual managers in firms except to monitor carefully new entrants and those who exit the industry. Other researchers, such as Porter (1980, 1985) and Miles and Snow

(1978), have reported on the existence of more than one kind of practice in an organization and on the difficulties this creates, particularly when firms make the transition from differentiator to cost leader as the industry matures, or to try to incorporate both defender and prospector qualities in the same firm. In the face of difficulties, like the ones described earlier, these researchers conclude that different practices need to be separated organizationally. Finally, Andrews (1980), exemplar of the rational approach, does not mention differences in styles of practice; Mintzberg (1982, 1985a, 1985b, 1987), exemplar of the natural approach, does not provide specific recommendations as to how to combine existing practices into a new practice in a close fit with a new environment.

An Action-based Research Agenda for Strategic Management

While the theory of action perspective can make a contribution to the field of strategic management, there are also several areas in which it needs to be developed in collaboration with practitioners and with other kinds of researchers, if it is to lead to maps for and repertoires of strategic inquiry and intervention.

First, the task of the consultant-researcher is likely to become far more challenging when an organization experiences escalating conflict as its environment shifts in a major way, when strategy designers are about to distance and disconnect themselves from the implementors, or when the organization's problems seem to its managers to put its survival at risk. The task is more challenging because the ante is raised, and the consultant-researcher's approach may be perceived by one or more groups as a trick and a continuation of politics in a different guise. This may be especially true if the organization has hired consultants in the past who overpromised and could not produce what they claimed.

The task may change in that instrumental problems present themselves with great urgency. When a firm's survival is threatened, politicking tends to decrease and may even be temporarily suspended. Under these conditions, managers may ask the consultant-researcher for a specific contribution in the instrumental realm before they are willing to engage in other learning-oriented activities. The consultant-researcher is asked to help bypassing the organization's defensive routines while at the same time pointing out areas for further work. Politicking may return as soon as the ante is lowered, but the consultant-researcher may be in an excellent position, based on his or her track record with managers, to ask them to address the politicking and to help them transform it into productive inquiry.

Second, in an organization whose members are relatively threatened by or dismissive of organizational inquiry and intervention, the surfacing and legitimizing of different kinds of practices, the theories of practice involved, and their incompatibility may be an intermediate step toward developing a reflective organizational competence that encompasses interpersonal skills patterned on Model II.

Third, when the consultant-researcher is successful in helping senior managers develop interpersonal behavior more nearly patterned on Model II, these managers may then help other managers in the organization to learn Model II skills. However, as the efforts spread in the organization, there are two dangers:

1. other managers may take the efforts to be a new gimmick to be learned quickly (on an espoused-theory level, Model II sounds like motherhood and apple pie), only to be taken aback when they begin to understand it and to see aspects of it as threatening, and

2. some groups may feel extremely threatened and put up the organizational equivalent of Type B defenses (Argyris, 1982, 1993).

Fourth, how can senior managers monitor the development of an ability to conduct inquiry in large organizations, beyond their immediate reports? What kinds of tools might they use? How can they intervene so as to improve the quality of organizational inquiry?

Fifth, apart from highly skilled interpersonal behavior patterned on Model II, a consultant needs a set of other skills tightly integrated with interpersonal ones. For instance, in order to be effective, consultant-researchers need skills in helping executives to appreciate and frame their theories of practice and to see how their espoused theory and theory-in-use are consistent or inconsistent with each other, alerting them to the need to reflect on their practice. Also, as in the case of Citadel, consultants could help managers see how practices build on one another and that their struggles are similar to struggles in previous episodes of strategic change.

Sixth, consulting and research are integrated in an action science. Consulting to practitioners on their specific problems is simultaneously research into the problems managers have in realizing a new strategy and probing a new environment. Such an activity is also the realization of a new strategy for scholarly consultants, a probe in a new environment, up to now mostly avoided by academics and practitioners alike. What are the dilemmas such scholarly consultants will face in their own professional lives when they are confronted, for example, with the simultaneous demands of on-line consulting and legitimate academic research and of teaching within a university system?

Afterword

The Learning Paradox

Our argument can be reformulated in terms of a **learning paradox**: the actions we take to promote productive organizational learning actually inhibit deeper learning.

Most organizational "fixes" are of the single-loop variety, even if they are undertaken by intervenors who espouse double-loop learning. This is illustrated by the organizational reforms we have described in the Mercury and GE cases, as well as the ones discussed in Chapter 9 and the structural fixes adopted by Citadel in Chapter 10. Such reforms and fixes tend to be subverted, over time, by a generic defensive pattern derived from O-I learning systems in interaction with Model I theories-in-use and Model I social virtues. This self-reinforcing defensive pattern not only undermines single-loop learning but also inhibits double-loop learning in organizational inquiry. It is found at interpersonal, group, and intergroup levels in most organizations. Here, in a simplified form, is the sequence of steps through which it tends to undermine organizational reforms and fixes:

1. *Problems are identified in discussable domains.* For example, organizational structures or information systems. The domains that are not discussable are bypassed, and the bypass is covered up. Variables in the undiscussable domain (associated with generic defensive patterns) may be recognized privately and discussed informally, but they are considered as externalities.

2. *Solutions are generated to deal with discussable features of the problems.* Important features in the undiscussable domain are excluded. This act of exclusion is covered up and often explained away by reasons ("human nature," for

example) that fall outside the responsibility of the participants, or go beyond what they can influence.

3. *During the early stages of intervention, the solutions do appear to correct some organizational errors.* Most of the solutions are single-loop in nature, and most of the participants have (or can readily be taught) the skills necessary for their implementation. But as error correction falls short of expected results, the importance of the undiscussable issues becomes increasingly apparent.

4. *The participants begin to experience a double bind.* If they face up to the issues they have treated as undiscussable, they will also have to make public how they have bypassed them or covered them up. If they do not make these issues public, they will know that they are preventing the correction of the errors they have detected and that they are doing so by design. If this becomes transparent, they could be accused of violating their managerial responsibility.

5. *The participants may deal with their personal causal responsibility by denying it or by assigning it to the domain of externalities.*

Hence the entire pattern by which single-loop learning tends over time to be undermined and double-loop learning tends to be inhibited, is composed of multiple levels of interpenetrating and interdependent processes.

Overcoming the Learning Paradox

Surmounting the learning paradox means reflecting on these defensive patterns—especially the Model I theories-in-use we bring to organizational inquiry—and restructuring them. The following steps represent an idealized progress toward double-loop learning in organizational inquiry:

1. *Describe the defensive patterns that underlie the learning paradox.* Such a description will include relevant behaviors at individual, interpersonal, group, intergroup, and organizational levels. One way to accomplish this is to produce organizational action maps of the kind described in Chapter 5 (the case of the CIO). Another dimension of description is to help the agents of the organization make explicit and accept responsibility for their contributions to primary and secondary inhibitory loops.

2. *Design, jointly with the participants, ways to interrupt the circular, self-reinforcing processes that inhibit double-loop learning.* Our preference is to begin by listing organizational problems such as those described by the financial executives in Chapter 4 and the information executives in Chapter 5. Next, we ask the participants to write scenarios showing how they would begin to solve the problems, assuming they had the control they needed to design and implement what they consider to be sound solutions.

3. *Help the participants assess the degree to which their action strategies are likely to limit the implementation of the solutions they have designed.* Included in this step is help in assessing their degree of unawareness of the discrepancy between their espoused theories and theories-in-use and in seeing that their unawareness is due to their skillful execution of strategies consistent with Model I theories-in-use and organizational defensive routines.

4. *Help the participants realize how they have participated in creating and maintaining a behavioral world where the strategies they redesign to correct the situation are unlikely to be effective.* As they truly learn this lesson, the participants will begin to feel a sense of being stuck: they are damned if they do and damned if they don't.

5. *Involve the participants in sessions, such as the ones described in Chapter 7, where they can develop the concepts and skills they need in order to escape from this bind.* They soon discover that changing their action strategies is not enough. Model II action strategies (for example, illustrating attributions to other people or subjecting assumptions to public testing) must serve Model II governing values. When Model II action strategies serve Model I governing values, they are at best "this year's gimmick" and are at worst a sham. In both cases, they are likely to be recognized by other people, because gimmicks and shams are an integral part of the Model I and O-I world.

6. *Reduce the use of defensive reasoning, and increase the use of productive reason.* This means that individuals design and implement their designs in such a way as to make their premises and inferences explicit, crafting their conclusions so that their claims to validity are subject to rigorous tests.

7. *Reduce secondary inhibitory loops, especially organiza-*
tional defensive routines, and replace them with high qual-
ity inquiry, good dialectic, and double-loop learning.

As these steps take hold, they enlarge the domain in which productive organizational learning occurs. Areas that were not influenceable and alterable become so. Moreover, the capacity to learn how to learn also enlarges. The organization becomes increasingly self-sufficient and increasingly in control of its management processes and performance results.

The process is not a simple and uninterrupted progress in learning and competence. It includes regressions and the need to face up to issues previously not imagined. But both of these conditions become opportunities to strengthen and deepen learning competencies at all levels of the organization.

Accounting for Selective Inattention to the Learning Paradox

If we are right in our diagnosis of the learning paradox and our analysis of the causes of the subversion of fixes and reforms, then we have an interesting question: Why do we see this, whereas so many other researchers into organizational learning appear not to see it?

We believe that one explanation stems from our involvement in organizational practice. Practitioners who attempt to change organizations, especially to initiate productive organizational learning, inevitably run up against the O-I patterns that exist as consistent, ungetoverable features of their day-to-day worlds. Practitioners may respond to these patterns in a variety of ways—through flight, fight, resignation, or cynicism—but they cannot ignore them, although they can collude with them by *acting* as though they were not there and by excluding them from public discussion. In some instances practitioners may adopt none of these responses but may actually attempt to understand defensive organizational patterns and change them.

Scholars, however, *can* distance themselves from the O-I patterns that are characteristic of the real-world organizations they study. They can do so in an Olympian way, holding themselves aloof from the microphenomena of organizational life or in a Utopian way, by focusing exclusively on some desirable future state (see Gusfield, 1991). They can take cognizance of the existence of defensive patterns while treating them as relatively unimportant (as Van de Ven and Burgelman do).

It is worth pointing out that scholars tend *not* to remain selectively inattentive to the defensive patterns that exist in the organizational settings where they operate as practitioners—their own university departments, for example. By way of illustration, over the past several years Argyris has conducted research in which senior and junior social science researchers completed left-hand/right-hand cases, similar to the cases described in Chapters 4 and 5. Almost all of these cases were written because the scholars were experiencing defensive routines created by other people with whom they were interacting, and all the difficulties they were trying to overcome included features of primary and secondary loops. But although scholars cannot avoid defensive patterns in their own practice, they can and do exclude their own practice experience from the phenomena about which they theorize.

When we turn the practitioner/researcher relationship on its head, going back to the argument we made in Chapter 2, we then treat the world of organizational practice as the primary context for research on organizational learning. In this process, we try not only to explain something but to make something, that is, to create rare events of double-loop organizational inquiry that can be studied. In so doing, we join with practitioners and inevitably come up against the defensive O-I patterns that inhibit productive organizational learning, the patterns that undermine the persistence of single-loop solutions and double-loop changes in organizational theories-in-use. And we experience the need in our practice of intervention research to overcome our own Model I theories-in-use, to deliver in practice the Model II reponses that are most likely to enable people in the client organization to become aware of their O-I systems and their personal theories-in-use and to see how they might think and act differently. In short, we engage in collaborative research with organizational practitioners to create and reflect on double-loop organizational inquiry.

In a recent article, Miner and Mezias (1995) acknowledge the limited scholarly research on double-loop learning. They suggest that it is largely a matter of time before scholars get around to it. However, we doubt that time is really the dominant variable. Other important variables are operating, and if these are not changed, they will continue to keep scholars from engaging in the practice-oriented research that would bring them into contact with defensive patterns and point to the need for research on double-loop learning in organizational inquiry. It is our hypothesis that these variables are built into the norms that govern most normal social science research.

The majority of social scientists adhere to the rule that empirical research should be descriptive. They avoid taking perspectives that are normative or prescriptive (an attitude that reveals a normative stance in its own right). This attitude leads social scientists to treat the status quo as co-extensive with social reality. Changing the status quo is not part of their mission. But we suggest that this normative stance against changing the status quo makes it unlikely that social science researchers will see or try to close important gaps in their descriptive theories. A case in point is the research conducted by proponents of the "behavioral theory of the firm," which we discussed in earlier chapters. This research describes "relational" concepts, such as limited learning, quasi-resolution of conflict, and intergroup rivalries, all phenomena consistent with the primary and secondary inhibitory loops we have described (Argyris, 1996). Proponents of the behavioral theory of the firm treat such phenomena as *givens* of the organizational world, and this reinforces the disposition of practitioners who created these phenomena to see them as "natural."

Finally, we point out that if one examines the theory-in-use required to implement normal social science research, it is consistent with Model I (Argyris, 1980). Thus the practitioners of normal social science use a theory of action for rigorous research that is consistent with their interpersonal theories-in-use. This means that those who adhere to descriptive social science have chosen a field that is not likely to cause them to reexamine the bases of their skills or their confidence in dealing with individuals and in conducting research. The dilemma is that such skills and competencies are not effective in *creating* double-loop learning, and without helping to create it, scholars are unlikely to find opportunities to study it.

Directions for Future Research

The following are some of the research directions that seem to us to flow from the argument of this book which we have summarized above:

1. *Existence proofs.* There is a need to multiply existence proofs of the transformation of O-I to O-II learning systems, as illustrated by Argyris's work with the management consulting firm described in Chapter 7. This should include the development of new and more extensive ways of documenting both the outcomes and the constituent processes of such instances of intervention research.

2. *Analysis of change processes.* There is a need for further studies of the "anatomy" of the changes that occur in the shift from O-I to O-II learning systems. This should include both the processes by which organizations evolve O-II learning systems and the complementary processes by which their members develop M-II theories-in-use.

3. *Interactions between double-loop learning in organizational inquiry and interventions aimed at fostering "learning organizations."* It would be useful to conduct further studies of the effects of double-loop learning in organizational inquiry on the fate of organizational reforms such as TQM, Reengineering, Management Empowerment, and improvements in functional management, such as Activity-Based Costing and organizational learning to develop strategy for competitive advantage. How are the limitations of such interventions, some of which we have described in Chapter 9, affected by the development of enhanced capacity for double-loop learning?

4. *Relationships between double-loop learning in organizational inquiry and other theories of organizational learning.* How could collaborative action research, aimed at fostering double-loop organizational inquiry, provide more robust tests of the dominant theories of organizational learning? The following are examples of some relevant studies:

- Studies of cognitive capability for productive organizational learning. These would explore the effects of increased capacity for double-loop inquiry on such phenomena as competence traps and superstitious learning.
- Studies of relationships between double-loop learning in organizational inquiry and evolutionary approaches to the development of the firm. These studies would address the question of the negative and/or positive effects of organizational defensive routines. An item of particular interest: tracing the relationships between long-term organizational dialectics, as illustrated by our Mercury story and Burgelman's account of Intel's evolution, and the character of the organizational inquiry that occurs at crucial "joints" in the dialectic.
- Studies of relationships between the theory of action perspective on organizational learning and Hirschman's (1958)

view that behavioral change can be elicited and coerced over time through the introduction of new incentive structures such as pacing and forcing mechanisms.

5. *The methodology of collaborative action research.* This research would further develop the meanings of "appropriate rigor" and "objectivity" in collaborative action research on organizational learning. It would pursue the elaboration of design and pattern causality and their associated methodologies of causal inference, including causal tracing and on-the-spot experimentation.

6. *Ethical implications of the theory of action perspective.* This research would examine how ethical dilemmas arise in organizational practice and how they interact with O-I systems. It would address the problem of "organizational learning for evil ends," and it would explore the ethical significance of double-loop organizational inquiry.

7. *Research uses of educational settings.* In Chapter 6, the "classroom" chapter, we illustrated how the classroom setting can be used to conduct research on the theories-in-use held by participants and the primary and secondary inhibitory loops they tend to create in their interactions with one another. It would be useful to multiply examples of such inquiry, showing how the tasks of education and research can be fruitfully combined.

8. *A social science of rare events, possible worlds.* This research would explore further the meaning and implications for social science methodology of "creating rare events in order to study them." A topic of special importance would be envisioning and enacting organizational worlds characterized by O-II and M-II.

References

Ackoff, Russell (1981). *Creating the Corporate Future.* New York: John Wiley and Sons.

Ackoff, Russell (1974). *Redesigning the Future.* New York: John Wiley and Sons, Inc.

Andrews, Kenneth R. (1980). *The Concept of Corporate Strategy.* Homewood, Il: Richard D. Irwin, (originally published in 1970).

Ansoff, H. Igor (1965). *Corporate Strategy.* New York: McGraw-Hill.

Argyris, Chris (1996). "Unrecognized Defenses of Scholars." In *Organizational Science,* forthcoming.

Argyris, Chris (1994). "Good Communication That Blocks Learning." In *Harvard Business Review,* vol. 72, no. 4: 77–85.

Argyris, Chris (1993). *Knowledge for Action: A Guide to Overcoming Barriers to Organizational Change.* San Francisco: Jossey-Bass Publishers.

Argyris, Chris, and Kaplan, Robert (1993). "Implementing New Knowledge: The Case of Activity-Based Costing." Harvard Business School Working Paper, November 8, 1993.

Argyris, Chris (1991). "Teaching Smart People How to Learn." In *Harvard Business Review,* vol. 69 (3), pp. 99–109.

Argyris, Chris (1982). *Reasoning, Learning and Action: Individual and Organizational.* San Francisco: Jossey-Bass.

Argyris, Chris (1980). *The Inner Contradictions of Rigorous Research.* New York: Academic Press.

Argyris, Chris, and Schön, Donald A. (1974). *Theory in Practice: Increasing Professional Effectiveness.* San Francisco: Jossey-Bass.

Ashby, W. Ross (1960). *Design for a Brain.* New York: John Wiley and Sons, Inc.

Bardach, Eugene (1980). "On Designing Implementable Programs." In *Pitfalls of Analysis,* Giandomenico Majone and E.S. Quade, eds. Chichester, England: John Wiley and Sons.

Barker, Roger G., and Wright, H.F. (1954). *Midwest and Its Children.* New York: Row Peterson.

Barnard, Chester (1938; second edition, 1968). *The Functions of the Executive.* Cambridge, Mass.: Harvard University Press.

Bateson, Gregory (1972). *Steps to an Ecology of Mind.* San Francisco: Chandler Publishing Co.

Beer, Michael (1994). "Developing an Organization Capable of Implementing Strategy and Learning." Harvard Business School Working Paper, September, 1994.

Bendix, Reinhard (1956). *Work and Authority in Industry.* New York: Harper and Row.

Bower, Joseph L. (1970). *Managing the Resource Allocation Process.* Boston: Division of Research, Harvard Business School.

Bowman, Edward (1995). "Next Steps for Corporate Strategy." In Advances in Strategic Management, P. Shrivastava, C. Stubbart, A. Huff, and J. Dutton, eds. Greenwich, Conn: JAI Press, Inc.

Burgelman, Robert (1994). "Fading Memories: A Process Theory of Strategic Business Exit in Dynamic Environments." In *Administrative Sciences Quarterly,* March, 1994, vol. 39: 24–56.

Burgelman, Robert A. (1983). "A Process Model of Internal Corporate Venturing in a Major Diversified Firm." In *Administrative Science Quarterly,* March, 1983, vol. 28: 223–244.

Campbell, Donald T., and Stanley, J. C. (1963). *Experimental and Quasi-Experimental Designs for Research.* Skokie, Ill.: Rand McNally.

Campbell, Donald (1969). Variation and Selective Retention in Socio-Cultural Evolution. In *General Systems,* vol. 16: pp. 69–85.

Cohen, Michael D., and March, J.G. (1974). *Leadership and Ambiguity.* Princeton: Carnegie Foundation for the Advancement of Teaching.

Crozier, Michel (1964; original publication, 1963). *The Bureaucratic Phenomenon.* Chicago, Ill.: University of Chicago Press.

Cyert, R.M., and March, J.G. (1963). *A Behavioral Theory of the Firm.* Englewood Cliffs, N.J.: Prentice Hall.

DeMonchaux, Suzanne (1992). "The Loss of the Innocent Eye." Mimeo, Cambridge, Mass.

Devereaux, Georges (1967). *From Anxiety to Method in the Behavioral Sciences.* The Hague: Mouton.

Dewey, John (1938). *Logic: The Theory of Inquiry.* New York: Holt, Rinehart and Winston.

Doz, Yves, L., and Prahalad, C.K. (1987). "A Process Model of Strategic Redirection in Large Complex Firms: The Case of Multinational Corporations. In A.M. Pettigrew (ed.), *The Management of Strategic Change.* Oxford: Basil Blackwell.

Doz, Yves L., and Thanheiser, H. (1992). "Regaining Competitiveness: A Process of Organizational Renewal." INSEAD Working Paper N-92/10/SM, January.

Fiol, C.M. and Lyles, M.A. (1985). "Organizational Learning." In *Academy of Management Review,* 10, pp. 803–813.

Garvin, David (1993). "Building a Learning Orgnization." In *The Harvard Business Review,* July–August, vol. 71, no. 4; pp. 78–91.

Gusfield, Joseph (1979). "'Buddy, Can You Paradigm?' The Crisis of Theory in the Welfare State." In *Pacific Sociological Review,* vol. 22, no. 1: 3–22.

Hamel, Gary, and Prahalad, C.K. (1989). "Strategic Intent." In *Harvard Business Review,* May–June, vol. 67, no. 3.

Harre, R., and Secord, P.F. (1972). *The Explanation of Social Behavior.* Oxford: Basil Blackwell.

Hayes, R.H., Wheelwright, S.C. and Clark, K.B. (1988). *Dynamic Manufacturing: Creating a Learning Organization.* New York: The Free Press.

Herbst, Philip G. (1974). *Socio-Technical Design: Strategies in Multidisciplinary Research.* London: Tavistock Publications.

Hernnstein, R.J. (1991). "Experiments on Stable Suboptimality in Individual Behavior." In *Learning and Adaptive Economic Behavior,* vol. 81, no. 2: pp. 360–364.

Hirschman, Albert (1970). *Exit, Voice, and Loyalty: Responses to Decline in Firms, Organizations, and States.* Cambridge, Mass.: Harvard University Press.

Hirschman, Albert O. (1958). *The Strategy of Economic Development.* New Haven: Yale University Press.

Holland, John H., and Miller, John H. (1991). "Artificial Adaptive Agents in Economic Theory." In *Learning and Adaptive Economic Behavior,* vol. 81, no. 2: pp. 365–370.

Huber, George P. (1989). "Organizational Learning: An Examination of the Contributing Processes and a Review of the Literature." Prepared for the NSF-sponsored Conference on Organizational Learning, Carnegie-Mellon University, May 18–20, 1989.

Hughes, Everett (1959). "The Study of Occupations." In R.K. Merton, L. Broom, and L.S. Cottrell, Jr. (eds.), *Sociology Today.* New York: Basic Books.

Jacques, Elliott (1951). *The Changing Culture of a Factory.* London: Tavistock.

James, L.R., Mulaik, S.A., and Brett, J.M. (1982). *Causal Analysis: Assumptions, Models, and Data.* Beverly Hills, Calif.: Sage Publications.

Jones, Alan M., and Hendry, Chris (1992). *The Learning Organization: A Review of Literature and Practice.* Coventry, U. K.: Warwick Business School, University of Warwick.

Kim, Daniel (1993). "Creating Learning Organizations: Understanding the Link Between Individual and Organizational Learning." OL&IL Paper v3.5, MIT Sloan School of Management, Massachusetts Institute of Technology, Cambridge, Massachusetts.

Kunda, Gideon (1992). *Engineering Culture.* Philadelphia: Temple University Press.

Lanzara, Gian-Francesco (1983). "Ephemeral Organizations." In *Management Studies,* vol. 20, no.1. (issue on organizational learning).

Levitt, Barbara, and March, James G. (1988). "Organizational Learning." In *Annual Review of Sociology,* 14:319–40.

Lewin, Kurt, and Grabbe, P. (1945). "Conduct, Knowledge, and Acceptance of New Values." In *The Journal of Social Issues,* vol. 1, no. 3, August.

Lounamaa, P., and March, J.G. (1987). "Adaptive Coordination of a Learning Team." In *Management Science,* vol. 33, pp. 107–123.

Mallinger, Mark (1993). "Ambush Along the TQM Trail." Mimeo, Pepperdine University, Malibu, Calif.

March, James, and Olsen, Johan (1995). *Democratic Governance*, forthcoming, The Free Press, 1995.

March, James G., and Olsen, J. (1989). *Institutions Rediscovered.* New York: The Free Press.

March, James G., and Olsen, J. (1976). *Ambiguity and Choice in Organizations.* Bergen, Norway: Universitetsforlaget.

Marin, Dalia (1993). "Learning and Dynamic Comparative Advantage: Lessons from Austria's Postwar Pattern of Growth for Eastern Europe." Paper prepared for the 17th Economic Policy Panel, Copenhagen, 22–23, April, 1993.

Miles, R.E., and Snow, C.C. (1978). *Organizational Strategy, Structure, and Process.* New York: McGraw-Hill.

Mill, John Stuart (1949; originally published 1843). *A System of Logic.* London: Longmans, Green.

Miner, A.S., and Mezias, S.J. (1995). *Ugly Duckling No More: Pasts and Futures of Organizational Learning Research.*

Minsky, Marvin (1987). *The Society of Mind.* New York: Simon and Schuster.

Mintzberg, Henry, (1987). "Crafting Strategy." In *Harvard Business Review,* July–August, vol. 64, no. 4.

Mintzberg, Henry, and McHugh, A. (1985). "Strategy Formulation in an Adhocracy." In *Administrative Science Quarterly,* 30: 160–197.

H. Mintzberg, and Waters, J.A. "Tracking Strategy in an Entrepreneurial Firm." In *Academy of Management Review,* 25 (1982): 465–499.

Nelson, Richard, and Winter, S.G. (1982). *An Evolutionary Theory of Economic Change.* Cambridge, Mass.: The Belknap Press of Harvard University Press.

Olafson, Frederick A. (1967). *Principles and Persons: An Ethical Interpretation of Existentialism.* Baltimore: The Johns Hopkins Press.

Overmeer, W.J.A.M. (1995). "Strategy Design, Learning and Realization: Exploring Designing Under Conditions of Major Change. In H. Thomas, D. O'Neal and J. Kelly (eds.), *Strategic Renaissance and Business Transformation,* Chichester, England: John Wiley and Sons.

Overmeer, W.J.A.M.(1989). *Corporate Inquiry and Strategic Learning: The Role of Surprises and Improvisation in Organizing Major Strategic Change.* Cambridge, Mass.: MIT Doctoral Dissertation, School of Architecture and Planning.

Padgett, John F. (1992). Learning from (and about) March. In *Organization Science,* vol. 3 (February): pp. 744–748.

Perrow, Charles (1979). *Complex Organizations: A Critical Essay.* New York: Random House.

Pettigrew, Andrew M. (1973). *The Politics of Organizational Decision Making.* London: Tavistock.

Polanyi, Michael (1958). *Personal Knowledge.* Chicago: University of Chicago Press.

Polanyi, Michael (1967). *The Tacit Dimension.* New York: Doubleday (Anchor).

Popper, Karl (1969). *Conjectures and Refutations.* New York: Harper and Row.

Porter, Michael E. (1980). *Competitive Strategy: Techniques for Analyzing Industries and Competitors.* New York: The Free Press.

Porter, Michael E. (1985). *Competitive Advantage: Creating and Sustaining Superior Performance.* New York: The Free Press.

Pressman, Jeffrey and Wildavsky, A. (1973). *Implementation.* Berkeley: University of California Press.

Quinn, James B. (1980). *Strategies for Change: Logical Incrementalism.* Homewood, Ill.: Dorsey Press.

Rodwin, Lloyd, and Schön, Donald A., eds. (1994). *Rethinking the Development Experience: Essays Provoked by the Work of Albert Hirschman.* Washington, D.C.: The Brookings Institution.

Ross, J., and Staw, B.M. (1986). "Expo 86: An Escalation Prototype." In *Administrative Science Quarterly,* vol. 31: 274–297.

Roth, George (1993). *Business Process Re-Engineering in Business Service Companies.* Doctoral Dissertation, Sloan School of Management, Massachusetts Institute of Technology. Cambridge, Massachusetts.

Ryle, Gilbert (1949). *The Concept of Mind.* London: Hutchinson.

Schein, Edgar (1985; second edition, 1992). *Organizational Culture and Leadership.* San Francisco: Jossey-Bass Publishers.

Schneiderman, Arthur M. (1992). Are There Limits to Total Quality Management? Mimeo, Analog Devices.

Schön, Donald A., and Rein, Martin (1994). *Frame Reflection: Toward the Resolution of Intractable Controvesies.* New York: Basic Books.

Schön, Donald A. (1983). *The Reflective Practitioner.* New York: Basic Books.

Schön, Donald A. (1967). *Technology and Change: The New Heraclitus.* New York: Delacorte Press.

Scribner, Sylvia (1984). "Studying Working Intelligence." In B. Rogoff and J. Lave, eds., *Everyday Cognition: Its Development in Social Context.* Cambridge, Mass.: Harvard University Press.

Senge, Peter (1990). *The Fifth Discipline: The Art and Practice of the Learning Organization.* New York: Doubleday.

Simon, Herbert (1973). "Applying Information Technology to Organization Design." In *Public Administration Review,* vol. 33: 268–278.

Simon, Herbert (1976). *The Sciences of the Artificial.* Cambridge, Mass.: MIT Press.

Thorsrud, Einar (1981). *Organization Development from a Scandinavian Point of View.* AI-doc. 51/80, Oslo: Work Research Institutes.

Trist, Eric, and Bamforth, K.W. (1951). "Some Social and Psychological Consequences of the Longwall Method of Coal-Getting." In *Human Relations,* vol. 4, 3–38.

Ulrich, David, Jick, Todd, and Von Glinow, Mary Ann (1993). "High-Impact Learning: Building and Diffusing Learning Capability." In *Organizational Dynamics,* Autumn: 52–66.

Van de Ven, Andrew and Polley, D. (1992). Learning While Innovating. In *Organization Science,* vol. 3, no. 1, February: pp. 92–115.

Van Maanen, John (1988). *Tales of the Field.* Chicago: University of Chicago Press.

Veblen, Thorsten (1962; originally published, 1918). *The Higher Learning in America.* New York: Hill and Wang.

Vickers, Geoffrey (1968). *Value Systems and Social Process.* London: Tavistock.

Von Hayek, Friederich (1967). *Studies in Philosophy, Politics, and Economics.* Chicago: University of Chicago Press.

Weber, Max (1946; original publication, 1910). "Bureaucracy." In *From Max Weber: Essays in Sociology,* edited and translated by Hans H Gerth and C. Wright Mills; pp. 196–230. Oxford, England: Oxford University Press.

Weick, Karl (1979). *The Social Psychology of Organizing,* Second Edition. Reading, Mass.: Addison-Wesley.

Whitehead, Alfred North (1929). *The Aims of Education and Other Essays.* New York: Macmillan.

Zajonc, R.B. (1989). "Styles of Explanation in Social Psychology." In *The European Journal of Social Psychology,* September–October.

Name Index

Ackoff, Russell, 233

Andrews, Kenneth R., 251, 252, 278

Argyris, Chris, 27, 76, 85n, 95, 150, 152–153, 157, 204, 214, 224, 225, 231, 249, 274, 275, 279, 286

Ashby, W. Ross, 21n

Baker, George P., 224

Bamforth, K. W., 45

Bardach, Eugene, 192, 195

Barker, Roger, 12

Barnard, Chester, 10

Bateson, Gregory, 29

Beer, Michael, 231–232, 240–243, 245

Bendix, Reinhard, 194

Bowman, Edward, 182

Brett, J. M., 39

Burgelman, Robert, 189–190, 192, 201, 211–220, 221n, 242, 243, 245, 246, 252, 284, 287

Campbell, Donald T., 39, 189

Clark, K. B., 182

Cohen, Michael D., 195

Cordiner, Ralph, 222, 223, 243

Crozier, Michel, 29, 192, 195

Cyert, R. M., 197, 198, 256

Deming, W. Edwards, 231

Devereaux, George, 49

Dewey, John, 11, 30–31, 45

Doz, Yves L., 253, 254n

Eichman, Adolph, 19, 193

Emery, Fred, 181

Fiol, C. M., 189, 194, 197

Forrester, Jay, 183, 184

Frohman, Dov, 212

Garvin, David, 180–181

Goffman, E., 194

Grabbe, P., 44

Grove, Andy, 215, 217

Gusfield, Joseph, 284

Hamel, Gary, 253

Harré, R., 49

Hayes, R. H., 182

Henderson, A. M., 11

Hendry, Chris, 184–185

Herbst, David Philip, 181

Herrnstein, R. J., 189

Hirschman, Albert, 183, 192, 221*n,* 287–288
Holland, John H., 189
Huber, George P., 189
Hughes, Everett, 34
Jacques, Elliott, 45
James, L. R., 39
Jick, Todd, 181
Jones, Alan M., 184–185
Kaplan, Robert, 229–231
Kim, Daniel, 190, 197
Kunda, Gideon, 194
Lanzara, Gian-Francesco, 9, 10
Leavitt, Barbara, 189, 194, 195
Lewin, Kurt, 44
Lounamaa, P., 196
Lyles, M. A., 189, 194, 197
Lynch, Kevin, 45
Mallinger, Mark, 234–236
March, James G., 19, 189, 194–198, 248, 256
Marin, Dalia, 189
Marrow, Alfred, 44
Mezias, S. J., 285
Miles, R. E., 277–278
Mill, John Stuart, 39
Miller, John H., 189
Miner, A. S., 285
Minsky, Marvin, 192
Mintzberg, Henry, 251, 252, 278
Moore, Gordon, 215
Mulaik, S. A., 39
Nelson, Richard, 189, 192
Olafson, Frederick A., 39
Olsen, Johan, 195
Overmeer, W.J.A.M., 182, 263*n*

Padgett, John F., 197
Parsons, Talcott, 11
Peirce, Charles, 30
Perrow, Charles, 195
Polanyi, Michael, 193, 252
Polley, D., 201–211, 242, 245
Popper, Karl, 37
Porter, Michael, 251, 277–278
Prahalad, C. K., 253, 254*n*
Pressman, Jeffrey, 192
Quinn, James B., 254–255
Rein, Martin, 197
Rittel, Hurst, 159*n*
Rodwin, Lloyd, 183
Ross, J., 204
Roth, George, 236–239
Ryle, Glebert, 189
Scheffler, Israel, 31
Schein, Edgar, 185–187, 192
Schmiddy, Harold, 223
Schneiderman, Arthur M., 232–234, 243
Schön, Donald A., 19, 34, 53*n,* 95, 183, 197, 204, 207, 252, 274
Scribner, Sylvia, 12–13
Secord, P. F., 49
Senge, Peter, 184, 187
Simon, Herbert, 38, 197, 198
Sloan, Alfred, 222
Snow, C. C., 277–278
Stanley, J. C., 39
Staw, B. M., 204
Thomas, Howard, 263*n*
Thorsrud, Einar, 181
Trist, Eric, 45

Ulrich, David, 181
Van de Ven, Andrew, 201–211, 242, 245, 284
Van Maanen, John, 194
Vickers, Geoffrey, 36, 189
Von Glinow, Mary Ann, 181
Von Hayek, Friederich, 39
Webber, Melvin, 159n

Weber, Max, 10–11
Weick, Karl, 16
Wheelwright, S. C., 182
Whitehead, Alfred North, 122
Wildavsky, A., 192
Winter, S. G., 189, 192
Wruck, Karen H., 224
Zajonc, R. B., 47

Subject Index

Action maps
    in comprehensive intervention
        study, 158–165
    construction of, 156–158
    example of, 160–161
    for feedback sessions, 154–155
    interdependence of compo-
        nents in, 157
    testing validity of, 155–156
Action research
    collaborative, 46–51,288
    practitioner/researcher collabo-
        ration in, 43–46
    strategic management and
        agenda for, 278–280
Action science, 50
Activity-based costing,
    229–231, 243
Adaptive learning model,
    202–211
Agencies, 10–11
Agents-experient, 36–37
Aggression, 200, 202
American Pragmatism, 30
Apheresis, 203
Behavioral world
    instrumental theories-in-use
        and, 69, 93

    of organizations, 28, 29, 69
Business Process Reengineering,
    236, 249
Case approach, 79–80
Causal inference, 41
Causal reasoning, 157–158
Causal tracing, 40–41
Causality
    concern with, 37–38
    covering laws and, 38–39, 42
    design, 39, 40, 187
    efficient, 39, 40
    explanations for human behav-
        ior and, 107
    variables and, 38
CIO case
    CIO's reaction and, 87–88
    description of, 85
    immediate reports and, 85–87
    Model I theories-in-use and,
        92–96
    primary inhibitory loop and,
        89–92
    reflections on action of CIO
        in, 88–89
    secondary inhibitory loop and,
        97–103
Citadel case
    conclusions regarding, 273–277

disconnected probing during shift in environment in, 266–267

inside-out view of, 264–266

overview for, 260–264

probing environment, strategic learning, and organizational defensive routines in, 270–273

realizing strategy and emergence of defensive routines in, 267–270

Coherence, 246

Collaborative action research, 46–51, 288

Collectivities, 6–8, 191

Competence trap, 213

Comprehensive intervention
explanation of, 150
limited *vs.*, 111

Comprehensive intervention study
action map construction in, 156–158

analysis of case discussion in, 172–175

conducting learning experiments in, 175–176

directors' action map in, 158–165

feedback process in, 154–156

feedback session discussions in, 165–168

feedback session purposes in, 153

first seminar in, 168–171

framing problem in, 152–153

goals of, 151–152

overview of, 150

second seminar in, 171–172

Conditions for error
explanation of, 90–91
fragmented learning outcomes and, 198

list of, 91

Covering laws
causality and, 38–39, 42
normal social science research and, 41

Decentralization study, 222–229

Defensive reasoning, 75, 283

Defensive routines
cynical attitude about, 102
organizational rigidity due to, 101
reactions to, 101–102
technical-objective dimension of organizational life and individual-organizational, 103–106

Design causality, 39, 40, 187

Deuterolearning, 29

Double-loop learning
example of, 22–25
explanation of, 21
Model I and Model O-II and capacity for, 112
Model II and, 119, 246, 245, 246
requirements for, 96, 103
research on, 285, 287
single- *vs., n,* 25–27, 200–201
theories-in-use and, 76, 124
values and norms and, 22

Double-track research, 75–76

DRAM (dynamic random access memory) study, 211–221, 243, 246

Dynamic conservatism, 221

Ecological adjustment, 66

Economic development, 183

Ephemeral organizations, 9–10

Error
conditions for, 90–91

detection and correction of,
31–33, 216–217
explanation of, 32
first-order, 28, 248, 187–188
reducing conditions for, 68
second-order, 28
single-loop learning correction
of, 22

Espoused theory, 13

First-order errors
capacity for productive learning and, 248
explanation of, 28
learning organization and,
187–188

Garbage can theory, 195

Gatekeeper, 44

General Motors study,
222–229, 243

Helplessness, 172

Hiding hand principle, 221n

Human resources, 184–185

Individual learning, 4–6

Industrial Democracy Movement,
181

Inference
causal, 41
rational, 195–196

Inquirers, types of, 36

Inquiry, *See also* Organizational
inquiry
Deweyan, 30–31, 33
end-view of, 33
importance of interpersonal,
200
influence of, 49, 191, 197

Instrumental learning
explanation of, 4
uses for, 18–19

Instrumental theory-in-use
behavioral world of organiza-

tions and, 69, 93
explanation of, 14

Intel study, 211–221, 243

Intervention, *See also*
Comprehensive interven-
tion study
based on introduction of organizational enablers, 201
comprehensive, 111, 150
comprehensive, *See also*
Comprehensive interven-
tion study
limited, 67–71, 111
strategic human resource management, 240, 241

Intervention classes
conclusions regarding,
147–149
focus of testing in, 122–124
overview of, 122
a setting for relevant tests,
124–125
transcript of class discussion
in, 125–147

Language, influence of computers
on, 5

Leadership, 185

Learning, *See also* Organizational
learning
double-loop, *See* Double-loop
learning
as drawing lessons from history, 196–197
individual, 4–6
instrumental, 4, 18–19
product/process ambiguity of,
3
signs of, 173–175
single-loop, *See* Single-loop
learning
study of technological innovation and, 202–211
superstitious, 19, 196,
248–249

Learning experiments, 175–176

Learning leader, 185–186

Learning organizations
economic development and,
183
human resources and, 184–185
organizational culture and,
185–187
organizational strategy and,
181–182
overview of literature on,
180–181, 194
production and, 182
second-order errors and, 188
sociotechnical systems and,
181
systems dynamics and,
183–184

Learning paradox
explanation of, 281–282
selective inattention to,
284–286
steps to overcome, 282–284

Limited intervention, 111

Limited learning systems, 50
example of limited intervention into, 67–71
explanation of, 99
individual and supraindividual
unities and, 102–103
reasons for, 187–188
responsibility for creating,
166–167

Management empowerment, 249

Mercury Corporation
corporate development
dilemma of, 64–66
inquiry into process of new
business development by,
53–64
limited intervention into limited learning system in,
67–71

organizational dialectic and,
71–72
overview of, 52–53

Misplaced concreteness, 122

Model I
causal reasoning and, 157
ineffectiveness of, 96, 123
interpersonal inquiry and, 209
results and prevalence of, 96
schema of, 92, 93
shifts to Model II from, 29
shifts to Model II from, *See
also* Intervention classes
social virtues of, 96, 120, 123,
229
technical theories and defenses
of, 104–107
theories-in-use and, 92, 94–96
as used in intervention class
discussions, 122–124
as used in intervention class
discussions, *See also*
Intervention classes
values and action strategies of,
117

Model II
causal reasoning and, 157
double-loop organizational in
quiry and, 245, 246
explanation of, 117–119
as final state, 112
shifts from Model I to, 29
shifts from Model I to, *See
also* Intervention classes
social virtues of, 119–121, 123
as used in intervention class
discussions, 123, 124
as used in intervention class
discussions, *See also*
Intervention classes

Model O-I, 100, 103

Model O-I, 111

Model O-I, *See also* O-I learning
systems

Model O-II, 112

Model O-II, *See also* O-II learning systems

O-I learning systems
  counterproductive nature of, 123
  learning sequence of, 106
  O-II learning systems evolved from, 111–112, 286, 287
  O-II learning systems evolved from, *See also* Comprehensive intervention study
  organizational inquiry and, 111, 209

O-II learning systems
  case examples of early, 112–116
  components of, 112–113
  explanation of, 111–112
  moving from O-I learning systems to, 111–112, 286, 287
  moving from O-I learning systems to, *See also* Comprehensive intervention study

Organizational action
  conditions for, 11
  explanation of, 8–11
  threats to coherent, 246

Organizational adaptation and learning
  Burgelman study of, 211–222
  Van de Ven and Polley study of, 202–211

Organizational culture
  controllability of, 186–187
  explanation of, 185
  management of, 185–186

Organizational decentralization theory, 223

Organizational defensive routines
  defensive reasoning and, 107

secondary inhibitory loops and, 99–103

Organizational dialectic
  explanation of, 71–72
  suppression of good, 107

Organizational enablers
  intervention based on, 201, 247
  outcome of, 249

Organizational inquiry, *See also* Inquiry
  Dewey and, 33–34
  explanation of, 11, 191–192, 259–260
  individual and, 11–12
  O-I learning systems and, 111
  outcomes of, 16–18
  as political process, 49
  as productive organizational learning, 20, 200
  requirements for, 259

Organizational knowledge
  conditions for, 12
  tasks and, 13

Organizational learning, *See also* Learning; Productive organizational learning
  contradictory nature of, 188–193
  controversial issues of, 200–202
  early views of, 4
  examples of near misses in, 17–18
  explanation of, 15–17, 189
  individual *vs.*, 5–6
  instrumental, 4
  as meaningful notion, 193–194
  paradoxical nature of, 244–245
  requirements for, 258–260
  research needs for, 286–288
  scholarly literature on, 45–46, 188–198

types of literature on, 180
ways of hindering productive,
19–20
ways of hindering productive,
See also Mercury
Corporation

Organizational strategy, 181–182

Organizational structures, 28

Organizations
behavioral world of, 28, 29, 69
as collectivities, 6–8, 191
explanation of, 10
learning within, 3–5
as pluralistic systems, 195
political aspects of, 9

Polis, 9

Practitioners
action research and, 43–46
causality and, 39–40, 46
recommendations for, 250
relationship between re-
searchers and, 34–37

Primary inhibitory loops
counterproductive dialogues
and, 92, 99, 98
explanation of, 90–91
reinforcement of, 99
transition to secondary inhibitory loops from, 97

Problems, wicked, 159

Production process, 182

Productive organizational learning, *See also* Organiza-
tional learning
explanation of, 194–198–201
meaning of, 194–198–201
organizational learning and,
194–198
overcoming impediments to,
249–250
study illustrating limited, 221
threats to, 246–249

Quality of Work Life, 181

Rational inference, 195–196

Reasoning
causal, 157–158
defensive, 75, 283
dilemmas in research on,
75–78
explanations for human behavior and, 107

Reflective transfer, 42–43

Researchers
action research and, 43–46
recommendations for, 250
relationship between practitioners and, 34–37

Secondary inhibitory loops
CIO case and, 97–99
explanation of, 97
organizational defensive routines and, 99–103

Second-order errors
explanation of, 28
learning organization and, 188

Self-fulfilling processes, 171–172

Self-sealing processes, 171–172

Sidewinder missile, 17–18

Single-loop learning
double- *vs.*, 4, 21*n*, 25–27,
200–201
ecological adjustment in, 66
error correcting and, 22
explanation of, 20–21

Skilled incompetence, 217

Skilled unawareness, 217

Social virtues
model I, 96, 120, 123, 229
model I and, 96, 120
model II and, 119–121

Sociotechnical systems, 181

Spectator-manipulator, 36

Strategic Human Resource Management (SHRM) intervention, 240, 241, 243

Strategic intent, 253

Strategic management
action-based research agenda for, 278–280
gap between intent and realization in, 253–256
splits in field of, 251–253
theory of action perspective and, 273–278

Strategy making
encompassing realization as well as intent, 256–258
natural process of, 251–252
as probe into environment, 258–260
as probe into environment, *See also* Citadel case
rational process of, 251, 252

Superstitious learning, 19, 196, 248–249

Systems dynamics, 183–184

Tavistock Institute, 44–45, 181

Technical theories
explanation of, 103
features of, 103–104
Model I defenses and, 104

Technological innovation study, 202–211

Theories-in-use
changes in, 18
construction of, 15, 16
double-loop learning and, 76, 124
examples of, 14–15
explanation of, 13–14, 25–26
first- and second-order errors in, 28
inconsistencies in, 66
individual, 29
instrumental, 14, 69, 93
public testing of, 95
technical, 103

Theory of action
ethical implications of, 288
explanation of, 50, 75–76, 254
inconsistencies in, 64
obtaining valid information about individual, 78–79
strategic decisions and, 254, 255
strategic management and perspective of, 273–278
usefulness of, 260

Therapeutic Apheresis Program (TAP), 203–210, 246, 247

Total Quality Management (TQM)
learning produced by, 27
life cycle of, 249
studies of, 27, 231–236, 243

Trust, 226–228

Unlearning, 3–4

Wicked problems, 159